MARITIME REGIME BUILDING

Publications on Ocean Development

Volume 36

A Series of Studies on
the International, Legal, Institutional and Policy Aspects
of Ocean Development

General Editor: Shigeru Oda

The titles published in this series are listed at the end of this volume.

Maritime Regime Building

Lessons Learned and Their Relevance for Northeast Asia

edited by

MARK J. VALENCIA

Senior Fellow, East-West Center, Honolulu, Hawaii, U.S.A.

MARTINUS NIJHOFF PUBLISHERS
THE HAGUE/BOSTON/LONDON

Published by:
Kluwer Law International
P.O. Box 85889, 2508 CN The Hague, The Netherlands
sales@kli.wkap.nl
http://www.kluwerlaw.com

Sold and Distributed in North, Central and South America by:
Kluwer Law International
101 Philip Drive, Norwell, MA 02061, USA
kluwerlaw@wkap.com

Sold and Distributed in all other countries by:
Kluwer Law International
Distribution Centre, P.O. Box 322, 3300 AH Dordrecht, The Netherlands

Library of Congress Cataloging-in-Publication Data is available

Printed on acid-free paper

ISBN 90-411-1580-3

Kluwer Law International incorporates the publishing programmes
of Graham & Trotman Ltd, Kluwer Law and Taxation Publishers
and Martinus Nijhoff Publishers

Typeset by BookEns Ltd, Royston, Herts
Printed and bound in Great Britain by Antony Rowe Limited

TABLE OF CONTENTS

FOREWORD

The past few decades have witnessed the emergence of a vast array of regional arrangements and institutions dealing with all aspects of ocean management. The level of cooperation ranges from minimal dispute avoidance to relatively comprehensive ocean governance at the regional level. As concrete examples, reasonably successful and comprehensive regional regimes have been created for the Baltic, the North, and the Mediterranean Seas as well as the South Pacific Ocean. And attempts at regional regime building are ongoing in Southeast Asia, the South China Sea and the Indian Ocean. Although there are broad similarities between many of these semi-enclosed seas and those of Northeast Asia, no regional maritime regime has yet been initiated in Northeast Asia.

This variety of experiences raises several questions. What factors are conducive to maritime regime initiation, expansion and positive evolution, and which constrain regime formation and growth? Why has maritime regime building been successful in Europe and largely unsuccessful in Northeast Asia? And which, if any, lessons learned in other contexts are applicable in Northeast Asia?

The papers in this volume describe and explain existing or incipient regional maritime regimes in an unusually broad comparative context, and extract lessons learned that may be applicable elsewhere, including Northeast Asia. Moreover, the case studies are neatly sandwiched between an introduction to concepts and principles on regional co-operation and concluding chapters on lessons learned and their applicability to Northeast Asia. Given the growing interest in regime formation and effectiveness in general, and in maritime regimes in particular, this book and its conclusions should be of considerable interest to both analysts and policymakers.

The papers are authored by leading authorities on not only the maritime affairs of their particular region of focus but on maritime policy in general. They were presented at a "Planning Meeting for a Possible Project on Maritime Regime Building: Lessons Learned and Their Relevance for Northeast Asia," supported and hosted by the East-West Center, 28–30 August 2000.

I would like to acknowledge the support of the East-West Center for the Workshop. Jenny Miller Garmendia, Degree Fellow, was extremely helpful in preparing for the seminar and taking notes of discussions therein. I also acknowledge the excellent assistance of Carolyn Eguchi, Program Officer, and Anna Tanaka, Secretary, as well as Irene Cadelina, Secretary who typed the initial draft of this manuscript.

Mark J. Valencia

LIST OF PARTICIPANTS

Mr. Steinar E. ANDRESEN
Senior Research Fellow
Fridtjof Nansen Institute
Fridtjof Nansens vei 17, Postboks 36
N-1326 Lysaker
Norway

Tel: (47) 671 1900/22
Fax: (47 671 1910
E-mail: Steinar.andresen@fni.no

Dr. Hanns J. BUCHHOLZ
Institute of Geography
Hannover University
Department of Human Geography
Schneiderberg 50
30167 Hannover
Germany

Tel: 49 511 762 4930
Fax: 49 511 762 3533
E-mail: buchholz@mbox.kusogeo.uni-hannover.de

Dr. Aldo CHIRCOP
Coordinator, Marine Affairs Program
Dalhousie University
Halifax, Nova Scotia
Canada B3H 3J5

Tel: 902 494 1988
Fax: 902 494 1001
E-mail: aldo.chircop@dal.ca

Dr. Hasjim DJALAL
Member of National Maritime Council of Indonesia/Special Adviser to Minister of Ocean Exploration and Fisheries
Jalan Veteran III No. 12
Jakarta Pusat, Indonesia

Tel: 62 21 325 2029/385 7009
Fax: 62 21 3858029

Dr. Hiran JAYEWARDENE
Secretary General
Indian Ocean Marine Affairs Cooperation Secretariat (IOMAC)
Bandarsanaike Memorial International Conference Hall (BMICH)
Suite 4–212, Bauddhaloka Mawatha
Colombo 7
Sri Lanka

Tel: 94 1 686329
Fax: 94 1 699691
E-mail: iomacs@lanka.ccom.lk

Dr. Douglas M. JOHNSTON
Emeritus Professor
University of Victoria
Centre for Global Studies
Victoria
Canada V9E 1J9

Tel: 250 472 4520
Fax: 250 472 4830
E-mail: dmjejohn@uvic.ca

Professor Phillip M. SAUNDERS
Associate Professor of Law
Dalhousie Law School
6061 University Avenue
HalifaxNova Scotia
Canada B3H 4H9

Tel: 902 494 6735
Fax: 902 494 6256
E-mail: psaunder@Kilcom1.UCIS.Dal.Ca

Dr. Jon M. VAN DYKE
Professor of Law
William S. Richardson School of Law
University of Hawaii, Manoa
2515 Dole Street, #239
Honolulu, HI 96822
USA

Tel: 808 956 8509
Fax: 808 956 5569
E-mail: jvandyke@hawaii.edu

Dr. Mark J. VALENCIA
Senior Fellow
Research Program
East-West Center
1601 East-West Road
Honolulu, HI 96844-1601
USA

Tel: 808 944 7247
Fax: 808 944 7399
E-mail: valencim@eastwestcenter.org

Phillip Saunders

MARITIME REGIONAL COOPERATION: THEORY AND PRINCIPLES

Introduction

The importance of the regional level to the study and practice of international ocean management is so well established that it appears at times to be almost an article of faith. Innumerable studies have focussed on the regional dimension of every conceivable ocean resource and use, and the past few decades have seen the emergence of a vast array of regional arrangements and institutions dealing with all aspects of ocean management, with the level of cooperation ranging from minimal dispute avoidance to relatively comprehensive ocean governance at the regional level.

The perceived benefits of a regional focus are both theoretical and practical. For the analyst, the regional level provides a convenient means of organizing the world into manageable units, for which information can be collected and digested in a sensible way, and through which patterns of behavior may be discernible which are not evident at the global level.[1] Beyond this descriptive advantage, explanatory possibilities arise, in that it may also be possible to identify regional characteristics which condition particular responses to ocean management issues. More significant than the analytical advantages, however, is the fact that states have so frequently resorted to regional action as they organize the international dimension of their ocean management efforts. The practical successes achieved (despite some failures) have also encouraged the *prescriptive* application of the regional approach, and regional solutions to ocean management challenges are frequently proposed by academics, governments, non-governmental organizations and, as discussed further below, in global multilateral agreements such as the 1982 *United Nations Convention on the Law of the Sea*[2] *(hereinafter "LOS 1982")*.

This collection of essays brings together the descriptive, explanatory and prescriptive functions of regional studies, and does so in an unusually broad comparative context. The extensive, and quite varied experiences of several regions are used to provide lessons which might assist in the development of regional

Mark J. Valencia (ed.), Maritime Regime Building, 1–16.

approaches to ocean management issues in Northeast Asia. This introductory chapter will briefly review the perceived benefits and challenges generally associated with the adoption of regional approaches to the development of ocean management regimes, and identify some of the questions which face decision-makers proposing to embark on the course of regional cooperation. It is hoped that this will provide the basis for defining some of the questions which might be asked about the experiences of the various regions, with the objective of structuring the "lessons learned" from past successes and failures to provide guidance for the effective utilization of regional approaches in the future.

Twenty-three years ago, the University of Hawaii hosted the annual conference of the Law of the Sea Institute, with the theme of regionalization and its impact on the anticipated outcome of UNCLOS III.[3] Although there was already significant experience with a number of regional marine institutions and arrangements in various parts of the world, and while many of the analyses put forward hold up well today, much of what was presented with respect to the role of regionalism in the emerging legal regime of the oceans was, of necessity, speculative. This collection of studies provides the opportunity to revisit many of the questions about the utility and appropriate place of regionalism in the global oceans regime, but based now on far more practical implementation experience.

Regions and Regimes

Before turning to the question of regional cooperation, however, it is useful to focus for a moment on the broader issue of just which phenomena we are considering within the regional context. For the purposes of this paper, the focus will be on the development of international ocean management *regimes* at the regional level. The concept of the international regime, familiar to political scientists since the early 1980s, emerged as an approach to describing and explaining complex sets of international arrangements dealing with the same or closely connected issue areas, and with a particular concern for the cumulative effect of the various arrangements.[4] Individual component parts may have been negotiated over time, with or without explicit reference to each other, but with interconnected functional concerns and broadly similar membership. The notion of a regime may have as many definitions as it does proponents, but it has been most broadly defined in Krasner's description of clusters of

> ... implicit or explicit principles, norms, rules, and decision-making procedures around which actors' expectations converge in a given area of international relations. Principles are beliefs of fact, causation, and rectitude. Norms are standards of behaviour defined in terms of rights and obligations. Rules are specific prescriptions or proscriptions for action. Decision-making procedures are prevailing practices for making and implementing collective choice.[5]

The content of a regime, as defined here, has obvious implications for lawyers, given its concern with norms and rules, but it opens the scope of inquiry through its extension to non-binding or "soft law" instruments,[6] and even more broadly through its inclusion of institutional and social elements and non-governmental actors. The approach also highlights the significance of knowledge (scientific and other) to the effective creation and maintenance of regimes, as well as the potential role in regime creation played by "epistemic communities", a term used in this context "to refer to a specific community of experts sharing a belief in a common set of cause-and-effect relationships as well as the common values to which policies governing these relationships will be applied."[7] Without recounting the development and refinement of regime theory in detail, it is sufficient to say that it offers the most inclusive approach to what might be considered as part of a regional system of ocean management, and as such is most likely to elucidate all elements of interest. In addition, it provides the possibility of expanding the range of relevant regional characteristics which might be employed in determining the suitability of a particular type of cooperative activity in a region.

One subset of regime theory which should be mentioned here is the "transformational approach" to regime formation, which argues for regimes designed to "generate increasingly greater commitment and deeper cooperation through a process of iterative, state-to-state negotiation that promotes identity convergence."[8] In one sense this argument differs from other regime proponents in emphasis rather than in the fundamental approach, in that regimes are generally seen as capable of improving and deepening the levels of cooperation among parties over time. The difference is still significant, however, in circumstances where the possibility of widespread adherence to an extensive set of obligations is unlikely, for "transformationalism" would support the watering down of the regime in exchange for broader membership, in the belief that the operation of the regime will, over time, increase the convergence of interests:

> To maximize this process [of promoting convergence] Transformationalism prescribes that regimes be highly inclusive, minimize the stringency of obligations, deemphasize enforcement, and utilize decsion-making rules requiring near unanimity. ... According to Transformationalists, it is the weak convention that is most likely to beget the strong regime.[9]

While one of the most important advantages of regime theory is its flexibility and adaptability, this comes with its own dangers, in that an overly broad definition of what constitutes a regime may lead to a lack of precision and attempts to cluster unrelated elements together in the creation of regimes by hindsight. Furthermore, there is the possibility that, in trying to explain everything at once, we end up explaining nothing. These issues are addressed further below, with respect to the research questions suggested for consideration.

Benefits and Challenges of Regional Cooperation

As is noted above, many states have found the regional level of organization to be an appropriate response to the challenges of managing their ocean resources and uses.[10] Some arrangements and institutions have been "independent" in the sense of being created within a region, while others have operated under the auspices of broader global programs sponsored by bodies such as FAO and IOC.[11] UNEP, through its extensive Regional Seas Programme, has promoted networks of framework conventions, action plans and other instruments in 13 regions.[12] Substantively, regional cooperation has extended to living resource management, scientific research, maritime transport, military activities, environmental protection, and non-living resource management, as well as more broadly based regional economic development activities[13]

Why has the regional level of organization been adopted so widely, albeit unevenly, with respect to the oceans, and why did the trend seem to accelerate as States expanded their maritime jurisdiction in the last three decades of the 20th century, when unilateral approaches might have become more feasible with the incorporation of vast new areas within national control?

Perhaps the simplest reason for turning to the region is found in recognition of the fact that many ocean resources and uses are inherently transboundary in nature, and that not all of these are functionally manageable at a global level.[14] The management of many living resources, whether joint, straddling or highly migratory stocks, cannot be approached in any coherent way without the cooperation of multiple parties. Control of shipping, particularly in congested areas such as multi-State straits, cannot be carried out unilaterally with any hope of success.[15] The exploration of new management approaches based on large marine ecosystems (LMEs) presupposes the possibility of adopting some degree of management cooperation for larger areas than are contained within national jurisdiction.[16] Even the problem of maritime boundaries, which might be thought of as a classically bilateral exercise, can necessitate multilateral approaches (if only for the sake of conflict avoidance), where several jurisdictional claims overlap.[17]

The international dimension of ocean management is, of course, subject to significant regulation and functional cooperation at the global level, through a myriad of agreements and other arrangements. The global approach has been particularly popular in the fields of environmental law and resource management, in recognition of the scale of the challenges and the need for some degree of consistency in principles. This breadth, however, is sometimes achieved at the expense of depth. Many of these agreements are negotiated on the basis of consensus, with the result that the nature of the obligations tends towards the lowest common denominator, in order to ensure that the largest possible number of parties might be brought on board. This has led to some "commitments" being effectively unenforceable, either because they are legally non-binding,[18] or because their imprecision is such that the ultimate effect is the same.[19]

The generality of global arrangements is further enhanced by the practical difficulty of defining detailed approaches which are appropriate to all possible situations, given the phenomenal diversity of uses, management challenges and national implementation capacities found in the various regions of the world. The global level serves an indispensable function in creating blueprints for action, and in defining general principles, but in many circumstances it is simply expecting too much to look to this level for obligations which are both binding and detailed, or for decision-making processes which would be appropriate to all parts of the world. This difficulty is clearest in the case of ambitious multi-sectoral law-making efforts such as the *LOS 1982*.[20]

In response to this problem, the region can provide an important mediating level between the generalities of global regimes and the specifics of national implementation. If a region contains a smaller number of states with more congruent interests and similar management concerns,[21] there may be a better chance of achieving more specific agreements, possibly of more binding effect, than could occur within a larger grouping. Further definition and "hardening" of global frameworks can thus be achieved through regional regime formation. This potential role for regions is explicitly recognized in the call for further regional action in the global multilateral agreements which provide the basic architecture of the international law of the sea, as well as other documents which contribute to the definition of international ocean management.

In the *LOS 1982*, the call for regionalization of various functions[22] was expressed most clearly in Article 122, which set out the obligations of states bordering enclosed or semi-enclosed seas:[23]

> 122. States bordering an enclosed or semi-enclosed sea should cooperate with each other in the exercise of their rights and in the performance of their duties under this Convention. To this end they shall endeavour, directly or through an appropriate regional organization:
>
> (a) to coordinate the management, conservation, exploration and exploitation of the living resources of the sea;
> (b) to coordinate the implementation of their rights and duties with respect to the protection and preservation of the marine environment;
> (c) to coordinate their scientific research policies and undertake where appropriate joint programmes of scientific research in the area;
> (d) to invite, as appropriate, other interested States or international organizations to cooperate with them in furtherance of the provisions of this article.

This functional concern with *coordination* of such activities as scientific research and the implementation of national rights to manage the various zones is repeated elsewhere in the Convention,[24] and is particularly emphasized in Part XII, *Protection and Preservation of the Marine Environment*. Articles 197 – 201 set out a number of obligations to cooperate both globally and regionally in research, pollution prevention and in the formulation and elaboration of "international rules, standards and recommended practices and procedures ... for the protection of the marine environment, taking into account characteristic regional features." (Article 197)

More recently, the *Agreement For The Implementation Of The Provisions Of The United Nations Convention On The Law Of The Sea of 10 December 1982 Relating To The Conservation And Management Of Straddling Fish Stocks And Highly Migratory Fish Stocks*[25] [hereinafter *Straddling Stocks Agreement*] reflects a similar recognition of the crucial importance of regional cooperation. For example, where there is a regional or subregional organization or "arrangement" with "the competence to establish conservation and management measures for a particular straddling stock", then states are to "give effect to their duty to cooperate" by joining the organization or applying measures imposed by it.[26] Chapter 17 of *Agenda 21* also includes repeated references to the need for regional and subregional action, as does the 1995 *Global Programme of Action for the Protection of the Marine Environment from Land-Based Activities*.[27]

The definition of the "region", whether for analytical or operational purposes, offers the same flexibility as for the definition of regimes. A region might be defined around existing patterns of cooperation (regardless of whether that cooperation is marine-related), if it is felt that building on prior experience and confidence with integration will increase the possibility of success in the marine sector. Managerial concerns could be dominant, with a combination of resource and use patterns forming the basis of a region tailored to ensuring the best possible chance of addressing a management problem shared by all members of the region. Other possible criteria include: geographic proximity and the presence of transboundary issues (as with some enclosed and semi-enclosed seas); cultural homogeneity; military alliances; and even *ad hoc* groupings intended to reflect a common position on a specific issue of special concern.[28]

This list is by no means exhaustive, but the point is that marine regions (or sub-regions) may be defined to suit the objectives of a study or to maximize the commonality of interests in the development of regional cooperation measures. Because of this, States might be considered to be members of a number of overlapping "regions" defined for different purposes and according to different criteria.[29]

Finally, and of particular relevance to developing States, the regional level of co-operation offers the possibility of improved capacity-building. Modern multilateral treaties such as the *LOS 1982* and the UNCED-related conventions encompass a huge range of positive obligations which will require a complex and expensive process of implementation before they can be fulfilled. This in turn presupposes the availability of significant scientific, managerial and enforcement capabilities, which may or may not be present.[30] Regional cooperation has been used as a means of addressing this general problem in at least three ways. First, some degree of regionalization of ocean governance tasks, whether in scientific research or enforcement activities, permits pooling and more efficient use of scarce resources, while at the same time extending the geographic scope of a unified set of management measures. Second, regional agencies can act as important sources of assistance in national capacity-building, whether through intra-regional transfers of knowledge and information, or by acting as a conduit for the delivery of development assistance programs in the region.[31] Finally, the presentation of a unified "regional front" allows States to increase their "leverage", whether in direct confrontations with external powers (as with DWFNs, for example),[32] or in the context of highly factionalized global negotiations.[33]

Despite these advantages, however, there are important limitations which must be considered. First, as with regime theory, flexibility in the definition of regions may be an asset, but it also presents challenges. For analysts, the possibility exists that they will obscure reality by imposition of an artificial and distorting regional template on patterns of behavior that are actually defined at the global or bilateral level, or within the context of another region than the one defined for the purposes of the study.[34] At the very least, we must always be alert to the possibility that the window through which we are currently looking at reality may only show one small part of a more complicated picture.

For practitioners, particularly those in government, this raises a more critical question – how to define the appropriate region for purposes of cooperation, given the possibility that there may be more than one option available. For example, in both the South Pacific and the Caribbean, regional fisheries organizations have had to deal with the involvement of metropolitan powers, including some involved in distant water fishing in the region. A typical trade-off in such a case might involve wider geographic coverage versus the degree of commonality of interest within the regional institution. Where the choice is made to work through existing regional organizations, this decision may be made by default. In other cases, the question of membership may be a functional question, in that the types of uses and management problems at issue (and their sensitivity) will define the scope of the appropriate membership.

This leads directly to the more general problem of the cost and durability of regional cooperation efforts. Regional cooperation, particularly where it involves the creation or expansion of regional institutions, can be an expensive business, and at the very least demands significant amounts of time and effort from individuals who may already by over-extended. There must be clear and demonstrated benefits to States if the commitment is to be maintained in the face of all the other demands on government resources,[35] especially as regional institutions are likely to be lacking in domestic political constituencies.[36]

This difficulty is most keenly felt in developing countries, and particularly in small island States, where the need for regional institutions is greatest, but the "spare" capacity to support them is least readily available. Apart from reliance on regional programs of UN agencies, which is not an answer to the need for "independent" regional institutions, the usual solution has been to seek development assistance funding to support regional efforts. However, this option has its dangers as well.[37] Over-reliance on donor support for regional institutions opens up the possibility of pressure, whether implicit or explicit, to avoid policies and programs which challenge the interests of funders.[38] At the very least, it is likely that the need to satisfy the priorities of funding agencies will influence the general direction of activities, possibly in ways which would not have been the first choice of member States.[39]

Apart from the possible warping of regional priorities to suit the availability of funding, there are more fundamental structural impediments to the use of development assistance in the creation of regional ocean management regimes. First, development agencies tend to operate on the basis of relatively short-term, project-oriented funding cycles.[40] Core institutional support, while it does exist, is usually frowned upon, and there is a general tendency to want evidence of institutional sustainability within some defined time period. The difficulty with regional institutions in developing regions is that they do not have the independent revenue base which is possible at the national level, and they may be well down on the priority list for funding by governments faced with many demands, especially as such funding decisions will typically be made by someone other than the people most directly concerned with the regional institutions. Second, the state-centric nature of many funding agencies means that there will be a natural focus on the national capacity-building elements of regional programs which, while useful in themselves, may lead to neglect of the equally important function of regional regime creation. This tendency is exacerbated by a desire for immediately quantifiable results to satisfy evaluation requirements, in that regime-level benefits may be more amorphous and evident over longer time periods than are taken into account in project planning.[41]

Regional Cooperation and the Problem of Choice

If there is a fundamental point to be made from this brief consideration of the advantages and disadvantages of regional cooperation, it is that the development of cooperative approaches to ocean management at the regional level involves a number of important choices, choices which may not always be made on the basis of what would be "ideal", but rather in light of what is possible, and which should be made with the most complete information available. It is possible to suggest a number of questions which must be addressed in deciding whether and how to engage in cooperative management approaches at the regional level.

The decision to cooperate at a regional level on a particular issue area presupposes the identification of some potential benefit to be gained beyond what could be accomplished at the national or global levels. There may be few marine management issues for which such benefits cannot be identified, but if we assume limited resources available for these efforts, there should be a clear understanding of the *priority* assigned to the problem, the particular advantage sought by regional action and at least a preliminary assessment that the benefits justify the inevitable costs.[42]

The scope of membership and participation in regional arrangements and institutions is a significant question for resolution, and one which may need to be revisited from time to time as interests or levels of commitment change.[43] The notion of "membership" may also be variable across issues, as with the development of sub-regional arrangements or additional obligations which only attract some of the members of the broader grouping. As noted earlier, the scope of involvement of non-regional actors may be a particularly sensitive issue, especially where external access to regional resources is a concern.

The appropriate mode of cooperation is also a matter of choice. Johnston and VanderZwaag, in a study of cooperative management options for the Gulf of Thailand, noted at least 12 possible modes of cooperation, including: consultative mechanisms; task forces; cooperative research plans; establishment of coordinated management priorities; framework conventions; and creation of a permanent management commission.[44] The potential range of options is limited only by the creativity of the parties, and while it is not possible to consider all of the existing examples here (and indeed these will be brought forward in the regional studies in any event), two points should be noted. First, these different approaches can exist on a continuum, with incremental movements up the scale of regional integration being possible as confidence and experience grows. Second, the variety of modes of cooperation speaks to the need for explicit consideration of all likely options, no matter how minimalist, before regional cooperative measures are rejected as unrealistic.

When an institution or institutions form part of the cooperative approach adopted in a region, further questions arise. Is a new institution required, and is it realistic to believe that States will agree to its creation? If there are existing institutions covering the relevant region, can their functions be enhanced or adapted to assume the planned role? It is quite likely that this option will at the very least require consideration, especially in developing countries, in that the experience of recent years has seen a tendency to review and rationalize regional institutional arrangements, rather than to add new ones.[45] The decline in real levels of ODA adds to this problem, in that the new institutions will certainly not be cost-free to members, whether because they have to contribute directly or because development funding committed to the regional level will result in a decline on the bilateral front. Finally, the decision on any institutional option must involve careful consideration of how the new (or enhanced) agency will interact and possibly overlap with the functions of other regional institutions and arrangements.[46]

Beyond the general consideration of functions and objectives for regional cooperation referred to above, institutional development requires more explicit and detailed consideration as to which functions are appropriate, not only to the region, but to the particular institution. Even where the general mandate and objective for regional cooperation have been settled, it will most likely still be necessary to choose from among the possible management activities, those which are best suited to regional action, and which are within the capacity of the chosen institution or mechanism to achieve.[47] It is at this stage, as the magnitude of tasks and the likely costs take concrete shape, that reality is most likely to intrude on over-ambitious plans for regional cooperation. This is, moreover, a recurring process, as interests and issues change over time, and regional institutions in particular must be prepared to justify their continued involvement in any given sector or program.[48]

Closely related to the question of an appropriate mode of cooperation is the issue of extent of obligation or commitment that might be sought from participants in a regional regime. Is there the need and the basis for formal and binding commitments through international agreements, or is the issue area more appropriately addressed through some other form of document? Is there a requirement for any document at all, or is it more appropriate in the circumstances to exchange views or perhaps pursue informal functional contacts in the hope that increasing confidence will ultimately lead to more explicit commitments? The options are virtually unlimited, but the point is that resort to something other than a traditional binding agreement should not be considered a "failure", for what matters to management is what actually happens in practice, and that is not necessarily dependent on the presence of formal obligations.[49]

The problem of funding and other support for regional programs and institutions was referred to above, but it should be noted that this is an issue which should be addressed early in the process of regime development, and not left to be dealt with once commitments are in place. In addition, the potential impact of the funding option on the content and direction of a programme dictates that it should be considered at least in part as a substantive question, and not merely as the neutral means by which other objectives are met.

Regional Ocean Management Regimes: Research Questions

The preceding section outlines the types of practical choices facing decision-makers engaged in the development of ocean management regimes at the regional level, choices which should be made in light of their best assessments of the likely outcomes. In reviewing the experience of the five regions represented in this collection, what kinds of questions might be asked which could be expected to assist in such an assessment? Allowing for the limitations of comparative studies dealing with very different regions, there are some general issues which should be kept in mind.

First, what are the *conditions* that make possible the development of durable regional ocean management regimes? This fundamental question has been a continuing concern for theorists and practitioners,[50] and it is an extraordinarily difficult one to answer, given the *sui generis* nature of every regional experience and the virtual impossibility of showing direct causal links in the development of such complex systems. Nonetheless, it is an inquiry that must be undertaken, and which should at least be assisted by a comparative review of experience in a number of regions, even allowing for all the *caveats* about the unique nature of each case and the problem of causation. The list of possible contributing factors will certainly be added to in this book, but the following are some of the elements which have been raised as potentially determinative:[51]

- pre-existing habits of cooperation and institutional development, whether in the same sector or more generally, and possibly extending to the presence of relevant functioning institutions;
- national and regional leadership;
- clearly defined benefits to be gained through regional cooperation, which may be based on the presence of significant management challenges with clear regional dimensions;
- the need for capacity-building, whether at the national level or through regional sharing of management capabilities;
- the presence of external threats (e.g., DWFNs) which may consolidate the regional position, and which may require a united front for an effective response;
- intra-regional maritime disputes which threaten security generally, and which motivate a regime for conflict avoidance and/or dispute resolution;
- cultural and political homogeneity;

the existence of significant transnational networks of scientific or other communities which can provide both information on management issues,and the stimulus for action;
public awareness and concern with a given issue or range of issues; and levels of economic development and availability of funding sources.

A related but distinct question concerns the *effectiveness* of regimes once created. Based on experience in other regions (both positive and negative) what factors might be seen as contributing to the successful operation of regional regimes? This does, of course, involve the difficult preliminary question of how we define and assess success for fairly amorphous things like regimes, but it is possible to suggest some fundamental issues which might be pursued.

- Is it possible to determine the impact of regimes and, if so, how? What indicators might be used (e.g., national policy compliance, improved conservation, enhanced revenues, a reduced conflict)?
- How has "compliance" been defined in the regimes under examination?
- Are there particular modes of cooperation and institutional options which have a better chance of success?
- If, as has been suggested, no one mode is necessarily preferable, is it possible to suggest criteria by which the choice may be made in such a way as to increase effectiveness?

Further, are there particular types of issues, or even identifiable sectors, which are more amenable to regime development (beyond the core issue of urgency and possible benefits noted earlier)? For example, has regime development been more effective when restricted to single-sector issues, within which like-minded individuals are likely to have a higher degree of confidence in operating together, and for which a constituency can more readily be built?[52] Where multi-sectoral management is essential, has there been success in achieving it directly, or is it better to proceed through linked and overlapping sectoral regimes?

Part of the promise held out by regime proponents has been the potential contribution to conflict avoidance and dispute resolution. Has the experience in practice borne this out, or do regional regimes fade into the background as soon as national interests make a conflict real rather than potential? Are there steps that can be taken to enhance this element of regime development?

A critical issue for the future concerns how different regimes interact. This could include inter-regional and inter-sectoral connections, but the interaction between the regional and global levels is of particular interest. Twenty years ago the regional level was seen as a means of defining and enhancing the emerging global regimes. Has this happened in practice, and if so, to what effect? To what extent have global patterns been altered by regional developments, especially as new global arrangements and institutions have continued to emerge, often with regional groupings as important players in negotiations?

A final and perhaps slightly heretical question is whether we can "build" regimes at all in a conscious way. The possibility for deliberate planning of a regime seems greatest for single-sector issues with relatively well-defined parameters, but for more complex multi-purpose regimes we may wish to ask whether they were planned in their entirety, or just identified *ex post facto*? The answer to this question may assist in determining the usefulness of model or "ideal" regimes in a prescriptive sense.[53] The feasibility of planning and promoting regimes in a systematic way also has implications for the purported role of epistemic communities. Has the regional experience to date validated the predicted contribution of such groups to regime creation, or are we perhaps guilty of optimistically over-stating the role of academics and other non-governmental participants in this process?

NOTES

1. On this "perceptual" advantage, see D.M. Johnston and L.M. Enomoto, "Regional Approaches to the Protection and Preservation of the Marine Environment" *in* D. M. Johnston (ed.), *The Environmental Law of the Sea* (1981): 285.
2. UN Doc. A/Conf.62/122, Dec. 6, 1982, in force Nov. 16, 1994.
3. D.M. Johnston (ed.), *Regionalization of the Law of the Sea* (Cambridge, Mass.: Ballinger, 1978).
4. The concept has been extensively applied to international resource management, where the complexity of the instruments, institutions and actors made it particularly appropriate. See, e.g., Oran Young, *International Cooperation: Building Regimes for Natural Resources and the Environment* (Ithaca: Cornell Univ. Press, 1989). For similar reasons, the notion of regimes has been widely applied to the oceans; see, e.g., Peter Haas, "Prospects for Effective Marine Governance in the NW Pacific Region", *Marine Policy* 24 (2000): 341; see also Mark Valencia, Jon Van Dyke and Noel Ludwig, *Sharing the Resources of the South China Sea* (The Hague: Martinus Nijhoff, 1997): 199–222.
5. S.D. Krasner, "Structural Causes and Regime Consequences" *in* S.D. Krasner (ed.), *International Regimes* (Ithaca: Cornell Univ. Press, 1983): 2.
6. On the nature and importance of "soft law" instruments in environmental law see P.M. Dupuy, "Soft Law and the International Law of the Environment", *Michigan Journal of International Law* 12 (1991): 420.
7. Peter Haas, "Do Regimes Matter? Epistemic Communities and Mediterranean Pollution Control", *International Organization* 43,3 (1989): 384. As Haas notes, the term was brought into international relations from work done in the field of sociology of knowledge. This study of the Mediterranean considered the impact of like-minded scientists in developing the agenda and creating domestic support for international action on the environmental problems facing the region.
8. G. Downs, K, Danish and P. Barsoom, "The Transformational Model of International Regime Design: Triumph of Hope or Experience?, *Columbia Jourrnal of Transnational Law* 38,3 (2000): 467.
9. *Ibid.* It should be noted that a survey of environmental treaties carried out by Downs *et al.* cast doubt upon the supposed benefits of this approach, in part because of the equal or better success attributed to other strategies for alteration of state behavior, and because the empirical record was not promising. At the very least, they found that while the strategy could be "optimal in some contexts, there are others in which it will not yield all of the benefits that its advocates hope and still others where its application almost certainly will be counterproductive. The problem is that ... we do not know which context is which." *Ibid*: 508. On the issue of promoting convergence through the operation of regimes, see also Haas, *supra* n. 7: 377.
10. It is neither necessary nor possible here to recount the many efforts at regional marine cooperation which have taken place world-wide, many of which are the subject of the papers in this collection. Useful summaries, may, however, be found in the following sources: D.M. Johnston and D. VanderZwaag, "Toward the Management of the Gulf of Thailand: Charting The Course of Cooperation" *in* D.M. Johnston (ed.), *SEAPOL Integrated Studies of the Gulf of Thailand Vol.1* (Bangkok: SEAPOL, 1998): 96-113 (Mediterranean, Baltic, Arctic, Gulf of Maine); Valencia *et al*, *supra* n. 4: 150-153 (reference to UNEP Regional Seas, the Baltic, North Sea, Mediterranean); S.

Andresen, "The Environmental North Sea Regime: A Successful Regional Approach?" *in* E.M. Borgese, N. Ginsburg and J. Morgan (eds.), *Ocean Yearbook 8* (Chicago: University of Chicago Press, 1989); A. Chircop, "Participation in Marine Regionalism: An Appraisal In A Mediterranean Context" *in ibid*: 402. On a more prescriptive note, see, e.g., J.S. Warioba and E. Mrema, "Regional Cooperation: The Needs of the South" *in* E.M. Borgese, N. Ginsburg and J. Morgan (eds)., *Ocean Yearbook 10* (Chicago: University of Chicago Press, 1993): 90; P.M. Haas, "Prospects for Effective Marine Governance in the NW Pacific Region" *Marine Policy* 24 (2000): 341; B.M. Tsamenyi and K. Mfodwo, "South Pacific Island States and the New Regime of Fisheries: Issues of Law, Economy and Diplomacy" *in* J. Crawford and D. Rothwell (eds.), *The Law of the Sea in the Asian Pacific Region* (Dordrecht: Martinus Nijhoff, 1995): 121.

11. See L. Alexander, "Regionalism At Sea: Concept and Reality" *in* Johnston (ed.), *supra* n. 3: 10-12, for a summary of regional institutional arrangements existing prior to the *LOS 1982*. See also L. Kimball, "Part I: The UN Convention on the Law of the Sea: a Framework for Marine Conservation" *in* IUCN, *The Law of the Sea: Priorities and Responsibilities In Implementing the Convention* (Gland: IUCN, 1995), for a summary of global and regional arrangements post-*LOS 1982*.
12. For a review of this programme, see M. Jacobson, "The United Nations' Regional Seas Programme: How Does It Measure Up?" *Coastal Management* 23 (1995): 19.
13. See e.g., the activities listed in Alexander, *supra* n. 11: 10–12.
14. Alexander, *supra* n. 11: 3. The term transboundary is used here to include multiple zones and jurisdictions as well as the bilateral context.
15. For discussions of the status and practical issues surrounding the regime of international straits under the *LOS 1982*, see e.g.: J. Van Dyke, "Legal and Practical Problems Governing International Straits" *in* E.M. Borgese, N. Ginsburg and J. Morgan (eds.), *Ocean Yearbook 12* (Chicago: University of Chicago Press, 1996): 109; Tullio Scovazzi, "Management Regimes And Responsibility for International Straits With Special Reference to the Mediterranean Straits", *Marine Policy* 19 (1995): 137.
16. As noted by Lee Kimball, this concept dates from the 1970s and "has been promoted and refined as a means for ensuring that environmental factors affecting marine species and habitat are considered together with conservation measures, which themselves must take account of interactions among dependent and related species." Kimball identifies the *Convention on the Conservation of Antarctic Marine Living Resources* (CCAMLR), Canberra, 1980, as the first attempt to implement the concept in international law. Kimball, *supra* n. 11: 103.
17. See e.g., the initiatives surrounding the jurisdictional disputes in the South China Sea: I. Townsend-Gault, "Brokering Cooperation in the South China Sea" *in* L. Kriworken, M. Haward, D. VanderZwaag and B. Davis (eds.), *Oceans Law and Policy In The Post-UNCED Era: Australian and Canadian Perspectives"* (London: Kluwer, 1996): 313; Ted McDorman, "The South China Seas Islands Dispute in the 1990s: A New Multilateral Process and Continuing Friction", *International Journal of Marine and Coastal Law* 8 (1993): 263.
18. As, for example, with the following instruments: *Rio Declaration on Environment and Development*, June 13, 1992, UN Doc. A/Conf.151/5/Rev.1 [hereinafter *Rio Declaration*]; *Agenda 21: Programme of Action for Sustainable Development*, UN Doc. A/Conf.151/26/Rev.1, June 14, 1992 [hereinafter *Agenda 21*].
19. As is arguably the case with large portions of the *LOS 1982*, as well as the more recent UNCED – related treaties: *United Nations Convention on Biological Diversity*, June 5, 1992, in force Dec. 29, 1993 [hereinafter *Biological Diversity Convention*]; *United Nations Framework Convention on Climate Change*, May 5, 1992, in force March 21, 1994 [hereinafter *Climate Change Convention*]. On the weakening of substantive obligations as a result of consensus negotiations, see: Mary Ellen O'Connell, "Enforcing the New International Law of the Environment" *German Yearbook of International Law* 35 (1992): 301; John T. Lang, "Biological Conservation and Biological Diversity" *in* G. Sjostedt (ed.), *International Environmental Negotiation* (1993): 185; David Ardia, "Does The Emperor Have No Clothes? Enforcement of International Laws Protecting The Marine Environment" *Michigan Journal of International Law* 19,2 (1998): 497.
20. The failure of the global level to achieve both consensus and binding obligations on contentious issues

has nonetheless led to a certain amount of disillusionment among environmentalists who expected rather more. This attitude was concisely expressed in the context of forests by an observer who referred to the non-binding *Forest Principles* as the "regressive development of international law". A. Szekely, "The Legal Protection of the World's Forests After Rio '92" *in* L. Campiglio et al (ed.), *The Environment After Rio: International Law and Economics* (1994): 68.

21. And possibly, though not necessarily, more closely shared political and legal cultures.
22. For early considerations of the relationship between the Convention (as it was then being negotiated) and regional cooperation, see: L.D.M. Nelson, "The Functions of Regionalism in the Emerging Law of the Sea as Reflected in the ICNT" *in* Johnston, *supra* n. 3: 17; and E. Miles, "On The Utility of Regional Arrangements in the New Ocean Regime", *in ibid*: 255.
23. The term "enclosed or semi-enclosed seas" is defined in Art. 121 as "a gulf, basin or sea surrounded by two or more States and connected to another sea or the ocean by a narrow outlet or consisting entirely or primarily of the territorial seas and exclusive economic zones of two or more coastal States."
24. See e.g.: Art. 118, which mentions regional and sub-regional organizations as one approach to the management of the living resources of the high seas; Art. 63, dealing with straddling stocks; Art. 66(5), on the role of regional organizations in management of anadromous stocks.
25. A/Conf.164/37, Sept. 8, 1995; adopted Aug. 4, 1995, opened for signature Dec. 4, 1995, not in force.
26. *Straddling Stocks Agreement*, Article 8(3). See also Arts. 8(4) and 17. For a general discussion of the relationship of this agreement to the regionally-based dispute between Canada and the EU/Spain, see P. Saunders, "And Now That The War Is Over: Looking Back At The Canada-European Union Fisheries Confrontation Of 1995", *Canadian Law Newsletter* 31 (1996): 15.
27. UNEP (OCA)/LBA/IG.2/7, Dec. 5, 1995. See, e.g., Chapters 3 and 5.
28. The open-ended nature of the definitional criteria has been noted by L. Alexander, *Marine Regionalism In The Southeast Asian Seas East-West Center*, (1982): 3:

    > The distinguishing criteria for the region may be physical in nature, or may represent demographic, economic, political or other elements. In fact no limits exist to the categories that may be used in defining a region, so long as the criteria selected are valid ones and the area in which the criteria occur can be differentiated geographically from other areas

29. There are numerous examples of states which can be considered members of multiple overlapping "regions", including: EU members which are also Mediterranean states; Caribbean states which participate in complementary fisheries programs (with different memberships) through the Organization of Eastern Caribbean States (OECS) and CARICOM; South Pacific island states which have maintained functionally-distinct fisheries programs through SPC and FFA, again with different memberships. Once institutions are created or engaged for the purpose of cooperation, however, a certain amount of rigidity is probably inevitable if only out of convenience.
30. This problem is widespread, but nowhere more acute than in small island states such as those of the Caribbean, Southwest Indian Ocean and South Pacific, which often combine extensive zones with small populations and inadequate management resources.
31. See, e.g., the discussion of the relationship between the Canadian development assistance programme and the South Pacific regional institutions which functioned as executing agencies for many projects. R. Herr and P. Saunders, "The Management of South Pacific Marine Resources: Regional Institutions and Canadian Development Assistance" *in* Kriwoken *et al, supra* n. 17: 274–278.
32. The most notable success being the experience of the Forum Fisheries Agency (FFA) of the South Pacific in dealing with DWFN tuna fleets through cooperative programmes and ultimately through the mulitlateral treaty arrangement with the United States. For a summary of FFA activities in dealing with DWFNs in the 1980s and up to the early 1990s, see R. Herr (ed.), *The Forum Fisheries Agency:Achievements Challenges and Prospects* (Suva: ISP, 1990). See also J. Swan, "Highly Migratory Species: The South Pacific Forum Fisheries Agency" *in* A. Soons (ed.), *Implementation of the Law of the Sea Convention Through International Institutions* (Honolulu: LSI, 1990): 318.
33. For a review of the role played by regional actors in the drift-net fishing dispute in the South Pacific, which had both regional and global aspects to the negotiations, see A. Wright and D. Doulman, "Drift-Net Fishing In The South Pacific: From Controversy to Management", *Marine Policy* 15 (1991): 303.

34. See e.g., M. Valencia, "Southeast Asian Seas: National Marine Interests, Transnational Issues, and Marine Regionalism" *in* Chia Lin Sien and Colin MacAndrews (eds.), *Southeast Asian Seas: Frontiers for Development* (Singapore: McGraw Hill, 1981): 354, with reference to the mischaracterization of general bilateral issues as regional in nature.
35. See e.g., Miles, *supra* n. 22: 261, on this issue and on the related problem of how "divisible" benefits are perceived to be distributed among participants.
36. The promotion of a compatible domestic political agenda is, however, a key role that might be played by epistemic communities (as noted earlier)and by NGOs in general. See Haas, *supra* n. 7: 397–399.
37. For an early discussion of the more general problems facing developing countries in the creation of regional responses, including the specific issue of asymmetries in power and influence within regions, see B. Johnson, "Regionalism and the Law of the Sea: New Aspects of Dominance and Dependency", in Johnston, *supra* n. 3: 103.
38. Thus an important consideration for the FFA in the South Pacific was to develop funding sources for surveillance and enforcement programmes which did not rely on donors from countries with direct interests in the region.
39. The early programs of CCOP/SOPAC (later SOPAC – the South Pacific Applied Geoscience Commission) were heavily concentrated on deep sea research of questionable relevance to many regional states. This was arguably related more to the scientific interests of the major donors of the time than to regional priorities. Later, with the growing independence of the organization, the focus shifted markedly to nearshore and coastal issues. On the origins of SOPAC, see Herr and Saunders, *supra* n. 31 at 261.
40. See the discussion *ibid*: 280.
41. *Ibid*: 273, 279-80.
42. See the comment at *supra* n. 35. See also Valencia *et al*, *supra* n. 4: 151–152.
43. An example of such flexibility is found in the Mediterranean, where the Barcelona Convention of 1995 was amended to allow for extension beyond the waters of the Mediterranean, and protocols can define geographical scope independently. See Johnston and VanderZwaag, *supra* n. 10: 101; see also A. Vallega, "Geographcial Coverage and Effectiveness of the UNEP Convention on the Mediterranean", *Ocean and Coastal Mangement* 31 (1996): 199, cited therein.
44. Johnston and VanderZwaag, *supra* n. 10 at 118–122. Other options included non-binding statements of principles, action plans and codes of conduct, and the development of specific dispute settlement procedures. For other examples of flexible approaches to the development of cooperatives measures, see Valencia *et al*, *supra* n. 4 at 111–122, on a range of options for the South China Sea, including, *inter alia*, informal workshops, an eminent persons group, "preventive" diplomacy, various confidence building measures and joint research activities.
45. In the case of WIOTO, it was decided to establish a stand-alone organization, motivated partly by the lack of any appropriate agency covering an area congruent with the fisheries management challenges at issue. The OECS Fisheries Unit was set up within an existing organization, but as a relatively independent operation.
46. The review should extend to independent regional organizations as well as regional progams of global agencies, which may have been carrying out some of the target functions in the past. See e.g., the review of this issue in: Western Indian Ocean Tuna Organization (WIOTO), *Background Paper: Development of A Recommendation To Bring WIOTO Into Operation On An Interim Basis* (Dec. 1993) This can become a highly politicized and sensitive process, given the natural tendency for institutions to resist incursions on what is perceived to be their own turf.
47. So, for example, despite a clear statement of mandate in its constitutive Convention, the Western Indian Ocean Tuna Organisation (WIOTO) still went through an extensive process of definition and selection of central functions, including the identification of six sectoral priorities, including harmonization of fisheries policies, relations with DWFNs and surveillance and enforcement, as well as over 20 groups of tasks within those sectors. See *ibid.*
48. For an example of such an exercise, see Herr, *supra* n.32. This collection of papers was the product of a ten year review and re-consideration of the agency's mandate and priority functions.

49. The willingness to take seriously the practical contributions of non-binding instruments is closely linked to the reconceptulaization of "compliance", away from traditional notions of treaty observance and towards a better understanding of how states participate in and, generally, abide by the norms and rules of more complex international regimes. On the issue of compliance, see, e.g., B. Kingsbury, "The Concept of Compliance as a Function of Competing Conceptions of International Law" *in* T. Schoenbaum, J. Nakagawa and L. Reif (eds.), *Trilateral Perspectives On International Legal Issues* (New York: Transnational, 1998): 9 see also N. Okuwaki, "The Changing Nature of International Obligations: Can Voluntary Compliance Overcome the Difficulties in the Present Nation-State System", *in ibid*: 61.
50. See e.g.: Miles, *supra* n. 22: 260-264; Valencia *et al*, *supra* n. 4: 151–153.
51. Haas, *supra* n. 4: 343 cites five key factors in the creation of environmental regimes: "national leadership, international institutions, transnational scientific networks, NGOs, and public concern".
52. Valencia *et al*, *supra* n. 4: 153.
53. See i*bid*: 199–219 for an example of the use of an "ideal" regime design for the South China Sea. With respect to the more ambitious "transformational" approach to regime formation, the question is whether there has been any significant evidence in practice that this is a productive course to follow.

Hanns J. Buchholz

THE BALTIC SEA: LESSONS LEARNED

INTRODUCTION

Before the Second World War, most people thought that the oceans were infinite and inexhaustible regarding fish resources and in their capability to absorb waste. Therefore a tendency appeared in Europe to locate polluting industries on the seacoast so that dangerous emissions could flow into the open ocean. Similarly incinerator platforms were built in the North Sea to dispose of poisonous waste. Sometimes these dangerous materials were simply dumped into the sea.

In fisheries, the catching techniques improved tremendously and many stocks were overfished. In the 1960s, scholars, then groups of environmentally engaged people, and eventually politicians became aware of the seriousness of the situations. They began to realize that the oceans were not endless and inexhaustible but that marine resources were limited and the oceans. capability to absorb solid waste, waste water and other environmentally dangerous materials was finite as well.

A benchmark in this awakening was the first United Nations Conference On The Human Environment, on which the decision was taken in 1969. Regarding the oceans it became clear that due to the high transport ability of seawater, only regional co-operation on environmenal protection could lead to solutions. Not only could actions by an individual state not solve the problem, the actions of an individual state could easily undermine all the positive actions of other coastal states in a specific region. Thus governments began to establish intergovernmental regional arrangements for fisheries management and marine environmental protection. These efforts were first taken in the marginal seas, because here the damage and threat was greatest. The results of these regional efforts have been very different, due to differing circumstances. Indeed, despite many obstacles, regional co-operation for the protection of the Baltic Sea has been quite successful.

Mark J. Valencia (ed.), Maritime Regime Building, 17–25.

Characteristics of the Baltic

The Baltic Sea – like The Sea of Japan (East Sea), the Yellow Sea or the East China Sea – is a semi-enclosed marginal sea. The connection between the Baltic Sea and the North Sea and consequently to the Atlantic Ocean is very narrow and consists of the Great Belt, the Little Belt and the Sound. The Baltic Sea covers 415,000 square kilometers or roughly 120,000 square nautical miles. Its south-north axis is about 1300 kilometers or roughly 700 nautical miles, and its west-east axis is about 1000 kilometers or 540 nautical miles. Its small size requires bilateral or even multilateral negotiations and agreements for the delimitation of maritime boundaries.

The Baltic Sea has a maximum depth of 459 meters (1500 feet), but its average depth is 50 meters (170 feet) in the western Baltic Sea, 250-300 meters (800 to 1000 feet) in the central part and in the Gulf of Bothnia, and about 120 meters (350 feet) in the Gulf of Finland. The Baltic Sea is important to the fisheries of the littoral countries. The total catch in 1995 was 755,000 tonnes of mainly cod, herring, sprats and salmon. The Baltic Sea is also severely endangered by pollution, mainly from land. In 1998 the pollutant input amounted to 1 million tons of nitrogen, 14,000 tons of zinc, 2500 tons of lead, 120 tons of cadmium as well as considerable amounts of copper, nickel, chrome and mercury.

The Political Environment

The political environment of the formation of the Baltic regime was that prior to about 1990, i.e., before the disintegration of the Soviet Union, before the re-unification of Germany, and before Sweden and Finland became members of the European Union. The Baltic littoral countries then included the following:

- Denmark: capitalist, member of European Union, member of NATO; physically controls the entrance to the Baltic Sea; recognized sovereign over the connection between the Baltic and North Seas.[1]
- West Germany: capitalist; member of European Union; member of NATO; economically strong but politically cautious because of its responsibilities for the Second World War.
- Sweden: neutral, but distinctly western-oriented.
- Finland: neutral, but politically cautious in relation to the Soviet Union.
- Soviet Union: communist; superpower.
- Poland: communist; but increasing its political distance from the Soviet Union.
- German Democratic Republic: communist; strongly influenced by the Soviet Union.

At first glance there are strong similarities between the pre-1990 Baltic Sea area and the Sea of Japan (East Sea) in Northeast Asia. Both are semi-closed marginal seas surrounded by states of differing political orientation. They both have divided countries (Germany and Korea) that contain boundaries between two political systems, two military blocks, and extreme differences in economic prosperity. Both seas have relatively narrow entrances which are easy to control. Both seas are important fishing grounds but seemingly limited potential for mineral resources. Both seas are environmentally endangered. And both seas are so small that the delimitation of maritime boundaries demands bi-lateral or multi-lateral negotiations and agreements.

However, on closer examination there are important differences between the Baltic and Northeast Asia. The first difference is the natural environment. The Baltic Sea is much more closed than the Sea of Japan, and this has important consequences for regional co-operation.[2] There is very limited water exchange between the Baltic Sea and the North Sea/ North Atlantic. Theoretically it takes about 23 years to renew the entire water volume of the Baltic Sea. In reality some Baltic water will never be renewed because there are several ridges in the Baltic Sea bottom which hinder the flow of the deep water, e.g. "Darss Rib" with a maximum depth of 18 meters. The very narrow and shallow entrances to the Baltic Sea, together with the shallow bottom ridges constrain the passage of vessels, particularly large navy vessels. This was a major concern of the Soviet Union. Consequently, Baltic seawater is low in salt and oxygen. The input of nutrients from land results in high productivity in the surface waters and the organic matter consumes oxygen as it decomposes. Thus large parts of the Baltic Sea bottom water has very little if any biological life and the boundary between the oxygen-rich surface water and the deoxygenated deeper water is rising. The low rate of water exchange results in extreme differences of salinity in the Baltic Sea. The westernmost part has a salinity of 15 to 35‰, the central part 10‰, and the eastern Baltic Sea, less than 5‰ Consequently some species like herring and cod cannot survive in the eastern part of the Baltic thus limiting the distribution of some fish populations. Additionally the stocks are endangered by the pollution pouring off the land. They have also been under stress since the 1970s from increased fishing activities of the Baltic Sea states after they proclaimed their Fishery Zones in the 1970s.

Differences in Political Environment Between the Baltic Region and Northeast Asia

The Soviet Union was a strong superpower, but this power was limited in the Baltic Sea, partly due to the constraints on navigation. The Soviet Union treated the Baltic Sea countries with caution because it did not want its connection to the open sea to be constrained. It was also limited by considerations regarding the highly respected neutral Kingdom of Sweden. Indeed the presence of two neutral states of good international reputation is a significant political difference between the Baltic area and Northeast Asia. The Soviet Union desired a neutral Baltic Sea, an "Ocean of Peace," in order to keep the extraregional NATO states like the United States out of the Sea. Sweden and Finland supported this position and thus played an important role in facilitating the strategic interest of the Soviet Union.

Another difference is the situation of the then German Democratic Republic (GDR). The GDR was a communist country, but it was never as isolated as North Korea. The reasons are that the two Germanies never fought a war, and the GDR more or less always followed the political advice of the Soviet Union. Further, in the

Baltic Sea area there is no state like the People's Republic of China which – quite different from the European states – does not make rapid decisions on political matters.

In most of the Baltic Sea littoral states, there was open discussion of political, economic and environmental themes. This discussion was also allowed in communist Poland because Poland wanted to show its relative independence from the Soviet Union. And even in Estonia, Latvia and Lithuania, discussion of environmental issues was carried on by informal groups which in reality were seeking to change the political system or to gain independence from the Soviet Union.

Another significant difference between the Baltic Sea area and Northeast Asia is the historic legacy of regional co-operation in the Baltic Sea area. In medieval times the Hanseatic League, an association of trading cities, was a significant institution. During the 12th to 15th centuries, the Baltic Sea was essentially an "inland lake" of northern Europe. At this time land travel was extremely difficult and the marginal seas and the navigable rivers were the most important means of trade. It was only after the 16th century that the main trade routes in Europe turned from the Baltic to the North Sea and then to the Atlantic because of the rising importance of America.

Moreover, the "International Council for the Exploration of the Sea" (ICES) was founded in 1902, due to the initiative of the Scandinavian states. After World War I new states appeared – Finland, Estonia, Latvia, Lithuania and Poland – and these states became members of ICES, the last being Poland in 1925. Interrupted by World War II, ICES began its work again in 1945. One of the consequences of the existence of ICES is that very early on, the Baltic Sea became one of the best understood seas in the world. In the 1960s ICES thoroughly analyzed the environmental situation of the Baltic Sea, and in 1969/70, revealed that it was heavily polluted and "dying." This caught the attention of both the public and political leaders.[3] Another significant example of cooperation on the Baltic Sea area is the "Nordic Council," founded in 1952 for cooperation among the governments and the parliaments of Denmark, Finland, Sweden, Norway and Iceland. And there are several other relevant associations in the Baltic Sea area such as the Conference of Baltic Oceanographers and the Baltic Marine Biologists. Even in the old Soviet Union there was an ocean-oriented community of scientists who participated in many regional organizations. But this interest did not go beyond science to policy. This has now changed dramatically.

In 1947 the "Economic Commission for Europe" (ECE) was created as a sub-organisation of the United Nations Economic and Security Council. The main task was the promotion of trade in Europe. But in 1967, "Environmental Protection" became the fourth priority of the ECE Work Program with the aim of diminishing environmental constraints on trade. One of the solutions was cooperation in environmental technology.[4] The Baltic Sea area thus has a history of a wide variety of networking and co-operation which was a pre-condition for a co-operative maritime regime.

The Creation of Maritime Regimes In The Baltic Sea Area

Maritime Boundary Delimitation

Despite of the varied interests of seven states (plus the political entity of the Åland Islands), the maritime boundary delimitation process has been relatively smooth.[5] Both Poland and the GDR were part of the communist block, but their relations were sensitive because the GDR did not want to reduce its own territorial sea area for the benefit of Poland. The approach to the Polish ports of Swinoujscie and Szczecin, including an important roadsted needed by Poland, demanded some sacrifice by the GDR.[6] At the end of the 1980s a solution was reached due to two reasons. The GDR had a burden of guilt from World War II and thus was inclined to compromise in Poland's favor. In the second half of the 1980s, Poland became more detached from the Soviet Union, and the GDR feared that if communism collapsed in Poland there would be no chance to reach an agreement regarding their maritime boundary. Thus in 1989 the GDR and Poland signed a treaty.

The maritime boundary between the Soviet Union and Finland did not create real difficulties, because Finland was very careful in its relations with the Soviet Union. And the boundaries between the three Scandinavian states in the Baltic Sea were resolved without great difficulties because of the traditionally close transboundary cooperation of these Nordic countries. The maritime boundary between the two Germanies was not resolved but with the re-unification of Germany this problem disappeared.

In general the delimitation of the maritime zones in the Baltic Sea was not difficult because of political interdependencies. Moreover, there were no significant petroleum or mineral resources known in the Baltic Sea. Also it is easier for a state to agree on new boundaries than on other bi- or multi-lateral regimes because fixed boundaries stabilize the sovereignty of a state.

Maritime Environment Regimes

Agreements regarding cooperation to protect the maritime environment were more difficult but were achieved.[7] However, before 1968, there was not much cooperation regarding the Baltic Sea and its environment. The Cold War hindered cooperation across the block boundaries and to make matters worse, in 1968 the Warsaw Pact members marched into Czechoslovakia. Also, there was little awareness regarding the environmental problems of oceans. The UN Conference on the Human Environment took place in 1972, in Stockholm, with 1200 participants from 113 states and 400 international organizations. However, the GDR could not participate because it was not a member of the United Nations. Although the motto of the Conference was "one world"[8] all the other communist countries, except Romania, did not send delegates. Among many other matters, the Stockholm Conference asked all countries to take steps to combat the pollution of the oceans.[9] Sweden also invited all littoral countries of the Baltic Sea to a conference at Visby in Gotland. This conference elaborated a "Treaty for the Control and Prevention of Oil

Pollution". Unfortunately, the final draft was not ratified because West Germany would not agree to East Germany becoming a party to this treaty.

At this point the creation of the "Organization for Security and Cooperation in Europe" (OSCE) had an important effect on the region. The idea for this organization goes back to the 1950s when the Soviet Union asked for a collective security system in Europe. The Soviet Union intended to abolish NATO and to keep the United States out of Europe. After several unsuccessful attempts, the Warsaw Pact made a new proposal for an OSCE in October 1969 and at the end of 1969 the NATO-states accepted it.[10]

This OSCE Conference was the main political impetus for successful cooperation of the states around the Baltic Sea. Although environmental policy was not the main task of the OSCE Conference, it assumed a strategic importance among more politically important matters. The themes of the OSCE Conference were distributed into "three baskets":

- Basket 1: (inter alia) peaceful co-existence and security issues;
- Basket 2: (inter alia) economy, environment and science and technology; and
- Basket 3: (inter alia) human rights.

The positions of the participants – especially those of East and West – were far apart regarding the questions of security (Basket 1) and of human rights (Basket 3). Thus it seemed much easier to achieve positive results regarding Basket 2 issues. Since all participating states were interested in results, the relatively innocuous issues of environment were taken up, even if only general agreements could be reached. These discussions produced a political "umbrella" under which the more concrete conventions could grow.

In 1973 Finland organized a conference in Helsinki of experts from all Baltic Sea states. They developed the text of a draft "Convention On The Protection Of The Maritime Environment Of The Baltic Sea Area," the Helsinki Convention.[11] The Helsinki Convention came into force in 1980 with the deposit of the last ratification by the Federal Republic of Germany. The reason for this long ratification process was that in 1976 the European Community took responsibility for all matters concerning water. Therefore individual states of the EC/EU had to determine the proper diplomatic procedures for ratification. The European community developed a true sense of "community" which subsumed political and cultural differences. However, the real work began in 1975 with an Interim Helsinki Commission which became responsible for pollution from land; pollution from ships; waste dumping at sea; environmental regulations for submarine mining; principles for the control of pollution; and regulations for nature protection and biodiversity. However, all decisions are only recommendations. These rules and regulations were amended several times. In 1992 the area of responsibility was extended to include the inland waters landward of the base lines of the Baltic Sea states.[12] Although pollution input to the Baltic has certainly decreased since the Convention came into force, this may be due more to a decline in polluting industries sited at the coast rather than treaties and regulations.

A Polish initiative to manage fisheries has been fairly successful. Based on the alarming results of specific ICES research projects of ICES in 1969/70, the Polish government invited the other six Baltic Sea states to participate in a conference which eventually drafted a "Convention on Fishing and Conservation of the Living Resources in the Baltic Sea and the Belts." This Gdansk Convention was signed on 13 September 1973. Although the initial goal of this convention was economic, the theme was by necessity very much environment-oriented. Following Article 5 of the Gdansk Convention, the International Baltic Sea Fishery Commission (IBSFC) was established. This Commission provides recommendations for the Total Allowable Catch (TAC) and related matters. The European Community replaced Denmark and Germany in 1984, and Sweden and Finland in 1995 as a member of IBSFC. Other members include Poland, Lithuania, Latvia, Estonia and Russia.

Summary Of The Favorable Conditions For Maritime Regime Building In The Baltic Sea Area

- Awareness of the growing pollution and decreasing fish catch.
- Public pressure for action.
- Awareness that Baltic Sea states were both "originators" and "sufferers" of pollution and that a solution could only be found in collective agreement and action.
- The beginning of the end of the Cold War providing an opportunity for intergovernmental cooperation between "West" and "East."
- The long tradition of Baltic cooperation which positively influenced the demand for common action.
- The involvement of neutral states with high international reputation.
- The vulnerability of the Soviet Union in the Baltic Sea area because of geography.
- The Soviet Union's restraint of the German Democratic Republic.
- The interest of the Soviet Union in a collective security system which led to the OSCE.
- The strategic role of environmental matters in the OSCE negotiations.

Lessons Learned

Europeans tend to create very complicated, highly structured bureaucratic law-based regimes. Thus it is not possible to transfer structures and methods of the Baltic Sea area to Northeast Asia because the factors and situations are different and the actions and reactions of the respective governments will be different.

However, the Baltic Sea experience did generate some general lessons that may be applicable in Northeast Asia. For example, it seems possible to co-operate on "low" politics even when "high" politics are tense. Second, knowledge must be sufficient and made available to the public.[13] Third, activism by groups of knowledgeable people can formulate strategies and apply pressure that becomes politically effective. This was not very important at the beginning of the Baltic regime but became more of an impetus as the regime evolved. Now environmentalists are part of the government in Denmark, Germany, and Sweden. Cooperative networks on a subnational level are most helpful such as associations of cities like city-partnerships; conferences of tourist organizations; workshops of fishery associations; and scientific conferences. Finally, mixing of the political tasks of bi-lateral or multi-lateral conferences with seemingly "weaker" matters of environmental protection can facilitate a breakthrough in regime creation.

Research is needed in the following areas:

- Delineation of existing networks and cooperation, or at least preliminary contacts and whether networks already exist which could become the basis for a maritime regime.
- The significance of Agenda 21-groups and of other NGOs.
- Development of a legal framework combining the knowledge of public servants and the practical experience of ordinary citizens.
- Design of new systems of maritime governance for highly complex space-use-systems, i.e., comprehensive sea-use planning which integrates environmental protection and development.

NOTES

1. A.G. Oude Elferink, "The Regime of Passage of Ships through the Danish Straits." *NILOS Papers* (1999) Online no. 3. *http://www.law.uu.nl/english/isep/framenilos.asp*
2. H.J. Buchholz, "Baltic Sea and North Sea: Two Marginal Seas Under Stress/Il Mare Baltico e il Mare Del Nord: Due Mari Marginali Sotto Tensione" *in* H.D. Smith and A. Vallega (eds.), *The Management of Semi-enclosed Seas: The Emerging Global Pattern and the Liguarian Case* (Genoa, 1990): 41–70; F.B. Pedersen, "The Sensitivity of the Baltic Sea to Natural and Man-made Impact" *in* J.C.J. Nihoul (ed.), *Hydrodynamics of Semi-enclosed Seas* (Amsterdam, 1982): 385–399; A. Voipio, *The Baltic Sea* (Amsterdam, 1981).
3. H.J. Buchholz 1990, *supra* n.2.
4. J. Bruch, *Umweltkooperation im Ostseeraum*. (Doctoral dissertation, Mainz University, 1999).
5. G. Jaenicke, "Cooperation in the Baltic Sea Area" *in* Proceedings of the Law of the Sea Institute (Honolulu: Law of the Sea Institute, 1980): 493–513; U. Jensch, Nordsee-Seerecht und Umweltschutz *in Außepolitik* (1987): 81–98; U. Jensch, Die Ostsee als Wirtschafts-und Lebensraum. Wirtschaft, Umweltschutz, Seerecht *in Jahrbuch des Internationalen Rechts* (1990): 349–382; R. Wolfrum. "Kie Küstenmeergrenzen der Bundesrepublik Deutschland in Nordund Ostsee" *in Archiv des Völkerrechts* (1986): 247–272.
6. H.J. Buchholz, "Sea Use and Environmental Security as Factors in the Delimitation of German-Polish Maritime Boundaries" *in International Boundaries and Environmental Security. Frameworks for Regional Cooperation* (London, 1997): 139–146.
7. R. Dieter, *Das Umweltregime der Ostsee. Völker-und europarechtliche Aspekte* (Bonn, 1993); Industrie-und Handelskammer Lübeck, "Umweltschutz für die Ostsee, Lübeck", (Ostsee-Jahrbuch 1992/93); H.J. Koch and R. Lagoni (eds.), *Meeresumweltschutz für Nord-und Ostsee. Zum Zusammenspiel von Völkerrecht und nationalem Umweltrecht* (Baden-Baden, 1996); M. List, *Umweltschutz in zwei Meeren. Vergleich der internationalen Zusammenarbeit zum Schutz der Meeresumwelt in Nord-und Ostsee* (Munich, 1991).
8. W. Skupnik, "Konferenz der Vereinten Nationen über die menschliche Umwelt" *in Vereinte Nationen* 4 (1972): 111–113.
9. A. Vallega, "Towards the Post-Modern Ocean" *in European Review*, 8 (2000): 201–213.
10. W.V. Bredow, Der KSZE-Prozeß. Von der Zähmung bis zur Auflösung des Ost-West-Konfliktes (Darmstadt, 1992).
11. J. Koschwitz, "Das Übereinkommen über den Schutz der Meeresumwelt des Ostseegebietes" *in*

Jahrbuch des Internationalen Rechts, (1975): 223-240; T. Palmowski, "An der Schwelle der zweiten Dekade des Helsinki-Abkommens. Der polnische Beitrag zum Schutz der Ostsee" *in* K. Tudyka (ed.), *Umweltpolitik in Ost-und Westeuropa* (Opladen, 1975): 143–154.

12. P. Ehlers, "Meeresschutz – eine eigenständige Staatsaufgabe" *in Natur und Recht* (1983): 129–30; P. Ehlers, "Zehn Jahre Helsinki-Übereinkommen. Ein Bericht" *in Natur und Recht* 4 (1984): 138–143; P. Ehlers, "Das neue Helsinki-Übereinkommen. Ein weitere Schritt zum Schutz der Ostsee" *in Natur and Recht* 5 (1993): 202–212; P. Ehlers, "Jahre Helsinki-Übereinkommen: Kritische Ztwischenbilanz" *in* I. Lozan, et al. (eds.), *Warnsignale aus der Ostsee* (Berlin, 1996): 291–296.
13. Vallega, 2000, *supra* n. 9.

Aldo Chircop

THE MEDITERRANEAN: LESSONS LEARNED

INTRODUCTION

Mediterranean regional environmental cooperation is frequently cited as a model regional seas program. In 1975, when the Mediterranean Action Plan (MAP Phase I) was adopted, it was the United Nations Environment Programme (UNEP)'s first Regional Seas Programme.[1] Since then, regional cooperation has evolved into a complex regime addressing broader environment and development issues, with a growing emphasis on integrated coastal area management. The regime is currently mid-way in a MAP Phase II covering the period 1996 to 2005.[2] Consistent with the spirit of Rio, MAP's current focus has evolved from the narrow confines of pollution issues to broader environment and development concerns.

There are differing, if not contrasting views on what MAP has achieved since its inception. It is arguable that today the Mediterranean is not necessarily any cleaner than it was in 1975, although the current environmental cooperation was unthinkable two decades ago. Even the Action Plan for the Protection of the Marine Environment and the Sustainable Development of the Coastal Areas of the Mediterranean (MAP Phase II), the region's new action plan, grants that "it is difficult to assess progress achieved ..."[3] And yet, the way Mediterranean environmental cooperation was engineered and re-engineered over time has been used as inspiration for sister regional sea programs and other regional intergovernmental programs. What maintains global interest in the "Mediterranean model" is the dynamic character of a regime that maintains problem-oriented communication in a region characterized by high diversity and co-existence of conflict and cooperation. It has evolved significantly in response to changing political relations in a post-Cold War era, a better and growing understanding of environmental problems, demands for inclusive processes and realization of the utility of employing common standard-setting and integrated management approaches. Today this regime involves 21 states and numerous intergovernmental and non-governmental organizations which are active to different extents.[4]

The purpose of this chapter is to provide an analytical overview of how and why

Mark J. Valencia (ed.), Maritime Regime Building, 27–49.

the MAP was established, how it has evolved over a quarter century and what new directions it might or should take. Analysis is offered on the functioning and/or success or otherwise of the various elements in the regime in view of identifying opportunities, constraints and lessons learned which could be of interest to other regions aspiring to build similar regimes. The principal focus will be on the macro MAP system, rather than on individual MAP components or the larger subject of regional cooperation in marine affairs that would include, among others, the General Fisheries Commission for the Mediterranean (formerly General Fisheries Council for the Mediterranean, GFCM), the International Commission for the Scientific Exploration of the Mediterranean Sea (ICSEM) and the Euro-Mediterranean dialogue. However, elements of these will be referred to where appropriate in the discussion on regional environmental regime-building.

The principal tenet advanced in this chapter is that cooperation may thrive in the context of diversity and conflict, if the issues and fora around and in which expectations converge are widened, rather than narrowed. This may sound paradoxical, but is evident. Mediterranean cooperation has thrived through pluralism and complexity.

The Mediterranean Context

Couched between Africa, Asia and Europe, the Mediterranean Sea is a body of water stretching from the Strait of Gibraltar to the Levantine coast. Its only outlets to other seas are to the Atlantic through the Strait of Gibraltar, the Black Sea (itself a semi-enclosed sea) through the Turkish Straits (Bosporus and Dardanelles and the interconnecting Sea of Marmara), and the Red Sea through the Suez Canal. It is a semi-enclosed water body with several semi-enclosed sub-seas.[5] This geography has shaped the physical properties and ecosystem of the region. Much of the coastal Mediterranean, in particular the eastern and southern littorals, tends to be arid with active desertification processes. There is high evaporation in the eastern basin which is not fully compensated by precipitation in and freshwater runoff from the region's watersheds. As a result, old Mediterranean water becomes highly saline in the eastern basin, causing it to "sink", migrate to the western basin and eventually exit through the Gibraltar sill. The cycle starts again with surficial fresh seawater flowing from the Atlantic into the western and eastern basins. Of all three outlets, only the Strait of Gibraltar is of major hydrological significance. It takes an average of 80 years to recycle Mediterranean waters.

The coastal and marine areas of the Mediterranean are habitats to numerous rich ecosystems in varying conditions of health. Historic and modern human intervention in inland and coastal areas has had long-term impacts. For instance, the opening of the Suez Canal in the 19th century led to migration of numerous species from the Indo-Pacific region into the eastern and central Mediterranean, displacing many local species and introducing new fisheries. The construction of the Aswan Dam and reduction of the Nile flow in the second half of the 20th century affected entire fisheries in the Levantine region. Nonetheless, the region still supports significant commercial and artisanal fisheries. The catch amounts to 2 to 3% of the world total and is insufficient to meet the nutritional demands of the peoples of the region and of tourism.

The region has a total population exceeding 350 million, and receives more than 100 million tourists a year. This heavy human presence is not evenly distributed, with the largest concentrations being in European coastal cities and major urban centres of the Levantine and North Africa. There are several megacities which, in some cases, account for 25 to 33% of the total population of the country. Athens and Cairo are two examples. The pressure on infrastructures is considerable. The supply of energy, fresh water and food tax coastal and marine resources. In particular, the coastal area is being urbanized in many areas, frequently at the expense of habitats of fragile species, agricultural land and forested areas.

The management challenges are many at both domestic and international levels. The narrow geographical limits place additional pressures on maritime neighborliness. The level of environmental, economic and social interdependence is necessarily high. For these reasons, although the international law of the sea has conferred obvious benefits to coastal States, it has also exacerbated the challenge of managing maritime neighborliness in the context of expansive claims to national maritime space at the expense of neighbors. As a result, there are relatively few maritime boundaries that are fully resolved. Moreover, the emphasis on national marine spatial allocation has also biased regime-building in favour of the region's coastal States, irrespective of ecosystems and the transboundary nature of management problems.

The definition of national maritime territory and cooperative environmental management have also had to take place in a situation of high linguistic, cultural, social, economic, and ultimately, political diversity. Capabilities, in terms of power, wealth, knowledge and skill in the region are distributed very unevenly. These differences are not theoretical; indeed they are real and pose far-reaching management implications. There are historic burdens and a colonial heritage within living memory. There are ongoing political, and sometimes military conflicts between neighbors. As a major market, the European Community and its Mediterranean states heavily influence economic and social development in Levantine and North African States. Wealthy States have tended to attract labor migrants in large numbers, sometimes leading to social and political tension in host countries. Uneven scientific and technological capabilities continue to affect regime implementation. This complex and highly interconnected backdrop has heavily influenced regime-building.

Conception And Germination

In this context, the question of how this regime was initiated is intriguing. The foundation blocks were not laid by States or the UNEP as the initiator of the Regional Seas Programme. Rather they were the work of international organizations, scientific institutions, non-governmental organizations, and individuals concerned about the state of the Mediterranean Sea in the 1960s and early 1970s. Thus, Maltese Ambassador Pardo's famous speech to the First Committee of the

General Assembly in 1967, which sensitized the international community to ocean problems and led to the Third United Nations Conference on the Law of the Sea, made no comment on Mediterranean pollution problems.[6] The initial concerns may have romanticized the Mediterranean and grossly misunderstood the actual state of its ecosystem, but as well-intentioned concerns they served to mobilize knowledge-building processes, the elites in the public, and ultimately decision makers. The initial concerns were over the impact of pollution on marine resources. The pollution concern was driven to a great extent by perceptions of the extent and impact of vessel-source pollution in the wake of the Torrey Canyon accident.

The now almost forgotten Cooperative Investigations of the Mediterranean (CIM), a scientific program of the Intergovernmental Oceanographic Commission (IOC), was adopted in 1967 as a result of an earlier enquiry by this organization on the desirability of cooperative research. The programme involved joint execution by the GFCM, as an FAO regional fishery body, and ICSEM. Although this program did not achieve much of what it had intended, it focussed on marine pollution. It served to highlight two important challenges: first, mobilizing regional cooperation was not going to be a simple affair because there were uneven capabilities and non-Mediterranean participation posed political difficulties; second, given the insufficient scientific understanding of the Mediterranean, a scientific component to build a knowledge base would be essential. The subject of participation in Mediterranean regime-building would become a continuing concern and cooperation in science would eventually materialize in MEDPOL as part of MAP Phase I.

GFCM played an early important role in regional discourse. GFCM responded to conferences in Rome in 1968 and Milan in 1969 to address marine pollution problems in the region with the establishment of an Ad Hoc Working Party on Marine Pollution in the Mediterranean and its Effects on Living Resources and Fishing. Because of its mandate, GFCM intended to cover the Mediterranean *and* the Black Sea. It was recognised that there was little information on contamination of coastal areas and high seas from land-based sources. There was little response from Black Sea States so that the intended comprehensive study could not cover this sea and therefore had to exclude it.[7] The information gathered on the Mediterranean was useful for a subsequent FAO-sponsored Technical Conference on Marine Pollution and its Effects on Living Resources and Fishing in Rome in 1970. This meeting, together with an Intergovernmental Working Group on Marine Pollution meeting in London in 1971 urged close international cooperation in combatting Mediterranean marine pollution.

The Eleventh Session of GFCM in 1972 was cognizant of the role it should play and went further by recommending that the FAO Director-General "consult with Member Governments of GFCM with a view to convening a meeting of these governments for discussions aimed at preparing a Convention to control the discharge into the sea of pollutants that would affect its living resources, bearing in mind the economic effects of such control."[8] This led to a Consultation on the Protection of Living Resources and Fisheries from Pollution in the Mediterranean in 1973 and 1974.

In the meantime, there were other pre-UNEP initiatives in the early 1970s which were inspired by the United Nations Conference on the Human Environment in 1972. There was an influential study on environmental degradation and pollution commenced in 1972 by the Organization for Economic Cooperation and Development (OECD). This study, which highlighted the limitations of sectoral ocean development, lack of comprehensive scientific information and the need for international cooperation brought together major polluting States France, Italy and Spain with Greece and former Yugoslavia, two States which played important brokering roles in facilitating regional cooperation with developing States.[9] This was followed in 1974 by a conference of the Inter-Parliamentary Union supported by the newly formed UNEP, and FAO, UNESCO, WHO and IMO (IMCO at the time). The meeting proposed a holistic approach that would reconcile environment and development, anticipating in a number of ways the Bruntland Report and the thinking in Rio, and in the process, recommended ratification of the IMO conventions, development of regional and subregional environmental protection agreements, establishment of a scientific research fund in liaison with UNEP, information and training, and the convening of an intergovernmental conference.[10]

The GFCM's Twelfth Session took place in Varna in 1974 almost at the same time as UNEP's Governing Council gave the green light for a regional program for the protection of the Mediterranean marine environment. What was originally a request to UNEP to support FAO efforts on this initiative turned into second thoughts on an FAO-led initiative. The resumed FAO Consultation eventually felt that a multi-sectoral approach was going to be needed to address the protection of the marine environment and all its uses, rather than an instrument limited to living resource protection. At this stage there was broad regional support for a regional regime, but the question as to who would take the initiative was re-opened as a result of UNEP's establishment. Egypt, Israel, Lebanon, Libya, Malta, Tunisia, Turkey and former Yugoslavia saw FAO, in cooperation with other organizations, as the institution to be entrusted with the preparation of a draft framework convention. France, Italy, Monaco and Spain were in favor of UNEP as an organization qualified to ensure coordination of Mediterranean initiatives.[11]

In the autumn of 1974, UNEP assumed leadership after much of the groundwork was prepared by FAO. It convened an important International Workshop on Marine Pollution in the Mediterranean in Monaco in 1974, with co-sponsorship from the initiators, GFCM, ICSEM and IOC. UNEP would eventually lead the development of the regime with multi-agency support. By the end of that year, a task force of scientists, experts, international organizations and government representatives met to draft an action plan for the forthcoming intergovernmental conference to be convened in early 1975. UNEP was well-placed to do this. It was the "Stockholm child" and much hope was placed on its role as a program with a holistic function not limited by narrow sectoral interests. It had resources which were still uncommitted, whereas FAO's resources were stretched and Mediterranean states were unwilling to commit any new funding. It was a new institution with no political commitments and with a responsibility to play a coordinating and stimulating role (later referred to as "catalytic") in a UN system having overlapping functions among its constituent parts.

MAP In Operation

Policy and Management Direction

From its establishment and well into the 1990s, the MAP Phase I was primarily directed at combating marine pollution of the Mediterranean Sea proper. The first Intergovernmental Meeting on the Protection of the Mediterranean was convened in Barcelona by the Executive Director of UNEP, and 16 out of the 18 Mediterranean States at the time attended together with several international organizations for the sole purpose of adopting the Mediterranean Action Plan.

The six-page MAP Phase I was a simple document with four resolutions having action items addressing the socio-economic dimension (integrated planning), scientific research and monitoring, legal framework and institutional and financial aspects.[12] These were seen as necessarily interdependent elements in addressing the marine pollution problem of the region. The broader concern with marine environmental protection in a wider-than-pollution sense would emerge gradually. The socio-economic component inevitably led to the need for the regime to re-orient towards environment and development. This would happen during Phase I and before the United Nations Conference on Environment and Development (UNCED) in Rio in 1992. UNCED would serve to consolidate the re-direction and propel change in the formal legal and institutional framework.

In reality, the simplicity of MAP Phase I belied the complexity and difficulties to be encountered in its mobilization and implementation. A rolling planning process was started which would see gradual and often bumpy implementation, but which enabled regional States to assume incremental responsibilities as the regime grew. The 29-page MAP Phase II document was drafted at the outset in 1995 as a complex series of responses to a *problematique*. The MAP Phase II confirmed the shift "from a sectoral approach to pollution control to integrated coastal zone planning and management as the key tool through which solutions are being sought."[13] There is now greater recognition of regional and national shortcomings in the inappropriate management of coastal areas, including inadequate planning and management, inadequate legislation and its enforcement, weak institutional structures and inadequate human resources, lack of adequate financial resources and ultimately lack of clear political commitments.[14] This assessment does reflect in part what Phase I failed to achieve on these grounds, although it can be said that MAP Phase I had fewer and less specific objectives. MAP Phase II leaves no doubt as to the explicit multi-sectoral commitment that would require integrated approaches. Its principal components are advanced with sub-components as follows: (1) sustainable development in the Mediterranean (integrating environment and development; conservation of nature, landscape and sites; assessment, prevention and elimination of marine pollution; information and participation); (2) strengthening of the legal framework; (3) institutional and financial arrangements.

The central sustainable development component speaks to issues of agriculture, industry, energy, tourism, transport, urban management, natural resource management, water resources, soil, living marine resources, forest and plant coverage and the needs of integrated coastal area management. This broad integrated approach is further reflected in the Barcelona Resolution and Priority Fields of Activities, where spatial references are displaced by functional concerns underlying commitments.[15]

At the same time as the areas of activities are already significantly more comprehensive than in MAP Phase 1, the objectives are even more far-reaching. Social and economic development and land-use policies are targeted. Pollution receives a secondary place to the need to reconcile environment and development. It is accompanied by nature and culture conservation concerns. The final purpose of the plan is to "contribute to improvement of the quality of life."[16] The MAP Phase II, Amended Barcelona Convention and related instruments are guided by the Rio principles of sustainable development.

Principles guiding MAP Phase II implementation are also set out. Clearly, Mediterranean States "are responsible for the implementation of the Barcelona Convention, its Protocols and MAP" and consequently regime tasks are decided at regular meetings of State parties. Other interesting and useful developments are a commitment by State parties to involve local, provincial and regional authorities in activity formulation and implementation, and the active involvement of NGOs. Capacity-building is to be pursued at regional, provincial and local levels.[17] MAP Phase II is attempting to engage the deeper reaches of national decision-making and implementation, and those civil society groups that tend to participate in these processes. In this regard, State parties now have a duty to give their publics an opportunity to participate in decision-making processes relevant to the regime.[18]

The nascent participation of civil society groups is promoting greater transparency at regional and national levels. The statements of NGO participants at the last biennial meeting of contracting parties in 1999 are telling in this regard.[19] Considerable criticism has been forthcoming from participating NGOs, as well as some State parties, at the slow national action in fulfilling regime responsibilities. The duty to report on national implementation action and compliance monitoring now reflected in the Amended Barcelona Convention has forced State parties to provide lengthier and somewhat more thoughtful reports on progress over the biennium.[20]

Geography of the Regime

The geography of the regime might not appear to have changed much since 1975. But in reality, there has been important change. When the Barcelona Convention for the Protection of the Mediterranean Sea against Pollution (Unamended Barcelona Convention) was adopted in 1976, Mediterranean States were clear on its regional and national application. On the regional side, the Mediterranean Sea Area was defined as "the maritime waters of the Mediterranean Sea proper, including its gulfs and seas bounded to the west by the meridian passing through Cape Spartel lighthouse, at the entrance of the Straits of Gibraltar, and to the east by the southern limits of the straits of the Dardanelles between Mehmetcik and Kumkale lighthouses."[21] This provision ensured that the Black Sea would not be covered, even though it was included in the management area of GFCM for fisheries purposes. From a national application perspective, "Except as may be otherwise provided in any protocol to this Convention the Mediterranean Sea Area shall not include internal waters of the Contracting Parties."[22] State parties were defensive of their territoriality, but were conscious at the same time of the inevitable application to areas of sovereignty. They thus conceded application to the territorial sea and at the same time tried to maintain control over the regime's gradual application to other areas of sovereignty for specific protocols. They did consent in 1976 to the application of the Protocol Concerning Cooperation in Combating Pollution of the Mediterranean Sea by Oil and other Harmful Substances in Cases of Emergency (Emergency Protocol) to activities in coastal waters, ports and estuaries.[23]

This limited application was an initial constraining factor. At the Intergovernmental Meeting on the Blue Plan in 1977, it was decided that

> ... the "Blue Plan" should cover the entire Mediterranean Basin, namely the Mediterranean Sea, as defined in the Barcelona Convention, and the adjacent coastal zones. The coastal zones might vary in territorial depth from one area to another, depending on the problems to be considered and the nature of the disciplines involved. The Mediterranean region is recognized in this respect as constituting not a single ecosystem but, rather, a complex of ecosystems of varying dimensions, displaying certain comparable ecological and climatic features, but differing from one another according to latitude and altitude. In all cases, the states concerned are the 18 coastal states of the Mediterranean region.[24]

While on the one hand this re-affirmed regime application exclusively to coastal States (in itself a potential constraint in relation to interregional issues), it highlighted the need to move from rigid spatial applications. Thus, for the purposes of the Protocol for the Protection of the Mediterranean Sea against Pollution from Land-Based Sources (Unamended LBS Protocol) in 1980, Mediterranean States consented to an application that included internal waters to the freshwater limit in the case of watercourses and saltwater marshes communicating with the sea.[25] But these were discharge areas, and the Protocol addressed direct discharges from land-based areas in the territories of State parties and indirect discharges "through rivers, canals or other watercourses, including underground watercourses, or through run-off," and also through atmospheric sources in a subsequent additional annex.[26] The Protocol Concerning Mediterranean Specially Protected Areas (Unamended SPA Protocol) in 1982 also had a similar freshwater limit, but provided for States to individually increase protected areas to include wetlands and coastal areas.[27]

In effect, initial concerns with the extent of spatial application of the regime would be superseded by recognition of the needs of a functional application which would still leave State parties some control over areas of application. The report on the first phase of the Blue Plan rightly noted that to "limit the Blue Plan to the Mediterranean Sea and to its immediate shores would be to limit the concept of 'environment' much too narrowly."[28] Regime management areas needed to be defined in response to problems, and not the other way around. Thus regime participants would restrict the definition of area exclusively with reference to membership, and what that membership was willing to concede on a domestic level. Therefore the concept of sovereignty in classical international law was indeed a constraint!

In the 1990s, the regime, and its participants, went through a process of maturity that enabled a more flexible approach. As shown earlier, the MAP Phase II document is functionally, not spatially-oriented. On the legal front in the now re-renamed Convention for the Protection of the Marine Environment and the Coastal Region of the Mediterranean 1995 (Amended Barcelona Convention), a hint of a withdrawal symptom remained in the retention of the original definition from the Straits of Gibraltar to the Dardanelles, but at the same time there was provision for a discretionary extension to coastal areas as defined by individual State parties in their own territories and the possible extension of the coverage area in specific protocols.[29]

There was change in the re-named Protocol Concerning Specially Protected Areas and Biological Diversity in the Mediterranean (Amended SPA Protocol) that extended the geographical coverage to include the seabed and subsoil, including those in internal waters up to the freshwater limit, and terrestrial coastal areas designated by individual parties.[30] A provision similar in intent was adopted in the Protocol for the Protection of the Mediterranean Sea against Pollution Resulting from Exploration and Exploitation of the Continental Shelf and the Seabed and Subsoil (Seabed Protocol).[31] Not unexpectedly, the major change occurred in the re-named Protocol for the Protection of the Mediterranean Sea Against Pollution from Land-Based Sources and Activities (Amended LBS Protocol) through the inclusion of the hydrological basin of the Mediterranean Sea Area. Hydrologic basin is defined as the "entire watershed area within the territories of the Contracting Parties" draining into the Mediterranean.[32] The Protocol's application was further clarified in relation to direct and indirect discharges in territories of State parties, including atmospheric and fixed offshore structures within national jurisdiction. More interestingly, State parties committed to inviting "states that are not parties to the protocol and have in their territories parts of the hydrologic basin of the Mediterranean Area to cooperate in the implementation of the Protocol."[33] This latter provision seems to include non-Mediterranean states, so long as they share the region's hydrologic basin, such as the Nile riparian States. This was a necessary extension of the management region for parties to be in a position to address marine pollution from land-based sources consistent with the Global Programme of Action for the Protection of the Marine Environment from Land-Based Activities (GPA).[34] Perhaps it also constituted sober realisation of the limits of regionalism!

Legal Framework

The original central legal instrument of the regime, together with the first two protocols, was adopted in 1976. The Barcelona Convention for the Protection of the Mediterranean Sea against Pollution (Unamended Barcelona Convention) noted that "existing international conventions on the subject do not cover, in spite of the progress achieved, all aspects and sources of marine pollution and do not entirely meet the special requirements of the Mediterranean Area."[35] At the time, the Third United Nations Conference on the Law of the Sea had only completed two years of a

10-year comprehensive negotiation marathon. There were few pollution conventions and those in existence were mostly concerned with shipping matters in the event of accidents. The 1973 Convention on the Prevention of Pollution from Ships was not yet in force. Conservation instruments, such as the constitutive agreements of GFCM and the International Commission for the Conservation of Atlantic Tunas (which applied to the Mediterranean) concerned living resources and were the realm of other arrangements. Hence the Barcelona Convention was conceived as a framework instrument, necessarily general in nature, and focussing on legal responsibilities in preventing and combating marine pollution. It also highlighted, again in a generic manner, specific pollution sources: dumping from ships and aircraft, vessel-sources, seabed activities and land-based sources. It provided a discretionary responsibility for parties to enter into bilateral or multilateral agreements on a regional or subregional basis. More preemptory, they were to take appropriate joint individual or joint measures and to cooperate in treaty-making. They would eventually do this through six subsequent protocols. They were also to cooperate in pollution emergencies, pollution monitoring, scientific research, exchange of information, technical and other assistance, procedures for treaty compliance, and the development of a liability and compensation regime. Parties were expected to do this individually and cooperatively, including cooperation with international organizations when appropriate.

Much of the proposed legal development was indeed accomplished, at least in a formal legal sense during Phase I. Protocols on dumping and emergencies were adopted in 1976, land-based sources of pollution in 1980, and on specially protected areas in 1982. Most of these instruments would be amended at the beginning of Phase II and a new Protocol on the Prevention of Pollution of the Mediterranean Sea by Transboundary Movements of Hazardous Wastes and their Disposal (Hazardous Wastes Protocol) would also be adopted in 1996.[36] However, the Seabed Protocol would be adopted only in 1994. Moreover, the process of ratification and accession to these instruments would prove to be a lengthy process. Even today, at the time of writing, the Amended Barcelona Convention (amended in 1995) and the protocols on land-based sources of pollution (amended in 1996), dumping (amended in 1995), and the new protocols on seabed activities and hazardous wastes are not yet in force as a result of insufficient numbers of ratifications. The Amended SPA Protocol entered into force in December 1999. An attempt to negotiate a generic liability and compensation regime, as mandated by the Barcelona Convention has been discontinued. There is a clear dragging of heels, suggesting the existence of a significant gap between the political will to enter into these agreements and the bureaucratic readiness to implement them in the face of the costs implied. This is an obvious weakness of the regime. The legal instruments themselves are laudable in the extent and manner of articulating responsibilities for problem management.

Socio-economic Dimension

If the notion of integrated planning proposed in Stockholm in 1972 is still ambiguous and taxing today, it was even more so in the 1970s. This was, and still is, the most ambitious component of MAP. The principal purpose was to promote integrated planning both at individual national and cooperative regional levels. It was recognized then that this component had a delicate and vital character and required both immediate and long-term activities. Two lines of activities would eventually emerge, Blue Plan and Priority Actions Programme (PAP), and both would take considerable time and effort to mobilize following initial discussion in 1977.

Commencing in 1980, the Blue Plan consisted of, at least initially, a comprehensive study that would be useful for reconciling development and environment. Given trends over the previous 20 to 30 years, regional projections for development and environmental degradation were made until the year 2025. But even with such a late start, it was soon close to a crisis because national participation was lacking, ironically even though funding was in place. Perhaps the novelty of integration and perceptions of encroachment on national sovereignty were major concerns. Following successful termination of the first two phases of the Blue Plan, the third phase, which was supposed to consist of preparation of national development and environment scenarios and the establishment of national inter-agency teams, never quite functioned as originally planned. One comment from a prominent UNEP official was as follows:

> . . . unfortunately, the Blue Plan was essentially developing in isolation from the other components of the Action Plan, the analysis of the trends in human activities went far beyond the original concept and the environmental considerations moved from the focus of the Blue Plan to its margins. Furthermore, the available tangible products of the Blue Plan (publications, reports, etc.) are far less impressive than its projected image and do not allow either for and objective evaluation of the results obtained until now or for an assessment of the potential usefulness of these results in the context of the Action Plan.[37]

In reality it was an imaginative, if not also ambitious project. This type of cooperative study today would be considered essential in the context of long-term impact of climate change and sea-level rise. Integrated coastal area management, which is a widespread management practice today, poses precisely the same challenge of issue integration and of inter-agency cooperation in national planning. In hindsight, despite criticisms levied at the Blue Plan, it anticipated at an early stage the need to reconcile development and environment at a regional level, and that this could only be accomplished by understanding the processes of how various pieces of a complex jigsaw puzzle with active variables interact over a long time frame. Clearly, regional coastal states constituted an intricate part of that puzzle and would need to address sustainable development internally, before they could envision this process at a regional level. The initiation of the Mediterranean Environment and Development Observatory, as a follow-up to the Blue Plan, and the establishment of the Mediterranean Commission for Sustainable Development (MCSD) would simply confirm the need for this approach.

In contrast, the PAP would prove to be much less ambitious, and therefore less controversial, although it would suffer from an initial ill-definition of activities and financial shortages. Originally, it consisted of projects with an action-oriented and more immediate character, including training and technical assistance aimed at sound environmental management practices in support of sustainable socio-economic development. The objective was the establishment of "a permanent network of continuous cooperation among the Mediterranean coastal states concerning practical actions for progressive, inter-sectoral planning."[38] Commencing with projects on issues such as soil protection, water resource management, fisheries and aquaculture management, human settlements, tourism and clean energy sources, it gradually and logically moved in the direction of integrated coastal area management. The Coastal Area Management Programme (CAMP) was initiated to look at these and other issues from an integrated planning perspective and in the context of specific local pilot sites. To date it has seven completed projects, two are in process and four are being prepared, all in all covering 13 of the region's 21 countries. As such, CAMP is not a program for regional integrated coastal area management, and although such a role might still be premature, it suggests a potential future direction for MAP.

Neither the Blue Plan nor the PAP were considered sufficient in addressing the technological gap that existed in the region. Initiatives outside MAP Phase 1 would be undertaken, with mixed success. The initiative to establish a Mediterranean Centre for Research and Development in Marine Industrial Technology (MEDITECH) was originally inspired by an NGO, co-opted by Malta and supported by the United Nations Industrial Development Organization (UNIDO).[39] This initiative fell victim to the competition of several states wishing to host the center. This type of competition among Mediterranean states would also be in evidence in the establishment and location of Regional Activity Centres (RACs) in the regime's institutional framework. Somewhat more successful was the initiative for the Centre for Environment and Development for the Arab Region and Europe (CEDARE), which led to its establishment in Egypt.[40] However, this institution was something less than what was foreseen for MEDITECH and operates outside the MAP regional regime.

A Ministerial Conference on Sustainable Development in the Mediterranean convened by Tunisia in 1994 gave regime-building another interesting twist. Regional ministers of the environment adopted a regional version of Agenda 21, Agenda MED 21.[41] Despite the weak drafting of this holistic instrument, it served to further open the discourse on environment and development in the region and lead to a widened MAP Phase II. It also provided the seminal idea for the establishment of the MCSD within MAP Phase II.[42]

Research and Monitoring

The research and monitoring component is easily the most successful in Phase I perhaps as a result of the emergence and functioning of what Haas called "epistemic communities."[43] The Coordinated Pollution and Monitoring Programme in the Mediterranean (MEDPOL) was conceptualized before MAP and MEDPOL Phase I and eventually consisted of the scientific programme proposed by the International Workshop on Marine Pollution in Monaco in 1974. This had also capitalized on earlier efforts discussed above. So in a sense the regime's epistemic communities were in formation before the formal initiation of the regime.

To date, MEDPOL has operated in three phases: Phase I (1975–1980) focussed on research, followed by a prolonged Phase II (1981-1995) concentrating on monitoring. The general objective of MEDPOL Phase I was to establish a knowledge base built on a series of cooperative baseline studies, which would provide governments with the scientific and technical capability to implement MAP, especially for environmental assessment and management, informed policy-making and development and implementation of agreements.[44] In its first phase this programme involved over 200 groups from 83 institutions in 16 countries in a common knowledge-building effort.[45] Difficulties were encountered as a result of the large number of unequal participants, but these were overcome. The projects were well-conceived and executed under strong and decentralized scientific leadership. A number of UN bodies involved were assigned leadership roles or assigned goal-specific responsibilities, but within the overall coordination of the UNEP Regional Coordinating Unit.[46]

MEDPOL Phase II emphasized monitoring using baselines established in Phase I.[47] It provided scientific information for implementation and further development of the legal framework, indicators and evaluation of pollution prevention measures, information useful for national and international management decisions, and periodic assessment of the state of pollution. The structure and participation developed in Phase I was maintained in large part. MEDPOL Phase III (1996-2005) continues monitoring, but at the same time assists with the scientific and technical aspects of implementing legal responsibilities and management measures in the combating of pollution from land-based activities and sources, and in assisting the CAMP.[48]

The success of MEDPOL can be measured in various ways. In addition to the research, there were capacity-building activities, inter-calibration of analytical techniques and provision of common maintenance services to enable scientists to maintain data quality control and comparability. A periodic state of the Mediterranean report has been produced. Ultimately, the success of this initiative may have boiled down to three major contributions: a better understanding of the state of environmental problems to enable problem-oriented responses; the establishment of a region-wide scientific network; and scientific support for regime implementation and further development. The counterpart weakness is not related as much to the international cooperation in place, but rather to the slow development and implementation of subsequent national monitoring programs. As late as 1987, not all national programs were in place or fully operational.[49] This may have been due to the large scientific and technological gap to be expected between the developed north and the developing south, providing a useful insight on how regional inequities may impact on regime efficiency and effectiveness.

Pollution from Land-based Sources and Activities

The manner in which the regime has attempted to address pollution from land-based sources and activities deserves additional attention. In the Barcelona Resolution on the Environment and Sustainable Development in the Mediterranean Basin 1995, Mediterranean States agreed "to the reduction by the year 2005 of discharges and emissions which could reach the marine environment, of substances which are toxic, persistent and liable to bioaccumulate, in particular the organohalogens, to levels that are not harmful to man or nature, with a view to their gradual elimination ..."[50] These policy decisions are backed by both the legal framework and management instruments of the regime.

The general obligation in the Amended Barcelona Convention is stated as a requirement to "take all appropriate measures to prevent, abate, combat and to the fullest extent possible eliminate pollution of the Mediterranean Sea Area and to draw up and implement plans for the reduction and phasing out of substances that are toxic, persistent and liable to bioaccumulate ..."[51] These measures are to apply to point and non-point sources that are marine, coastal and watershed based, and whether the pathway is terrestrial or atmospheric. The Amended LBS Protocol further elaborates on these measures, highlighting the key principles of precaution, polluter pays, EIA based on Best Available Technology (BAT) and Best Environmental Practice (BEP), including the utilization of clean production technologies.

A central obligation of State parties is to develop and implement a regulatory, inspection and sanction system.[52] This individual obligation is accompanied by a complementary collective obligation in support of the adoption of common guidelines, standards and criteria, especially with reference to the following:

- length, depth and position of pipelines for coastal outfalls, taking into account, in particular, the methods for pretreatment of effluents;
- special requirements for effluents necessitating separate treatment;
- quality of sea-water used for specific purposes that is necessary for the protection of human health, living resources and ecosystems;
- control and progressive replacement of products, installations and industrial and other processes causing significant pollution of the marine environment; and
- specific requirements concerning the quantities of the substances discharged ... their concentration in effluents and methods of discharging them.[53]

Despite the commonality of such standards, a differentiated application is foreseen, especially with reference to local physical and ecological conditions, existing pollution, absorptive capacity of the marine environment and developmental conditions and concerns of parties.[54] The latter differentiated application, although motivated by equitable considerations, may be viewed as a potential weakness in the system. After all, all coastal States contribute to marine pollution, although to different extents. This potential weakness should be also viewed in the context of the two-thirds majority among State parties that is required for the adoption of action plans, programs and measures, including timetables.[55] The majority decision is not weighted, meaning that less politically-committed states have significant power in the setting of standards and timelines.

The general obligation to phase out toxic, persistent and bioaccumulating substances is further defined in Annex I. This annex provides a framework for the parties in addressing specified sectors of activity (30 in all), the characteristics of such substances in the environment and categories of substances. Clearly, priorities are to be established by the parties and based on the "relative importance of their impact on public health, the environment and socio-economic and cultural conditions."[56] Annex II further defines the elements to be considered in the authorization of waste discharge in the form of characteristics and composition of substances, characteristics of discharge constituents with respect to their harmfulness, characteristics of discharge site and receiving environment, availability of waste technologies, and potential impairment of marine ecosystems and sea-water uses. Each one of these elements is accompanied by a set of criteria. Two additional annexes to the Amended LBS Protocol address conditions of application to pollution transported through the atmosphere and criteria for the definition of BAT and BEP.

The Priority Fields of Activities address toxic pollutants and sewage, directly or indirectly, through several of the proposed sectoral or thematic strategies, including integrated water management, waste management, agriculture, industry and energy, transport, urban development and environment and assessment, prevention and control of marine pollution.[57] Waste management, in particular, singles out urban waste management, the installation of controlled discharges or treatment plants in coastal towns of over 100,000 inhabitants (including appropriate outfalls and treatment plants for towns with more than 10,000 inhabitants),[58] treatment plants for hazardous wastes and the banning of toxic waste exports to non-OECD Mediterranean states. Fertilizer and pesticide use is specifically addressed in the agriculture component. The urban development component promotes policies for energy control, non-polluting transport and waste management.

On a more concrete level, since 1985 common measures have been adopted periodically in the context of LBS Protocol implementation. These have included quality criteria for bathing waters (1985), quality criteria for mercury (1985), measures to prevent mercury pollution (1987), quality criteria for shellfish (1987), pollution from used lubricating oils (1989), pollution by cadmium and cadmium compounds (1989), pollution from organotin compounds (1989), pollution by organohalogen compounds (1989), pollution from organophosphorus compounds (1991), pollution from synthetic materials (1991), pollution from pathogenic micro-organisms (1991) and pollution by carcinogenic, teratogenic and mutagenic substances (1993).[59] As a result of the Barcelona Resolution intent to reduce toxic pollutants, in particular organohalogens, further common measures were agreed to in 1996.

More recently in 1997, Mediterranean states moved closer to concerted action with the adoption of the Strategic Action Programme (SAP) for regional and national activities to eliminate pollution from land-based sources and activities. As described by the current MEDPOL coordinator, "the key issues of concern include sewage, urban solid waste, air pollution from mobile sources, and the release of toxic, persistent, and bioaccumulative substances into the marine environment. Also addressed are the release of harmful concentrations of nutrients into the marine environment, activities that contribute to the destruction of the coastline and coastal habitats, and the storage, transportation, and disposal of radioactive and hazardous waste."[60] SAP serves as a strategic plan for the systematic implementation of the LBS Protocol over a 25-year period. Accordingly, a schedule of targets is set. Its success will depend to a significant extent on the adoption of national programs consistent with the regional commitment.

Institutional and Financial Aspects

The institutional framework was bound to be complex in a region where inter-bureaucratic penetration tends to be low and where international relations tend to use diplomatic channels. This may be less true of European Community States, but for other States in the region, perceptions of sovereignty and control tend to guide external relations. Accordingly, the decision-making processes of the regime are built around the biennial, extraordinary, intergovernmental review and plenipotentiary meetings of contracting parties to the Barcelona Convention. Regular policy-making and budgetary decisions are the responsibility of biennial meetings. In between sessions, the Bureau, which consists of elected state parties, guides and advises the UNEP Regional Coordinating Unit (RCU), the secretariat of the regime.

Following lengthy coordination by UNEP from Geneva, the RCU was established in Athens in 1982. This was important for regional ownership of the regime, and also to gradually elicit more regional commitment, and encourage less financial dependence on UNEP. The RCU is the critical pivot point of the regime, providing leadership to regime parties and key meetings, coordinating and pulling together, and often coaxing, the various regime activities. Although the RCU is led by UNEP, it has worked closely with UN and other institutions responsible for specific aspects of the regime. In fact, the WHO and FAO have had personnel residing and undertaking regime activities at the RCU itself.

The geographical location of regime institutions provides an interesting insight on how compromises were worked out, political visibility assuaged and regime benefits spread among lobbying states. Greece was a good candidate for the RCU because of its political middle ground policy between north and south. A series of Regional Activity Centres (RACs) would be spread around the region. The first was the Regional Oil Combating Centre (later changed to Regional Environmental Emergency Response Centre, REMPEC), established in Malta in 1976. This was followed by the Blue Plan Regional Activity Centre in Sophia Antipolis, France, and the Priority Actions Programme Regional Activity Centre in Split, formerly Yugoslavia, now Croatia, in 1977. The first center outside a European country was the Specially Protected Areas Regional Activity Centre, established in Tunis, Tunisia, in 1981. This trend to spread around regional centers in a politically equitable manner would not last long. In 1987 the secretariat for 100 Mediterranean Historic Sites would again be in France, Marseilles this time, perhaps reflecting the heavy French contribution to the regime. The Environment Remote Sensing

Regional Activity Centre would be established in Palermo, Italy in 1993, followed by the Cleaner Production Regional Activity Centre in Barcelona, Spain in 1995. The northern leadership seems to be evident. The fact that States hosting RACs are expected to make a substantial contribution over and above the regular assessed contribution to MAP might explain the geographical spread. France, Italy and Spain are Mediterranean European states with responsibilities for larger European interests in the region. Using their power, wealth, knowledge and skill, they have sought new relationships with their southern neighbours on various political and economic fronts. Against this backdrop, it will be interesting to see if a current Turkish proposal for the establishment of an RAC for education and training, located in Turkey, will be endorsed in the near future.

Except for MEDPOL, which is serviced through the RCU in Athens, the RACs are the front line of the regime. This is where the bulk of regime activity takes place. In those cases were the RACs are national institutions with a regional function, they also serve as showcases of know-how. Because of its preponderant shipping content, REMPEC is somewhat more sectoral than the others and is consequently run in concert with the International Maritime Organization (IMO). Over time, the RACs have developed a system of national focal points, normally bureaucratic contact points.

Continued development of regional institutions continued in 1996 with the establishment of the Mediterranean Commission for Sustainable Development. It is a forum of 36 members from all 21 states undertaking a regional discourse and providing advice in pursuit of a sustainable development strategy for the region. Serviced by the RCU as secretariat, and despite the rationale built for it through the socio-economic component and Agenda MED 21, it remains to be seen how it might affect the direction of regime-building. An innovation on the otherwise formalistic nature of the decision-making levels of the regime is the presence of representatives of local authorities, socio-economic actors and NGOs. This development is healthy in view of the fact that delegations to meetings of contracting parties have historically been led by ministers of the environment. Prior to the MCSD, the regime was slow in responding to the institutional implications of developmental, as well as environmental concerns.

The domestic implementation of regime activities is ostensibly coordinated through national focal points. This is the weakest link, for regional efforts often find political, technological and socio-economic stumbling blocks in domestic implementation. And indeed, it is at this level that this regime needs strengthening, more than at the regional institutional level. The regional superstructure works. The domestic challenge is both political and financial. Now there are more efforts at this level with new resources to be committed through the Euro-Mediterranean dialogue and programs under way with the support of the World Bank and European Investment Bank. But unless the need to reconcile environment and development receives tangible domestic prioritization beyond political 'lip service', including allocation of domestic resources and mobilization of inclusive local initiatives, this external infusion of resources can hardly be expected to lead to "locally-owned" sustainable development.

The ongoing debate on national contributions to MAP is a case in point. With national contributions assessed according to UN Scales of Assessment, France, Spain and Italy, together with the European Union, are the single largest contributors to the operating budget. Past arguments in support of the principal responsibility of industrialized States, the major polluters of the region as a result of their development, wear thin over time as major urban and industrial centers in the south continue to grow and increase their toll on the region's environmental protection budget. The principle of common but differentiated responsibilities is hardly a static concept in the context of change.

Conclusion: Lessons Learned

As a laboratory for regime-building, the Mediterranean offers many useful insights into how the environmental 'prisoners' dilemma' might be managed over time. The MAP still functions and continues to grow 25 years since its inception, despite criticism from scholars and practitioners. While it may be true that the Mediterranean is not cleaner today and it is true that objectives and standards have frequently not been met or postponed, the process of cooperation has attained value *per se*, whether it produces results or not. Moreover that process is evolving further and becoming more inclusive of non-governmental interests. Perhaps MAP is illustrative of a new type of process of communication that regional States hope will replace a troubled past. The regime provides principal and subsidiary fora in which regional States can address common issues with discrete 'arm-wrestling'. This might explain why regime members continue to be active members, periodically renew vows of regional solidarity, participate and stake their claim to benefits generated, commit resources, and more recently commit to a new type of governance characterized by less *dirigisme* and more civil society participation, both regionally and domestically. This suggests that one way of resolving the 'prisoners' dilemma' is by keeping it in check through focus on the common interest amid the diversity.

Diversity. Diversity has many faces in the Mediterranean. The cultural diversity is considered regional heritage, to be protected and fostered. The Mediterranean environment is also cultural and provides people and public institutions with a strong sense of regional identity. This is a unifying factor that has a higher profile in this regime than any other. There is political diversity, pitting different systems of thought supported by varying political and economic weight in the same decision-making process. More challenging are diverse capabilities to support initiatives. Diversity helps broaden issues and pool knowledge and skill. There is more room for trade-offs with more issues on the negotiating table. The playing field of power and wealth may never be level, but through multilateralism these values are toned down, certainly more so than in a situation of bilateralism. Consensus is important in moderating views.

Regime initiation and Leadership. The birth of MAP was possible because of political will and the groundwork in place. The preliminary scientific groundwork enabled a convergence of perceptions of the problems and the common interest in addressing them. This required leadership and highlighted the value of UN agencies in providing this in a region ready to accept it. Both GFCM at the beginning, and UNEP eventually, were highly respected and expected to work with regional States, and other supporting international organizations. It is essential for the lead organization to coordinate its efforts closely with other organizations and be responsive to a collective regional will. Because of their multilateral and non-partisan character, UN agencies have also had the merit of enabling States in conflict to sit at the same table.

Treaty-making. MAP is a formal regime, backed by formal instruments and institutions, with a formal way of conducting business. This may be contrasted to the informality of the Gulf of Maine Action Plan, but comparable to other Regional Seas Programmes. However, treaty-making is a slow process that may slow regime-building and give the impression of inefficiency. The process of convening groups of experts to conduct preparatory work, negotiation and adoption of the treaty in a diplomatic forum, securing the necessary number of ratifications to bring it into force, and hopefully having it implemented, can take many years. Moreover, there is always the danger, as is the case in the Mediterranean, of different States being subject to different legal regimes in relation to the same issue. There is no question that a legal framework to govern expectations in a multilateral context has great long-term value. To counter these disadvantages, it is necessary for regime institutions to assist member States in anticipating formal commitments through a gradual process of preparation and capacity-building.

Regime Control. Although international environmental and trade law have worn thin the sovereign veil, at a regional level States expect to be in control. Regionalism allows them to do that. It is essential that regional States perceive ownership of their regime in their region, with extra-regional or international organization support coming across as facilitative. Thus the central decision-making center in a regional regime concerned with environment and development has to be a forum of States, with States making the final decision even though the process may have a broad range of intergovernmental and non-governmental organization input designed to influence the decision. Without this ownership, international organization alone may not be sufficient to build viable regional regimes.

National Focal Points. When the Stockholm Conference on the Human Environment advocated the establishment of ministries of the environment, it had in mind an integrating institution within national public administrations characterized by sectoralism. Unfortunately, in most countries the ministry of the environment is itself frequently a sectoralized and marginalized institution. At times it is simply a portfolio in a line agency. Unless environment is a responsibility of the highest level of decision-making or a responsibility of a cross sectoral agency (such as economic planning) or assigned as a responsibility to an inter-agency body with real power, it is natural to see its limitations in representing a State's interests in a regime aimed at environment and development. This is a weakness of the biennial meetings of contracting parties to the Barcelona Convention, in that the minister of the environment leads the delegation and the national focal point is located in that ministry. This was so at the beginning of MAP and has become a tradition, irrespective of the re-orientation of the regime. In this respect, the establishment of the Mediterranean Commission for Sustainable Development with its composite membership is a healthy innovation which de-sectoralizes the environment and development discourse. The MCSD's weakness lies in the fact that it is purely advisory.

Regional Accountability. Under MAP Phase I there was a generic national reporting requirement in the Unamended Barcelona Convention. This was tightened and spelled out in greater detail in the Amended Barcelona Convention. This type of reporting on national implementation action in the biennium as a legal obligation has promoted accountability *vis-a-vis* other regime participants, and now also towards civil society participants. Although in MAP Phase I this requirement was taken lightly, there is a discernible trend towards more national openness in MAP Phase II, especially at the last meeting of contracting parties in Malta.

Knowledge-building. Knowledge-building activities are at the heart of the regime. They serve to inform participation, develop common conceptions and perceptions, and ultimately steer the regime. These activities give a regime a dynamic quality and are critical for the setting of standards and timelines. The knowledge base tends to grow as epistemic communities grow in size, diversity and activity.

Public Information and Participation. A regime that does not provide for public participation at regional and national levels risks remaining a civil service club with little accountability to interested constituencies and thus minimizing its effectiveness. It is difficult to sustain over the long-term. Civil society participation has an important multiplier effect in broadening the popular support base. Hence, the MAP Phase II and Amended Barcelona Convention trend towards broader and more formal NGO involvement and commitment to public participation is important for increasing support for the regime, especially as it becomes more ambitious in implementing the GPA and integrated coastal area management. There will be tough domestic decisions that will need constituency support.

Challenge of Integration. The true integrated approach has an inevitable logic: complexity increases as knowledge grows. This may lead to difficult decisions on "boundaries" to assist with an otherwise unwieldy management process. Ecosystem-based integrated coastal area management, such as to include a full-range of activities in a drainage basin, will be a logical direction for MAP to take. But in doing so, it will have to re-examine current regime boundaries and regional participation, if true integration is to be pursued. This entails political difficulties of extra-regional participation, which Mediterranean States resisted in the past. The geographical constraints of regionalism may have already been reached with the Amended LBS Protocol and GPA commitments.

Capacity-building. Capacity-building has to play catch-up with the regime. In a regime where there are great disparities in critical knowledge and skill areas, capacity-building is as important as effective communication in problem-solving. The ability to convert common intent into effective concerted action requires a reasonably level playing field. The principle of common but differentiated responsibilities should be accepted only with the *caveat* that capacity to undertake regime commitments has to be built, because otherwise, this well-intentioned principle might risk becoming an excuse for ineffective participation.

Regime Financing. Regime-building costs, and core costs have to be borne equitably by regime participants to reinforce ownership and accountability. The UN Scales of Assessment, which were developed on a global scale, might not be equitable at a regional level, where there are fewer States to take into account. MAP has been very efficient in maximizing activities with a relatively small biennial budget. At the same time, the reluctance of the majority of States to increase their contributions beyond the nominal amounts has forced larger contributions from fewer States. This has served to reinforce the primary influence of a few States on regime development.

Dynamism and Perception of Benefits of Regime-building. MAP is a dynamic regime and member States perceive benefits not immediately visible to observers. MAP has grown and changed significantly since inception, and yet no regional State has withdrawn from an activity because of dissatisfaction with the regime.

NOTES

1. Mediterranean Action Plan (hereafter MAP Phase I) *in* UNEP, *Report of the Intergovernmental Meeting on the Protection of the Mediterranean*, Barcelona, 28 January–4 February 1975 (UNEP/WG.2/5, 11 February 1975).
2. Action Plan for the Protection of the Marine Environment and the Sustainable Development of the Coastal Areas of the Mediterranean (MAP Phase II) *in* UNEP, *Mediterranean Action Plan and Convention for the Protection of the Marine Environment and the Coastal Region of the Mediterranean and its Protocols (Informal Document)* (Athens: UNEP, 1997)(hereafter UNEP, *MAP Phase II Instruments*): 1–29. For ease of reference this informal consolidation of the amended MAP instruments will be used. The amendments were formally adopted in the Final Act of Conference of Plenipotentiaries on the Convention for the Protection of the Mediterranean Sea against Pollution and its Protocols, Barcelona, 9–10 June 1995 (UNEP(OCA)/MED IG.6/7, 1 July 1995). For the unamended MAP instruments, see UNEP, *Mediterranean Action Plan and Convention for the Protection of the Mediterranean Sea against Pollution and its Related Protocols* (hereafter UNEP, *MAP Phase I Instruments*)(Athens: UNEP, 1992).
3. *Ibid.*, MAP Phase II: 1.
4. The current coastal states in the region are the following: Albania, Algeria, Bosnia and Herzegovina, Croatia, Cyprus, Egypt, France, Greece, Israel, Italy, Lebanon, Libya, Malta, Monaco, Morocco, Slovenia, Spain, Syria, Tunisia, Turkey and Yugoslavia (Serbia and Montenegro). New coastal states might come into existence in the event that the Palestinian National Authority declares statehood and if Montenegro secedes from what is left of former Yugoslavia.
5. These are the following: Adriatic, Aegean, Alboran, Algero-Provençal Basin, Balearic, Ionian, Levantine, Ligurian and Thyrennian. Although the Black Sea is geographically a sub-sea of the Mediterranean, it has been subject to separate regime development, and is consequently not discussed in this paper.
6. Arvid Pardo, *The Common Heritage: Selected Papers on Oceans and World Order, 1967–1974* (Malta: International Ocean Institute and Malta University Press, 1975): 25–30.
7. GFCM, *The State of Marine Pollution in the Mediterranean and Legislative Controls*, GFCM Studies and Reviews no. 51 (Rome: FAO, 1972) 2. Only Romania and Turkey provided data and this was considered insufficient to provide a picture for the whole Black Sea.
8. GFCM, *Report of the Eleventh Session*, Athens, 6–11 March 1972 (Rome: FAO, 1972), Resolution XI/72/1: 9–10. A circular letter was sent by the Director-General to GFCM members on 25 September 1972.
9. Baruch Boxer, "The Mediterranean Sea: Preparing and Implementing a Regional Action Plan" *in* David A. Kay and Harold K. Jacobsen (eds.), *Environmental Protection: The International Dimension* (Totowa, N.J.: Allanhead, 1983): 279.

10. Acte Final de la Conference Interparlementaire des pays côtiers sur la lutte contre la pollution de la mer Méditerranée, Rome, 29 mars–3 avril 1974, in Maguelonne Dejeant-Pons, ed., *Protection et developpement du bassin méditerranéen: Textes et documents internationaux* (Paris: Economica, 1987): 292–294.
11. FAO, *Protection of the Marine Environment Against Pollution in the Mediterranean: Report of the Consultation Convened to Study the Protection of Living Resources and Fisheries from Pollution in the Mediterranean,* Rome, 23 February and 27–31 May 1974, FAO Fisheries Report No. 148 (Rome: FAO, 1974): 2–3, 15.
12. These were as follows: "Integrated planning of the development and management of the resources of the Mediterranean Basin;" "Co-ordinated programme for research, monitoring, and exchange of information and assessment of the state of pollution and of protection measures;" "Framework convention and related protocols with their technical annexes for the protection of the Mediterranean environment;" "Institutional and financial implications of the Action Plan." UNEP, *Report of the Intergovernmental Meeting on the Protection of the Mediterranean*, Barcelona, 28 January–4 February 1975, (UNEP/WG.2/5, 11 February 1975): 2–3.
13. UNEP, *MAP Phase II Instruments, supra* n. 2: 1.
14. *Ibid.*: 1.
15. MAP Phase II, UNEP, *MAP Phase II Documents, supra* n. 2: 3–10. Barcelona Resolution on the Environment and Sustainable Development in the Mediterranean Basin, 10 June 1995 *in MAP Phase II Documents, ibid.*: 30–33. Priority Fields of Activities for the Environment and Development in the Mediterranean Basin (1996-2005) *in MAP Phase II Documents, ibid.*: 34–39.
16. MAP Phase II, *ibid.*: 2.
17. *Ibid.*
18. Amended Barcelona Convention, Article 15, *ibid.* 46.
19. *Eleventh Ordinary Meeting of the Contracting Parties to the Convention for the Protection of the Mediterranean Sea against Pollution and its Protocols*, Malta, 27–30 October 1999, UNEP(OCA)/MED IG.12/9, 6 December 1999 (Athens: UNEP, 1999), 21 *et seq.*
20. Amended Barcelona Convention, Articles 26–27, UNEP, *MAP Phase II Documents, supra* n. 2: 51–52.
21. This provision remained unamended. Unamended Barcelona Convention, Article 1(1), *MAP Phase I Instruments, supra* n. 2: 11–12.
22. *Ibid.*, Article 1(2), 12.
23. Emergency Protocol, Articles 1 and 2(a), UNEP, *MAP Phase 1 Instruments, supra* n. 2: 34–35.
24. UNEP, *Report of the Intergovernmental Meeting of the Mediterranean Coastal States on the Blue Plan*, Split, Yugoslavia, 31 January–4 February 1977 (UNEP/IG.5/7, 21 February 1977): 11.
25. Unamended LBS Protocol, Article 3, UNEP, *MAP Phase 1 Instruments, supra* n. 2: 41.
26. *Ibid.*, Article 4(1).
27. Unamended SPA Protocol, Article 2, UNEP, *MAP Phase 1 Instruments, supra* n. 2: 54.
28. *Overview of the Mediterranean Basin (Development and Environment)*, (Mediterranean Action Plan, Blue Plan First Phase, 1987): 13.
29. Amended Barcelona Convention, Article 1, in *MAP Phase II Documents, ibid.*: 41.
30. Amended SPA Protocol, Article 2, in UNEP, *MAP Phase II Documents, ibid.*: 90.
31. Seabed Protocol, UNEP, *MAP Phase II Documents, ibid.*, 114–144: 117.
32. Amended LBS Protocol, Articles 2 and 3, UNEP, *MAP Phase II Documents, ibid.*: 73.
33. *Ibid.*, Article 4: 73.
34. UNEP(OCA)/LBA/IG.2/7, 5 December 1995. Paragraph 34 of the GPA foresees involvement of land-locked states whose river systems and drainage basin are closely linked to coastal and marine area degradation. Paragraph 35 also foresees interregional cooperation to coordinate efforts for marine environment protection. *Ibid.*: 20.
35. Unamended Barcelona Convention, Preamble, UNEP, *MAP Phase I Documents, supra* n. 2: 11.
36. Hazardous Wastes Protocol, UNEP, *MAP Phase II Documents, supra* n. 2: 145-166. This instrument was in effect a regional version of the 1989 Basel Convention on the Control of Transboundary Movements of Hazardous Wastes and Their Disposal.

37. UNEP, *Report of the Eighth Meeting of the National Focal Points for the Blue Plan*, Sophia Antipolis, 20–22 July 1987, UNEP/WG.171/5, 22 July 1987 (Athens: UNEP, 1987): 10.
38. UNEP, *Report of the Intergovernmental Meeting of Mediterranean Coastal States on the Blue Plan*, *supra* n. 24: 12.
39. UNIDO, *Report of the Meeting of Experts on the Establishment of a Mediterranean Regional Centre for Research and Development in Marine Industrial Technology*, Vienna, Austria, 18-21 April 1989 (IPCT.85(SPEC.), 16 May 1989).
40. For an overview of these two initiatives, see Aldo Chircop, "The Mediterranean and the Quest for Sustainable Development", *Ocean Development and International Law* 23 (1992): 17–30.
41. Agenda 21 for the Mediterranean Region, Tunis, 1 November 1994, in Republic of Tunisia, Ministry of Environment, Land Use Planning, *The Tunis Conference on Sustainable Development in the Mediterranean: Agenda MED 21* (Tunis: UNEP/MAP, 1994).
42. Resolution Related to the Creation of a Mediterranean Commission on Sustainable Development, Tunis, 1 November 1994, in Stefano Belfiore, Aldo E. Chircop and Chiara Della Mea (eds.), *The Sustainable Development of the Mediterranean: Selected Regional Policy Documents* (Genoa: International Centre for Coastal and Ocean Policy Studies, 1998): 17.
43. Peter M. Haas, *Saving the Mediterranean: The Politics of International Environmental Cooperation* (New York : Columbia University Press, 1990).
44. UNEP, *Co-ordinated Mediterranean Pollution Monitoring and Research Programme (MEDPOL) – Phase I: Programme Description*, UNEP Regional Seas Reports and Studies No. 23 (UNEP, 1984) 1–16.
45. *Ibid.* 3.
46. These included the Intergovernmental Oceanographic Commission (IOC), World Metereological Organization (WMO), General Fisheries Council for the Mediterranean (GFCM), World Health Organization (WHO), United Nations Industrial Development Organization (UNIDO), UN Economic Commission for Europe (ECE) and International Atomic Energy Agency (IAEA).
47. UNEP, *Long-Term Programme for Pollution Monitoring and Research in the Mediterranean (MEDPOL) – Phase II*, UNEP Regional Seas Reports and Studies No. 28 (UNEP, 1983).
48. UNEP, *MEDPOL – Phase III: Programme for the Assessment and Control of Pollution in the Mediterranean Region (1996-2005)*, UNEP(OCA)/MED.WG.89/5, 15 January 1995 (Athens: UNEP, 1995).
49. *Report of the Executive Director on the Implementation of the Action Plan and of the Genoa Declaration in 1986–87 and Recommendations for Activities to be Undertaken in the 1988-1989 Biennium with Related Budget Proposals*, UNEP/IG.74/3, 30 June 1987, (Athens: UNEP, 1987): 48–50.
50. Barcelona Resolution, UNEP, *MAP Phase II Instruments, supra* n. 2: 6.
51. Amended Barcelona Convention, Article 8, UNEP, *MAP Phase II Instruments*, *ibid:* 44.
52. Amended LBS Protocol, Article 6, UNEP, *MAP Phase II Instruments*, *ibid.*: 74.
53. *Ibid.*: Article 7, 74–75.
54. *Ibid.*: Article 7(2)(3), 75.
55. *Ibid.*: Article 15, 78.
56. *Ibid.*: Annex I, 80.
57. Priority Fields of Activities, UNEP, *MAP Phase II Documents, supra* n. 2: 34–39.
58. *MEDPOL Phase III: Programme for the Assessment and Control of Pollution in the Mediterranean Region (1996–2005)*, UNEP(OCA)/MED WG.89/5, 15 January 1995, (Athens: UNEP, 1995): 18.
59. See for instance the following compilation of measures: UNEP, *Common Measures Adopted by the Contracting Parties to the Convention for the Protection of the Mediterranean Sea Against Pollution*, MAP Technical Reports Series No. 38 (Athens: UNEP, 1990).
60. Francesco Saverio Civili (MEDPOL Programme Coordinator, UNEP), "Implementing the GPA in the Mediterranean", http://gpanews.unep.org, accessed on 23 May 2000. The priority areas include "the adoption of national regulations on sewage discharges into the sea and rivers, the establishment of a system of authorization for works that may cause alterations to the coastline or disturb natural habitats, the phase-out of the use of nine priority pesticides – DDT, aldrin, dieldrin, endrin, chlordane, heptachlor, mirex, toxaphene and hexachlorobenzene – except for those uses for which

WHO recommendations related to the safeguarding of human life suggest otherwise, the prohibition of the manufacture, trade, and new uses of PCBs, and the ratification and application of the Hazardous Waste Protocol." *Ibid.*

Steinar Andresen

THE NORTH SEA AND BEYOND: LESSONS LEARNED

INTRODUCTION

Scope and Purpose

In comparative terms, Northern Europe is often considered quite "advanced" regarding environmental policies and cooperation. As indicated by the Norwegian minister of Environmental Affairs in 1993: "This cooperation has in many respects served as a model for regional cooperation also for marine areas in other regions".[1] The "Northern Seas" are composed of three distinct though interrelated marine regions; the Northeast Atlantic, the Baltic Sea and the Barents Sea. The main focus of this chapter is on the North Sea/Northeast Atlantic (NEA). Its main purpose is to highlight lessons from this cooperation. Was the Norwegian Minister of Environment right that this is a "model region"? If so, can the lessons be applied successfully in other regions of the world, including Northeast Asia? In order to answer this question, we first have to know *what* has been achieved and *how* it has been achieved.

THE NORTH SEA AND THE NORTHEAST ATLANTIC

Characteristics of the North Sea

The North Sea has been formed by geological events over the past 20,000 years. It is a relatively enclosed and shallow basin. The water movement makes a long-term anti-clockwise circulation from the east coast of the United Kingdom throughout the central North Sea. Water discharged from continental estuaries is more confined to the eastern region. Water from these sources eventually leaves the North Sea via the Skagerak along the Norwegian coast. On average it takes about 36 months for water in the German Bight to leave the North Sea, whereas water in the northern North Sea may remain for only about 6 months. Though bottom waters may move in an

Mark J. Valencia (ed.), Maritime Regime Building, 51–72.

opposite direction, observations indicate that the coastal margins of the southern North Sea, the Skagerak, the northern Kattegat and the southern part of the Norwegian trench are the most important areas for transport and deposition of suspended matter. Physical features also shape the margins of the sea varying from the rugged cliffs of Norway to the dunes of lower areas and the sheltered inlets in the south.

The North Sea has a rich variety of natural resources, including one of the world's most productive fisheries. Birds use the North Sea for breeding sites and for feeding in winter. Seals and other mammals also exploit the biological production of the North Sea. All the living communities of the sea are in the end based on plants that create organic material. Thus, the North Sea is a complex system of physical, chemical and biological characteristics affected both by natural variations and by man. With the densely populated areas surrounding it, the North Sea is an area of intense human activity. The population in the drainage basin of the North Sea alone is approximately 150 million people. The North Sea has some of the heaviest marine traffic in the world, and many of Europe's major ports are located around it. Offshore oil and gas exploitation has also made the North Sea one of today's most important offshore sources of petroleum production. River input, direct discharge, atmospheric fall-out and dumping are among the major sources of pollutants to the North Sea.

Initiation and Development of North Sea Cooperation: The Institutional Framework

North Sea cooperation was triggered by dramatic accidents brought to the public's attention through the mass media. The wreck of the Torrey Canyon off the coast of Cornwall in 1967, resulting in 160 kilometres of oil-covered beaches, had considerable importance for the establishment of the 1969 Bonn Agreement for protection against oil pollution In 1971, the coaster "Stella Maris" left the port of Rotterdam with 650 tonnes of chlorinated hydrocarbons on board, destined to be dumped in the northern part of the North Sea. The incident caused immense public alarm and was met with protests from a number of European governments.

This incident was one of the reasons for the adoption in 1972 of the Convention for the Prevention of Marine Pollution by Dumping from Ships and Aircraft, (the Oslo Dumping Convention). It was signed by all 13 West European maritime states in 1972 – Belgium, Denmark, Finland, France, Germany, Iceland, Ireland, Netherlands, Norway, Portugal, Spain, Sweden and the United Kingdom. The Convention entered into force in 1974. A separate Convention for the Prevention of Marine Pollution from Land-based Sources was signed in Paris in 1974. The membership is the same as for the Oslo Dumping Convention, but the EU participates as a contracting member while Finland does not. This Convention entered into force in 1978.

The main objective of the Oslo Convention is to take all possible steps to prevent the pollution of the sea by substances that are liable to create hazards to human health, harm living resources and marine life, damage amenities, or interfere with other legitimate users of the sea. Geographically, the Convention covers the Northeast Atlantic and the North Sea including the high seas, territorial seas and internal coastal waters.[2] The Convention is structured around a black/gray annex system. Dumping of substances listed in Annex I (black list) is entirely prohibited, dumping of substances in Annex II (gray list) requires a specific permit, while other substances (Annex III) require approval from national authorities. Annex IV deals with incineration at sea.[3] The executive body of the Convention is the Oslo Commission (OSCOM) where the parties meet annually. Parties are required to submit records of dumping permits and approvals issued to the Commission for consideration. The Commission exercises overall supervision and reviews in general the condition of the sea and the effectiveness of control measures, and decides on other necessary measures.

The main objective of the Paris Convention is to take all possible steps to prevent pollution of the sea by adopting individually and jointly measures to combat marine pollution and by harmonizing the parties' policies in this regard. Like the Oslo Convention, the Paris Convention is structured around a "black/gray" list system. The Parties are required to implement measures for the elimination of pollution by substances listed in the "black list", and for the reduction or elimination of pollution by substances listed in the "gray" list. The Parties are required to inform the Commission of the legislative and administrative measures they have taken to ensure compliance with the provisions of the Convention. The Commission supervises implementation of the Convention. The geographical scope is the same as for the Oslo Convention. The main decision-rule in use within both bodies has been consensus, although this has changed somewhat more recently.

There are close institutional links between the two commissions. Both the Oslo and Paris Commissions are assisted by several scientific/technical bodies: the Standing Advisory Committee for Scientific Advice (SACSA) and the Technical Working Group (TWG) respectively, *ad hoc* working groups and the Joint Monitoring Group (JMG). Moreover, they share a permanent Secretariat in London with the Paris Commission, made up of five executive staff members and seven assistants. The annual budget for 1999 was £ 850 000[4] supplied by the Contracting Parties.

In the early 1980s, Germany called for a North Sea Ministerial Conference. The first International North Sea Conference (INSC) at ministerial level was held in Bremen in 1984. This conference was followed by those in London in 1987, in the Hague in 1990, and in Esbjerg, Denmark in 1995. The next conference will be in Oslo, Norway in 2002. Only the eight states directly bordering the North Sea proper participate in the ministerial conferences: Belgium, Denmark, France, Germany, Netherlands, Norway, Sweden and the United Kingdom. The only exception is Switzerland which participates because of its geographical position as a source of inputs to the river Rhine. Thus the geographical scope of this institutional framework is much more limited than that of the OSCON and PARCON. It includes only the North Sea, the English Channel and the Skagerak. In the wake of the 1987 London conference, the North Sea Task Force (NSTF) was established, as a reaction to gaps in knowledge of the state of the North Sea environment. The Task Force was an attempt to merge and coordinate the total scientific expertise of the

North Sea countries, the Oslo and Paris Commissions, and the International Council for the Exploration of the Sea (ICES). The NSTF published a Quality Status Report of the North Sea in 1993.

More recently the Oslo and Paris Conventions were merged into a single legal instrument. The OSPAR Convention for the Protection of the Northeast Atlantic was signed by ministers responsible for the marine environment in the Northeast Atlantic and the representative of the EC Commission during the fall of 1992. When it came into force in 1998, the new Convention replaced the Oslo and Paris Conventions. The Convention contains 34 articles and is supplemented by four Annexes and two Appendices. It establishes a Commission made up of representatives for each of the parties.

The Convention has been described as rather codifactory in nature taking into account the achievements of the existing Oslo and Paris Conventions and Commissions.[5] Codified elements include the precautionary principle, application of BAT (Best Available Technology) and BEP (Best Available Practices), but new principles such as sustainable management are included. The new Convention is a uniform regime for all substances and it does not distinguish between black and gray list substances, which have been united in Appendix 2. The creation of a uniform regime has had consequences for the regulation of radioactive substances, explicitly empowering the new Commission to adopt common measures. The dumping of low and intermediate level radioactive substances, not covered by the OSCOM, is – with some exceptions – prohibited. Furthermore, the new Commission clearly states that the decisions of the Commission are legally binding. Some believe that the provisions on compliance are an improvement in several respects. Finally, at the same time as the new Convention was adopted, an Action Plan for the Oslo and Paris Commissions was also agreed upon. It was also agreed to meet regularly to supervise the functioning and effectiveness of the new Convention. In short, there has been a considerable institutional development over time, from two issue-specific regimes to a more comprehensive legal regime – with the addition of a high level political component. But what has been the practical effect of this regime evolution?

What Has Been Achieved?

The question of *effectiveness* of regimes, or the measurement of the consequences of regimes is increasingly being addressed by students of international relations.[6] This chapter will not treat the shortcomings and merits of various approaches. The ultimate question we need to answer, of course, is the extent to which a regime has contributed to solving the problem it was set up to deal with. Unfortunately this is easier said than done. One way to deal with the issue of regime *effectiveness* is to differentiate between outputs, outcome and impact.[7] These concepts are frequently mixed, and the boundaries between them are not always clear. As used here, *output* is conceived as norms, rules and principles flowing from the regime, *outcome* as change in the target group's behavior as a result of the regime and *impact* as the tangible consequences affecting the physical problems at hand as a result of the working of the regime. Let us first look at the outputs.

More and Stricter Regulations Over Time

Rules and regulations adopted do not really tell us whether the regime is able to deal effectively with the environmental problems at hand, but usually they are necessary preconditions for subsequent implementation and problem-solving.

The North Sea regime started out slowly and the first decade was characterized by a gradual building up of administrative capacity, mainly to increase knowledge through research programs and monitoring. Measures to control and reduce pollutants were few in *number* and vague in *content*, especially in PARCOM. In a detailed study of the early years of the *Paris Commission*, Sætevik[8] observes that "during the period 1978 to 1987 the Paris Commission has only achieved a total of six binding decisions on regulation measures. Most of the decisions were recommendations containing vague and imprecise formulations, or non-committal recommendations". Also, policy outcomes were often close to the "least ambitious party" position and the parties were given high discretion on what pace to choose in implementing decisions.[9]

Overall the level of activity in the Oslo Commission during the first decade was higher. Still, procedural questions dominated and recommendations far outnumbered decisions. Until 1987 dumping problems were mainly dealt with through *control* rather than *reduction* of dumping.[10]

Starting in the latter half of the 1980s there was a strong increase in the level of activity and much "tougher" and far-reaching measures were gradually adopted within both sub-regimes. It all started with the second *North Sea Conference* in London in 1987. In relation to *land based pollution,* the Conference Declaration called for a substantial reduction (about 50%) between 1985 and 1995 in the total inputs to the North Sea of hazardous substances. The same applied to nitrogen and phosphorous inputs to sensitive areas where inputs were likely to cause pollution. National action plans to achieve these goals were to be elaborated.

The ambition of the ministers was even higher regarding *dumping* of waste as it was declared that dumping of industrial waste should be phased out and incineration should cease. Thus the focus changed from regulation of dumping to termination of dumping. *A precautionary approach,* the first one ever adopted internationally, was also agreed.[11] Finally, the London Conference decided to establish the North Sea Task Force.

The Ministerial Conference in the Hague in 1990 clarified and strengthened the London Declaration, especially regarding land based pollution. Thirty-six significant pollutants were designated for 50 percent reduction and a goal of 70% reduction was set for land based and *atmospheric* inputs of the most dangerous substances. The most far-reaching goal declared at the 1995 Conference in Esbjerg was a target of 25 years for the elimination of hazardous waste inputs. The North Sea Ministerial Conferences have a more limited regulatory scope than the two conventions, but most of these *policy declarations* were later adopted legally by the two commissions.[12]

Summing up, there has been a strong increase both in numerical and substantive output with the Oslo Commission being the most far reaching. The triggering effect in both cases was the INSC. But what has been the practical significance of these developments for *behavioral change* in the affected actors, i.e., have the recommendations and the decisions been *implemented*?

Increased Implementation But A Long Way To Go

The step from output to outcome is significant. Focusing on the output stage, as quite a few analysts do, can give the impression of an efficient, smoothly running organization which is making all the "right" decisions. By including behavioral change of key actors resulting from the regime, the outlook may be more uncertain and pessimistic.

By this criterion, OSCOM is a "success-story" and PARCOM more "mixed". Until 1987, the level of dumping of various materials was rather stable, with some exceptions regarding different substances.[13] In the 1990s, however, the Oslo Commission emerged as one of the most stunning success-stories in the history of international environmental regimes. Dumping of industrial waste and incineration has ceased. The Oslo Commission is probably the only example of an international environmental convention that has rendered itself superfluous, facilitating the subsequent merger between the two Conventions.[14]

Regarding the Paris Commission, a first observation is that during the first decade the issue was not very relevant as there was not much to implement. The few decisions and recommendations adopted were vague and mostly codified existing practice. Only marginal – if any – behavioral change was needed. Moreover, until well into the 1990s, aggregate information on the status of implementation was very limited.[15] More systematic attention, however, was given to implementation within the INSC approach. A "Progress Report" was presented at the 4th INSC in June 1995.

The Report reached several main conclusions. Regarding the 70% reduction targets for the *most hazardous substances,* "significant progress appears to have been made".[16] Regarding the 50% targets for the other heavy metals, many of the states will comply, but mainly regarding discharges from point sources. "Less success is reported in reducing emissions from diffuse sources"[17]. According to Maggs[18] the problem with diffuse sources was serious. "The 50% reduction target for atmospheric inputs of mercury, copper, zinc, chromium and nickel are not being met in several of the North Sea states ... and the 50% reduction target for pesticides, was met for only 3 of 16 pesticides listed". Regarding the call for a 50% reduction of nutrient emissions, all countries except France (25% reduction) were expected to achieve the goal by 1995. All North Sea countries, however, had serious problems implementing the 50% nitrogen goal and most expected to achieve only between a 20%–30% reduction.[19]

The Progress Report concludes that: "It is difficult to make an overall assessment of the effectiveness of the London and Hague Declarations in achieving a 50% or more reduction".[20] The bottom line seems to be that this is difficult partly because the picture is mixed, and partly because there has been a lack of common methodologies by which to calculate discharges. Considering the ambitious goals adopted in relation to these substances, it is hardly a surprise that quite a few of the goals were not achieved by 1995. Regardless of uncertainties, difficulties with data, baselines and comparability, there is no doubt that in contrast to the earlier period, *domestic implementation is well under way*. Nevertheless, there is still a long way to go in implementing many of these measures and the task ahead has not become easier in light of INSC's 25 years elimination target for the input of hazardous wastes.

But can we establish a causal link between the regime in question and the implementation taking place? This is necessary to decide regime effectiveness. The Progress Report is probably correct in observing that: "The reductions have been achieved as a result of a combination of measures taken nationally, some in consequence of international obligations from the EC and the Oslo and Paris Commissions".[21] In other words, the regime has had *some* impact on the behavior of key actors, private as well as public. Skjærseth[22] has studied this more closely in relation to three countries. Although uncertainties and methodological difficulties abound, he concludes that: "North Sea commitments have generated significant, although varying, substance at national levels in Norway, the Netherlands and the United Kingdom. They have generally been incorporated into national policy plans and there is a general match between actual behavioral change and national goals following from international commitments".[23]

Summing up, from a slow start, both regimes have triggered significant behavioral change over time, most notably regarding dumping, which stands forth as an undisputed 'success-story" Although the picture is more uncertain and mixed regarding land-based pollution, significant progress has been made in the 1990s.

Are Environmental Conditions Improving?

Has the marine environment in the North Sea and related ocean areas improved as a result of this regime? This is the real "bottom line", if we want to know if the regime has been truly effective. When deciding effectiveness in this sense, a two-step procedure is necessary. First we have to know the *evolution of environmental quality*; has it improved, has it deteriorated, are different trends observable or is there insufficient knowledge to determine this? Secondly, when and if such a determination can be made, we must establish a *causal link* between the relevant regime and the change in the environmental quality.

Three reports have been published on North Sea environmental quality (1984, 1987 and 1993). Although these reports are very different, the *broad substantive message* has not changed very much.[24] Generally, *uncertainty and lack of alarming indicators* characterize all of the Quality Status Reports (QSRs). In general, pollution has tended to be confined to certain regions, in the coastal margins or near identifiable pollution sources." In comparative terms, this ocean area is among the most studied in the world. Nevertheless, in the 1993 Quality Status Report for the North Sea it was stated that "a complete understanding of the North Sea as an ecosystem will probably never be achieved ... both natural variations and lack of understanding leads to scientific uncertainty as to the anthropogenic exploitation of, and effects on the natural ecosystem in the North Sea."[25] Maybe somewhat paradoxically, the fact that decision-makers are told that they have to accept uncertainty has contributed to strengthening the need for a precautionary approach.

In all probability the regime has had some positive effect, considering the energy, expertise and resources spent. Indeed, the quality of the environment in the region would probably have been poorer in absence of the regime. The point here is that when environmental trends are so uncertain, natural variations so strong and causal links so difficult to establish, the typical conclusion will be that; "yes, it probably had some positive effects".

This being said, we should not discard this yardstick altogether. If we cease our inquiry of behavioral change we may miss some useful observations. For example, due to a scientific dispute over the effect of the nutrient reduction off the coast of Norway, there has been a temporary halt in the Norwegian program. This illustrates that if basic causal links are not established it may be difficult to gather or maintain necessary public support for new costly measures. As social scientists, however, we have to use this approach with caution.

In short, quite a bit has been accomplished with regard to implementation and behavioral change, but there is considerable uncertainty. It may be argued that the real challenge is to *explain* how regimes perform, but this brief overview illustrates that it is not a trivial exercise to determine how regimes perform. Neither is this only a question of academic interest. As environmental regulations penetrate deeper into society, affecting more and new actors and become increasingly costly, the target groups as well as the public will want to know what the *effects* are of the measures introduced. If decision-makers are not able to demonstrate positive effect, it may be difficult to obtain or maintain the necessary legitimacy and support.

EXPLAINING PERFORMANCE

How then do we account for the difference in performance between the two sub-regimes and how do we account for their increased effectiveness over time? These two complex questions will be dealt with in a short and simplified manner. One way to deal with the issue is to differentiate between two different explanatory perspectives.[26] First, effectiveness is assumed to vary depending on the *type of the problem* and related actor preferences. Some problems are more "malign" than others due to differences in affectedness and asymmetries between the actors involved. The second perspective points to differences in the *problem solving capacity* of the regime in question, relating to differences in institutional structure, degree of leadership and distribution of power. That is, some regimes are more effective because the problems at hand are attacked with greater skills and energy

In this case, whereas the first approach is most relevant in relation to explaining the difference in performance *between* the two sub-regimes, the second approach is most relevant in explaining *development over time*. While problem structures tend to be rather stable over time, problem solving capacity may be more variable. The distribution of power may change, leaders may emerge or disappear and institutions may evolve. Thus, while the former perspective is important to establish a realistic benchmark as to what can be expected from various regimes, the latter is more important from a policy and an "institutional design" perspective.[27] Consequently, I will deal mostly with this perspective.

Problem Structures And Actor Preferences

The main reason for the higher effectiveness of OSCOM is simply that dumping in this area has been much easier to handle than the problem of land-based emissions. In general terms the dumping problem is easier to handle than the land based pollution problem. Dumping deals with a specific and conscious disposal operation. More specifically, the *number* of major dumping countries was *small* as the United Kingdom was the only state that dumped all categories of materials. Roughly half of the countries dumped one or more materials when cooperation was initiated. That is, some members had no material stakes whatsoever, some had moderate stakes, and one had large stakes.[28] Of equal significance was the fact that there were *alternatives* to ocean dumping, land-based storage and treatment. Moreover, from a "fairness" (focal point) perspective this made sense as it implied that instead of spreading potential risks to other countries, land-based storage implied an *internalization* of costs as well as risks.

Land-based emissions represent a more malign problem as these emissions flow from diffuse sources as a result of a wide range of human activities. Also, all members had large stakes involved, making it politically more difficult to address. A very large number of subnational actors would be affected, most notably industry, municipalities and agriculture. Moreover, no easy "technological fixes" were at hand and the possibilities for substitution were limited.

What were the actor preferences following from these problem structures? In this context there are similarities as well as differences between the two issues. On the dumping issue, it follows logically that the United Kingdom was the prime laggard, with Spain, Portugal and Ireland as more or less outspoken allies. The Scandinavian countries, with no dumping activities and anxious to be green, were the main leaders. Thus the conflict potential was far from insignificant, especially during the first period. For various reasons, France, West Germany, Belgium and the Netherlands chose to phase out their dumping activities, thereby increasing pressure on the remaining "laggards" and making the issue somewhat less politically difficult to deal with.

In relation to land based emissions, the picture initially was more elusive due to the lack of knowledge of the links between emissions and the level of pollution. Nevertheless, due to the anti-clockwise circulation pattern of the North Sea, there was some general knowledge about the "export/import" pattern that influenced the preferences of states. Roughly speaking this made the United Kingdom an exporter of pollution while she was not herself much affected by pollution from own sources or from that of other countries. The situation was quite different from "core" continental members like Germany, the Netherlands, Belgium and France. While they themselves contributed significantly to the problem, they were also significantly affected both by their own pollution and from that of others. These asymmetries in affectedness and difference in contribution to the problem help explain the slow moving progress in the Paris Commission initially. While the United Kingdom in general preferred the most lenient regulatory approach, the Netherlands, Sweden and to some extent Germany pushed for stricter regulations. Another rather pronounced laggard initially was the EU.[29] Still, the "leader/laggard" picture was less clear cut compared to the dumping issue as all were to some extent "sinners" and there were no true "saints".

Considering these rather "malign" problem-structures and conflicts, especially relating to land based emissions, how has it been possible to make so much progress over the last decade? First, there have been changes in *contextual factors*. Secondly, some important changes in *preferences* of main actors have taken place. Thirdly, and most important in our perspective is the *increased problem solving capacity* within the broader framework of the regime. Finally, *domestic constraints* are instrumental in explaining why not *even more* has been accomplished regarding land based emissions.

Infusion Of Political And Institutional Energy

We already know that the INSC approach in general and more specifically the London 1987 North Sea Conferences constitute the main explanation for increased effectiveness. But what elements of this approach had such a decisive impact? *Leadership* was important as Germany took the initiative for establishing the more limited North Sea Conference due to dissatisfaction with the working of the Convention system. Had this approach *not* been introduced, the course of events may well have been different. The precautionary approach was suggested by Germany at the 1984 North Sea Conference, but the time was not yet right for its wide adoption. Another innovation was an increase in *transparency* as for the first time in the history of North Sea cooperation, NGOs were invited to a hearing prior to the Bremen Conference to present their views. Although this did not have much practical effect at the time, some very important *seeds* were sown in Bremen.

But why was the London Conference so much more successful? At the general level *contextual factors* made a significant difference, as the level of *environmental awareness* was much higher in 1987 compared to 1984. This was linked to *external* shocks like the Chernobyl nuclear reactor accident and the "ozone hole" as well as the publication of the most important environmental document produced in the 1980s, the "Brundtland Report." These factors contributed to placing the environment high on the agenda, especially in Western European countries. As *demand* for green politics was increasing, policy makers were eager to *supply* it in order to secure future re-elections. The INSC was specifically designed for *Ministers,* eager to deliver results, in contrast to medium or low-level bureaucrats, who did not need to worry about results. The most important shift appears to have taken place in the United Kingdom, the main laggard.[30] The Conference took place in London and diplomatic "success" in the "home arena" is always important. The link between this contextual factor and institutional innovations such as adding the high-level component and increased transparency also secured good media coverage – in contrast to the more secluded and exclusive "commission'-approach. Probably contributing to speeding up the transformation of the ambitious INSC declarations to the Commission system was another *perceived* environmental shock in 1988, referred to as a *maritime Chernobyl* in the North Sea: the strong algae bloom and the massive death of seabirds and seals. Although research later indicated that cause/effect relations were highly uncertain and complex, it reinforced the perceived need for swift and strong action.

The fact that the process was strongly policy driven in this phase may be a reason why the dumping problem was so successfully attacked. Dumping, and even more so incineration, were *visible* activities – in contrast to the diffuse land-based pollution. As the United Kingdom stood out as the only main polluter within the North Sea context, this contributed to a very strong pressure from the environmental movement – which eventually had an effect. The United Kingdom gave in on important points during the North Sea Conference. Over time internal and external pressure made the United Kingdom realize that "the political costs of blocking the cooperation process were greater than the socioeconomic considerations."[31]

The picture was very different regarding land based pollution. All North Sea Countries would have to introduce costly and complex measures to comply with the ambitious goal adopted. Why, then, were such ambitious goals adopted in the first place? It may be that the Ministers were "captured by the momentum of the day". In a situation best characterized as a "green beauty contest", it appears that the Ministers from Sweden and Germany were particularly important in hammering out the 50% proposals. They agreed that forceful action was needed; 10% was insufficient and 90% was too much. Thus 50% seemed a reasonable "focal point".[32] In the same manner as most other suggested quantified emission reduction formulas in international environmental agreements, this figure *was political* and has been characterized as the "triumph of politics over ecology and economy". [33]

The Role Of Dominant Actors: the United Kingdom and the EU

Skjærseth[34] has shown that the United Kingdom initially did not have any intention of changing its practice in relation to dumping, even though it seemingly agreed to do so. The United Kingdom was even more "stubborn in relation to land based emissions. In general terms the United Kingdom has continued to be a "laggard", e.g., the party most frequently making reservations to decisions. Also, in relation to emissions of nutrients only at the insistence of the United Kingdom provision applies to "vulnerable areas." The United Kingdom has argued that this provision therefore does not apply to its waters and that no action was needed on its part. The United Kingdom has not reported nutrients emissions since 1992. This "stubborness" has been resisted by other State parties.

The changing role of the EU is important in this context. Recall that the EU was an initial laggard in the PARCOM. In the 1990s this changed, in part as a result of influence from the North Sea regime. In part a more pronounced environmental profile in the EU has developed over time. In relation to the North Sea regime, of particular importance is the adoption of the "dumping directive", introducing a ban on sewage sludge from 1998, the Nitrates and the Urban Waste Water Treatment

Directive (UWWTD) all in 1991. The fact that such a major player has gradually changed its position contributed to moving the North Sea regime in a more "progressive" direction, not the least by applying pressure on the United Kingdom. More generally, the EU can play an important role as the Directives have more of a binding effect than OSPAR decisions. Although the Directives are forceful when adopted, the process preceding their adoption is very complex and time-consuming. In this context, this problem is strengthened by the fact that there are members of the NS/NEA regime that are non-EU members: Norway, Iceland and Switzerland. Moreover, some EU members do not take part in the NS/NEA regional cooperation, e.g., Spain, Greece and Italy, which are not known for their support of "green" policies. Clearly this structural problem will make the streamlining of measures for the North Sea region a difficult and time-consuming procedure. If the EU ambition of expanding its membership in the future is implemented, the weight of this argument will increase. While the United Kingdom has tended to be an obstacle to co-operative environmenatal regimes, although decreasingly so overtime, overall the EU has had a more proactive role in the 1990s.

Domestic Constraints

Although the United Kingdom has been portrayed as a main laggard, many countries are having problems reaching the agreed goals. Considering the ambitious and somewhat arbitrary nature of the goals, it is not surprising that there has not been full attainment. Indeed, under real world circumstances, one cannot expect full compliance regarding land based pollution where so many different actors have to change their behavior so radically at so high costs within a fairly short time-span.

What are some of the more general domestic constraints making implementation difficult? Successful implementation is not only a question of *willingness* but also of *ability*. A government may be motivated and willing but problems of coordination abound. More specifically, there are *vertical* (between ministries and sub-national actors) and *horizontal* (between ministries) coordination problems.[35] In addition to the relevant ministries, municipalities, the agricultural sector and industry are also involved. The responsibilities of many of these organizations are quite removed from the international scene, but they all have to work together if the ambitious agreed goals are to become practical realities. Is it better to use "carrots" or "sticks" to induce subnational actors to change their behavior? In his seminal work Skjærseth,[36] shows that a complex interaction between local, state and international levels is crucial in explaining implementation performance. Industry has performed quite well in the North Sea context, but agriculture has not performed well. Probably this is because industry is accustomed to regulations of its emissions by various environmental regimes, but this is new for agriculture.[37] In terms of performance Skjærseth[38] ranks industry first, municipalities second and agriculture last. In terms of meeting the goals of the three countries under scrutiny, the United Kingdom is judged to be last, the Netherlands second and Norway first.

To summarize, North Sea/NEA cooperation has undergone significant development in its more than two decades of existence. It began with a low key legal approach in the 1970s that lasted through much of the 1980s. During this period, it was a forum for mid-level government officials, scientists and experts, mostly associated with the respective Ministries of Environment. Public attention and NGO pressure was marginal, and in its early years the PARCOM was described as primarily as a "travel club".[39] Then the politicians, the media, NGOs and other Ministries, became involved, vitalizing the process and applying pressure for cooperation. More recently concern about the environment has again been reduced and one of the key challenges is the implementation of the ambitious goals adopted – not to reach new and bold decisions. There are indications that implementation will be more difficult in the future as costs are increasing and environmental improvements may be smaller or uncertain. What then are the *merits* of the existing institutional design? And what are the lessons learned? Is NS/NEA cooperation a model for other regimes?

Lessons Learned

The Merits Of The Dual Approach

The most prominent successful lesson from this regime is the accomplishments made through the *dual approach, i.e., combining a "hard legal" regime with a "soft political" regime*. North Sea cooperation and Northeast Atlantic cooperation are quite distinct entities in formal and legal terms. While the North Sea regime is an intergovernmental political framework for cooperation, adopting goals and measures without any legal obligations, Northeast Atlantic cooperation is regulated by legal conventions, operating within established international law. While the legal approach has a *binding* effect upon the parties, policy declarations, which play a central role within many UN fora, have no such effect upon the parties. The latter approach has therefore been heavily criticized for lacking regulatory robustness or "bite". However, it seems that such *general* conclusions on the merits and shortcomings of either approach is very difficult to draw.

First, when scrutinized more closely, the legal approach may not always be so binding on the parties. In Northeast Atlantic cooperation for example, *recommendations* are not legally binding. Moreover, it has also been disputed whether in fact the *decisions* within the "old" PARCOM *are* legally binding on the Contracting Parties.[40] There is, however, no doubt that decisions of the new 1992 Convention are legally binding. Nevertheless legal measures have more "bite" than political declarations. This may provide opportunity for a more "responsible" and cautious policy by the parties, forcing the parties to calculate more carefully the practical effects and costs of decisions adopted. Such careful calculations have not always been prominent within the political approach. Thus, in general we would expect the distance between decisions and practice to be smaller within the legal approach as compared to the political approach.

On the other hand, although the ministerial declarations adopted for the North Sea have no legal effect, they have indeed been taken seriously by the parties. This political approach has been essential for what has been achieved in this region. Does this mean that the "softer" and often more ambitious political declarations are more effective than the more cautious but legally binding approach? On the face of it this may well appear to be the case. However, if we control for the different *political contexts* within which the two sub-regimes operate, this conclusion may not hold. The North Sea region is narrower, more homogeneous and composed of more affluent nations. Moreover, environmental problems have been more extensive here compared to the wider Northeast Atlantic. All these factors contribute towards the adoption of more forceful measures – as well as a willingness and ability to follow them up in this smaller region. Or, to borrow an expression from Skjæreth,[41] to *decouple* some of the main laggards, i.e., Spain and Portugal was essential for the success of the political approach. Thus to some extent it may be the difference in the *underlying scope of interests* within the two sub-regimes, rather than the *approaches* themselves that account for the difference in political energy. Any contrasting of these two approaches should therefore control for the political setting within which they operate. For example, political declarations adopted at the *global* level have usually little or no direct short-term effect due to the variety of interests represented and the absence of effective political pressure.

Rather than contrasting the two approaches, it is more fruitful to study the *interplay* between them. Two different approaches in a limited area may easily result in overlaps and dilute responsibilities, but in this case the two have clearly been *complementary,* creating synergies by achieving more than the two would have achieved separately. A main challenge – and achievement – has been to transform most of the ambitious political declarations from the more confined political setting to the broader legal setting. The main method to achieve this has been through *differential obligations*, an approach that has spread to other arenas, including broader global conventions.[42] That is, countries outside the North Sea area have sometimes obtained more lenient restrictions and/or more time to comply with decisions. The more narrow North Sea cooperation has acted as a "*motor*" within the wider regime while fine-tuning and specifications have developed within the wider legal context – turning soft declarations into hard obligations. On the one hand, without this political "motor" it may well be that NEA cooperation would not have been able to adjust to external demands for more action. On the other hand, in the absence of the established apparatus and expertise of NEA cooperation, the North Sea Conferences may have ended up like many high level initiatives characterized by much political "noise" and little lasting effect.[43]

The very slow start *may* to some extent have been avoided had the cooperation *started* in the key North Sea region and then spread to the more "peripheral" NEA countries. This would be in line with the lesson from the successful ozone regime where participation was initially limited to a relatively few key countries and subsequently expanded to include others. The logic behind this approach is that it makes sense to start out with those that are most heavily affected, contribute most to the problem and have the largest capacity to deal with it. If the differences between the parties are too large, it may prove too time consuming and cumbersome to initiate the process.

More recently there has been some question as to the continued need for the North Sea Conferences.[44] Since the 1992 Action Plan paved the way for a high level (ministerial) political component within OSPAR, this may seem logical. The "dual approach" is in a sense institutionalized in the established legal regime. The North Sea Conference approach may simply have "outlived" itself. It may be argued that it has played an important role as "*agenda setter*" and as the process of implementation is now at the forefront, the North Sea Conference may best be left to the traditional system. The intervals between the Conferences have also become longer over time (1984, 1987, 1990, 1995 and 2002). Perhaps the Conference in Oslo will be the last. But this institution may still have a role to play as a high profile and open forum. As the Ministerial meetings within the established system have now become routine and do not have a high profile, it is necessary to prevent NS/NEA cooperation from again disappearing from the agendas of the politicians and the public.

More emphasis, however, should be placed on the crucial implementation or performance issue. At the 1995 meeting two main issues were highlighted in the media: the adoption of the goal to stop the input of hazardous waste, and the dumping of platforms. The former fits into the "ambitious goal" category that always captures attention. Such goals, however, are convenient to adopt as the time-frames are so long and few of those adopting that goal will be in a responsible position to see if it is implemented or not.[45] The dumping issue is also a "classical high attention issue" – among the favorites for the activist NGOs. Both issues are certainly worthy of attention, but there was one essential component missing: exposure and focus on what had actually been *achieved.* If structured along these lines, the North Sea Conference could function as a form of *environmental performance review* as well as being a forum for long-term strategic thinking. Thus the dual approach may still have some untapped potential – at least in this region.

Building Institutional Capacity: Better Reporting Procedures And Increased Transparency

At crucial turning points, the development of this regime has been policy driven. Overall this has contributed to increased effectiveness. However, such pressure is rather cyclical, making the regime vulnerable to shifts in political priorities and public attention. It is therefore crucial that there is sufficient institutional capacity to keep the momentum going. A number of institutional dimensions may make a difference for regime effectiveness.[46] The decision-making rule clearly makes a difference, and is instrumental in explaining why the EU, with majority voting on many issues, is quite different from other international organizations and regimes. Some have pointed to the important role of knowledge and epistemic communities in regime effectiveness.[47] A number of analysts have singled out the significance of increasing transparency, not the least by opening up regimes to non-state actors. In the North Sea regime, transparency is particularly important and has increased over time.[48] One aspect of transparency that is particularly important when the question of domestic implementation is at the forefront is reporting procedures.

Reporting procedures were a weak point especially in PARCOM for a long time. The reasons are many: lack of good data on the part of a number of countries; reluctance to part with the data; insufficient compilation of data by the Secretariat; and methodological difficulties. According to the report made by Broadus et al[49] little was known about domestic implementation until the early 1990s due to the lack of compilation of data in any coherent form. It was also confirmed by the Secretariat, that until 1992, when an Action Plan for OSPAR was established, the procedures for reporting on implementation were very weak.[50] This situation changed significantly in the 1990s. According to the Secretariat: " the procedure for reporting on implementation has developed from virtually non-existent to what is now an integral part of each measure adopted by the Commissions ... This system is still not perfect but there has been a positive fundamental change in the Contracting Parties" attitude to implementation reporting ..."[51] Reporting procedures also improved following the adoption of the new Convention.[52]

The national reports submitted to the Secretariat are also subject to scrutiny at different levels. Before they are published, the Secretariat, or sometimes the lead country for the measures concerned, compiles the reports and prepares an overview which may then be examined at three different levels of the OSPAR hierarchy, culminating in the Commission's annual meeting. Since 1991, NGOs – from industry and the "green" lobby – have also been allowed to participate as observers at the Commission's annual meetings. All the documents produced for the Commission and its subsidiary bodies were formerly considered private unless the Commission specifically agreed to make them publicly available. Since 1993 documents prepared in the framework of the Commissions are available to all: NGOs, media and the public alike.

There is no doubt that the increased transparency, including better reporting procedures, has contributed to enhanced effectiveness of the regime. This does not mean that all is well. Just as there are instances of implementation failure, there are instances of reporting failure. There is little the Secretariat or NGOs can do to rectify this because procedures are in place and openness is secured. Essentially, a combination of mild pressure, convincing arguments and exposure, are the options. From a "green" perspective, "shaming" and "pressure" may seem tempting. But if used inappropriately it may result in even less enthusiastic participants and some parties may feel discredited. Lack of reporting and compliance may not be attributed only to willingness but also to ability. Therefore a balanced strategy for compliance may be preferable.

Comparison With Other Maritime Regimes

How does the North Sea compare to some other marine regional regimes like those for the Baltic and the Mediterranean? Using several criteria, Broadus et al.,[53] conclude that the Baltic program has been the most effective of these three regimes, followed by that for the North Sea, with that for the Mediterranean trailing far behind. One important reason that the Baltic regime is ranked first is that most attention in this analysis is on *outputs*. And the *procedural components* of the Baltic regime were well developed at an early time:" ... the Baltic region has in legal terms dealt with this problem in a most exemplary fashion, although somewhat more poorly to date in a practical sense".[54] In another comparative study between the Baltic regime and the North Sea regime, the conclusion is the same when output is used as an indicator. However, using a broader analytical perspective, including outcome (behavioral change), the North Sea regime is considered more effective.[55] In a large research project comparing 13 different international regimes in terms of effectiveness, OSCOM stands out as a high effectiveness regime, PARCOM is ranked in the middle, and the Mediterranean regime is considered to have low effectiveness regime.[56]

All of these rankings are certainly debatable. The key point is that the analyst must be *specific* regarding what criteria are used. Recall that for Haas[57] the Mediterranean regime stands out more or less as a "smashing success". What accounts for these differences in score assigned to the performance of the regime? Haas is essentially focussing on regime *formation* and the fact that cooperation is at all possible. Within the Miles et al project[58] the main emphasis is on behavioral change resulting from the regime. The regime may be a success in the former perspective and a failure in the latter. Ranking of regime effectiveness will also vary depending upon whether efforts are made to control for the differences in *type of problem* facing the various regimes.

Among the three regimes, the problems facing the regulators of the MEDPLAN are clearly the most difficult ones, considering the political, cultural and economic disparities between member countries. It is quite an accomplishment to create a regime under the given circumstances. The problems facing the regulators of the Baltic Sea were also more malign than the challenges facing the North Sea/NEA regime. Suffice it to mention that the environment was in worse shape in the Baltic and the disparities between the member countries were much larger; economically, politically and culturally. Considering especially the weak economies of the Eastern European states, their *ability* (but not necessarily their *willingness)* to cope with this problem was less developed.[59] Maybe as a result, the Baltic regime, at least for a long time, was better at producing papers and grand schemes rather than producing tangible results. In the latter half of the 1980s the Baltic regime *copied* the North Sea/NEA regime by adopting ambitious targets and adding a high level political component. This did not have the same decisive effect in the Baltic as it did in the North Sea – illustrating the futility of the "copying" approach. In the 1990s, the participants to the Baltic regime have become more creative, focussing more specifically on the pollution problems characteristic of the Baltic. Pollution "hot-spots" have been singled out, new financing institutions have been brought in and more cost-effective approaches are being tried.[60] In this sense, the Baltic Sea regulators may have been more creative than their colleagues in the North Sea regime where cost effectiveness has not been predominant. Uniform percentage wise reductions may be a good starting point, but such reductions are not efficient and also introduce an inequitable distribution of costs between countries.

It is thus difficult both to rank regimes and to borrow uncritically from one regime for another. There may be a few "good" general principles to be learned from previous experience, but the specifics of the various regions certainly need to be considered when regimes are created and subsequently developed.

Applicability Of Lessons Learned

What has been achieved over time within this regime? The severe methodological challenges of measuring regime effectiveness have been taken into account. Yet we can safely conclude that the effectiveness of the North Sea/North East Atlantic regime has increased over time in several ways. The level of activity has increased, measures have become more specific and stringent, domestic implementation has improved considerably and the environmental quality of this marine region has probably improved. Effectiveness, however, varies in relation to issue area. While the overall regime has been very successful in reducing and even terminating dumping, it is more of a mixed story when it comes to land-based pollution. Why is this so? Essentially it is because dumping is a problem that is easier to handle.

How do we account for increased effectiveness over time? The increase in problem solving capacity of the regime has been crucial for the overall positive development of the regime. Among the many factors, *the dual* approach, i.e., a combined soft political and hard legal approach has been particularly important in explaining progress.

Based on the lessons learned from this and the two other regimes briefly mentioned, are there any features that can and should be used in the Northeast Asia region?[61] A first observation is that simple copying or duplication is *not* advised. What may be a successful approach in one region may have little or no effect in another region. This was illustrated when comparing the North Sea regime with the Baltic regime. The same goes for the lessons learned concerning the relation between the ozone regime and climate regime. At the outset the ozone regime was used as a model for the climate regime, but this turned out to be too simple an approach as the two problems were so different.

A second observation is that there are probably more lessons to be learned from the Baltic and the Mediterranean regime than from the North Sea/NEA regime. The reason is simply that the first two regimes are somewhat more comparable to the Northeast Asia region due to the disparities between the members on a number of dimensions – including security issues. In comparative terms, it is difficult to think of regions that are more different that the North Sea/NEA region and the Northeast Asia region because the former is composed of affluent, Western countries essentially sharing the same political and cultural values. This is a very different story from Northeast Asia.

Does this mean that there are no lessons to be learned? There are lessons, but they should be related to various *stages* of the regime. As regards *regime creation*, which is most relevant for the Northeast Asia region, some important factors can be delineated. One is the importance of *leadership* – a crucial role was played by Germany in initiating the process of the North Sea Conferences. Another is the role of solid as well as consensual *knowledge* – also essential for the initiation as well as development of the regime. This should not be confused with the role of *epistemic communities*, as there has been little effect of such within this regime. A third factor is the crucial role played by *public opinion*, not the least in relation to perceived environmental disasters. It was an environmental disaster and resulting public opinion that triggered North Sea cooperation. A fourth relevant lesson is that "*cooperation takes time*". The North Sea regime was for a long time no more than a "travel club" for bureaucrats. Now it is considered a highly effective regime. Thus one should not give up on a regime even if almost nothing happens for a long time.

Finally a few words about lessons that stand out in the process of the *maturing of the regime and in its implementation phase*. First, the role of *public opinion* continues to be important. If interests and attention fade away, there is no pressure on politicians to act. The same is true for the importance of continued *knowledge building*. Overall it seems that *involving the ministers* is essentially a good approach. Although it is certainly not a simple solution to all problems, but for both this regime and the climate regime, adding a high level political component was essential to breaking political deadlocks. The *interaction between a high level policy component and a low level legal approach* – what has been referred to here as the "dual approach," is also worth considering. Again there is no guarantee of success, but this complementary approach has many merits. Many observers have pointed to the importance of *transparency* and this certainly has been confirmed in this regime. Finally, if a regime is to move from "paper to practice" there is a need for a strong and sustained institutional and political focus on *implementation*. It will be a long time before these factors have some applicability in the Northeast Asia region. But that does not mean that they should not be considered in a process of an open-minded intellectual approach to regime building in this region.

NOTES

1. *International Environmental Cooperation in the Northern Seas*, Booklet prepared by the Ministry of Environment in cooperation with S. Andresen, J.B. Skjærseth and O. Schram Stokke (Lysaker: The Fridtjof Nansen Institute and Environment Northern Seas (ENS) in connection with the ENS '93 Conference): 24.
2. For reasons of simplicity, I will often refer to "North Sea" cooperation, but the distinction between the Northeast Atlantic and the North Sea is an important one. The former area includes the North Sea but extends to Greenland in the west, Gibraltar in the south, and to the North Pole in the North. As the semi-enclosed North Sea is the key area of the cooperation, this will be most in focus.
3. This provision was added in 1983.
4. *Yearbook of International Cooperation on Environment and Development* 1999/2000 (Earthscan): 140.
5. E. Hey, T. Iljstra and A. Noellkaemper, "The 1992 OSPAR Convention for the Protection of the Marine Environment of the North East Atlantic: A Critical Analysis", *The International Journal of Marine and Coastal Law*, 8, 1 (1993): 1–49B.
6. D. Victor, K. Raustiala, and E. Skolnikoff (eds.), *The Implementation and Effectiveness of International Environmental Commitments* (MIT Press, 1998); E. Miles, et al., *Explaining Regime Effectiveness: Confronting Theory With Evidence* (MIT Press, forthcoming).
7. S. Andresen, J.B. Skjærseth and J. Wettestad, "Regime, the State and Society: Analyzing the Implementation of International Environmental Commitments", *IIASA Working Paper* 95–43 (June 1995): 66.
8. S. Sætevik, *Environmental Cooperation Between the North Sea States: Success or Failure?* (London and New York: Belhaven Press, 1988).
9. M. Pallemaerts, "The North Sea Ministerial Declarations from Bremen to the Hague: Does the Process Generate Any Substance?" *International Journal of Coastal and Estuarine Law*, 7, 1 (1992): 348–371.

10. J.B. Skjærseth, "Towards the End of Dumping in the North Sea: An Example of Effective International Problem-Solving?", *Marine Policy*, 16, 2: 133–140.
11. D. Freestone and T. Iljstra (eds.), "The North Sea: Perspectives on Regional Environmental Cooperation" Special issue of *The International Journal of Coastal and Estuarine Law* (London: Graham & Trotman, 1990).
12. For details, see J. Wettestad, "The 'Effectiveness" of the Paris Convention on Marine Pollution from Land-Based Sources", *International Environmental Affairs*, 4, 2 (1992): 101–121; P. Haas, Protecting the Baltic and the North Sea *in* P. Haas, R. Keohane and M. Levy, *Institutions for the Earth: Sources of Effective Environmental Protection (*MIT Press, 1993); S. Andresen, 1996, Effectiveness and Implementation Within the 'North Sea/Northeast Atlantic Cooperation': Development, Status and Future Perspectives, *in* Nordic research project on *The Effectiveness of Multilateral Environmental Agreements* Nord Environment, Nord 1996: 18. (Nordic Council, Copenhagen 1996): 60–63; and J.B. Skjærseth, *North Sea Cooperation: Linking International and Domestic Pollution Control* (Manchester University Press, 2000).
13. J.B. Skjærseth, "Effectiveness, Type of Problems and Problem-Solving Capacity: a Study of the Efforts of the Oslo Cooperation to Cope with Dumping in the North Sea and the North East Atlantic" (Fridtjof Nansen Institute, R:009–1991) (In Norwegian).
14. S. Andresen, *supra* n. 12.
15. J. Broadus et. al, *Comparative Assessment of Regional International Programs to Control Land-Based Marine Pollution: The Baltic, the North Sea and the Mediterranean*, (Woods Hole, Marine Policy Center, 1993).
16. Progress Report 95: 9; For none of the substances, however, was this goal reached by all. In some instances a majority had "complied", for others only a minority of the parties had reached the goal.
17. Progress Report 95: 10.
18. J.J. Maggs, 1995, "The Ministerial Declaration of the Fourth North Sea Conference," a review, *North Sea Monitor*, 13, 2: 4–24.
19. Progress Report 95: 12.
20. *Ibid*: 11.
21. *Ibid*: 10.
22. J.B. Skjærseth, *supra* n. 12.
23. *Ibid*: 90.
24. Generally, the tendency towards more thorough and independent research in the production of these status reports has increased over time. For an elaboration, see J.B. Skjaerseth, *supra* n. 12; and J. Wettestad, "Dealing with Land Based Marine Pollution in the North-East Atlantic: The Paris Convention and the North Sea Conferences *in* S. Andresen et al, *Science and Politics in International Environmental Regimes: Between Integrity and Involvement (*Manchester University Press, 2000).
25. North Sea Task Force, North Sea Quality Status Report (Oslo and Paris Commissions/International Council for the Exploration of the Seas, 1993).
26. See S. Andresen and J. Wettestad, "International Problem-Solving Effectiveness: The Oslo Project Story So Far," *International Environmental Affairs*, 7, 2 (Spring 1995): 127–150; and A. Underdal. "One Question, Two Answers" *in* E. Miles et al, *Explaining Regime Effectiveness: Confronting Theory With Evidence* (MIT Press, forthcoming). Other analysts apply different perspectives. See e.g., O. Young, et al., *The Effectiveness of International Environmental Regimes* (MIT Press, 1999).
27. The fact that the climate issue is so much more "malign" than the ozone issue explains much of why the latter is much more effective.
28. It is important to note, however, that such a distribution of stakes is no automatic recipe for success. For example, most countries have no material stakes in the whaling regime, but that does not mean that it has been very effective, see S. Andresen, The International Whaling Regime: More Failure Than Success, in E. Miles et al., *Explaining Regime Effectiveness: Confronting Theory With Evidence,* (MIT Press, forthcoming).
29. For further details on the role of the EU in this initial phase, see Saetevik, *supra* n. 8.
30. J. McCormick, 1991, *British Politics and the Environment* (Macmillan Press).
31. Skjaerseth, *supra* n. 10: 139.

32. Andresen, *supra* n. 12.
33. The reason for the latter is that equal emissions reductions runs counter to demand for cost effectiveness; P. Haas, *supra* n. 12.
34. Skjaerseth, *supra* n. 12.
35. A. Underdal and K Hanf, (eds), *International Environmental Agreements and Domestic Politics The Case of Acid Rain* (Ashgate Publishing Ltd, 2000).
36. J.B. Skjærseth, *North Sea Cooperation Linking International and Domestic Pollution Control* (Manchester University Press, 2000).
37. Andresen, *supra* n. 12: 73.
38. Skjaerseth, *supra* n. 12.
39. Andresen, *supra* n. 12.
40. E. Hey, T. Iljstra and A. Noellkaemper, "The 1992 OSPAR Convention for the Protection of the Marine Environment of the North East Atlantic: A Critical Analysis", *The International Journal of Marine and Coastal Law*, 8, 1 (1993): 1–49B.
41. Skjaerseth, *supra* n. 12.
42. This approach has been deemed crucial for the relative success of the ozone regime, and it is also an essential element of the climate regime.
43. There have not only been advantages associated with the dual approach but there has also sometimes been present an impression of "insiders" vs. "outsiders." For more on this and other problems, see Andresen, *supra* n. 12.
44. This question should also be seen in light of the role of the EU in the regime. Norway has been a driving force for the continuation of the INSC because as the only non-EU country in the North Sea region, it fears that the EU may eventually "swallow" the whole regime. For further discussion on this issue, see, Andresen, *ibid*; and Skjaerseth, *supra* n. 12.
45. To illustrate meaningless goal-setting, the Nordic Council some years ago declared that alcohol consumption should be reduced by 25% by the year 2000. In contrast, consumption has increased strongly – and the goal has long since been forgotten.
46. Wettestad, *supra* n. 24.
47. No epistemic community has been identified in the North Sea regime. This is not to say that scientific knowledge has not been important, but it has *not* been among the most decisive institutional factors; P. Haas, *Saving the Mediterranean: The Politics of International Environmental Cooperation*, (Columbia University Press, 1990); J. Wettestad, *Designing Effective International Regimes. The Key Conditions* (Edward Elgar; 1999); and Wettestad, *supra* n. 24.
48. At the last INSC more than 60 non governmental actors were present, representing target groups as well as the "green" movement.
49. J. Broadus et al., *Comparative Assessment of Regional International Programs to Control Land-Based Marine Pollution: The Baltic, the North Sea and the Mediterranean* (Woods Hole: Marine Policy Center, 1993).
50. Andresen, *supra* n. 12.
51. *Ibid*: 77.
52. Although it did not enter into legal force until 1998, on important points it was implemented much earlier.
53. Broadus et al., *supra* n. 49.
54. A. Westing (ed.), *Comprehensive Security for the Baltic: An Environmental Approach* (London: Sage, 1989).
55. Andresen, *supra* n. 12.
56. E. Miles, et al., *Explaining Regime Effectiveness: Confronting Theory With Evidence*, MIT Press, 2001.
57. Haas, *supra* n. 47.
58. Skjaerseth, *supra* n. 12.
59. I. Roginko, "Domestic Implementation of Baltic Sea Pollution Commitments in Russia and the Baltic States," in D. Victor et.al., *Effectiveness and Implementation of International Environmental Commitments* (MIT Press, 1998): 575–639.

60. O. Vakeva, "Financing of Environmental Investments in the Baltic Sea Area," the Convention on the Protection of the Marine Environment of the Baltic Sea Areas, Helsinki 1974 and 1992, Nordic Research Project on the Effectiveness of Multilateral Environmental Agreements, Nord Environment, Nord 1996: 18 (Nordic Council, Copenhagen): 47–60; Andresen, *supra* n. 12.
61. For a discussion of the application of lessons from one marine region to other(s), see M. Valencia, "Regional Maritime Regime Building: Prospects in Northeast and Southeast Asia," *Ocean Development and International Law* (2000) 31: 223–247; and P. Haas, Prospects for Effective Marine Governance in the NW Pacific region, *Marine Policy* (2000) 24: 341–348.

Douglas M. Johnston

SOUTHEAST ASIA: LESSONS LEARNED

Regional Ocean Management: Theory And Practice[1]

Regime theory has been developing (or "evolving") for over two decades.[2] From the beginning it has focussed chiefly on the contexts of natural resource development and ocean management.[3] One of the first full-scale applications of regime theory was oriented to the Arctic Ocean,[4] apparently in response to the challenge of combatting the special difficulties involved in imagining, promoting, designing and implementing cooperative arrangements in such a "heavily constrained" region.[5] The choice of such a "difficult" region for theory-building purposes is impressive, although there were benefits to be derived from thinking experimentally in a *tabula rasa* situation.

Similarly, the marine areas associated with Northeast Asia – the East China Sea, the Yellow Sea, the Sea of Japan, the Sea of Okhotsk, and adjacent areas of the North Pacific Ocean – have remained uncluttered with cooperative arrangements and negotiated settlements of the multilateral kind that could be characterized as experiments in regional ocean regime-building. In the past two decades the East-West Center has taken the initiative in organizing a series of workshops designed to explore the prospects of ocean regime-building in that other "difficult" region,[6] but, unlike the Arctic circumpolar region,[7] Northeast Asia continues to frustrate even the best-intentioned efforts to facilitate the establishment of cooperative ocean management "systems" there.[8]

In practice, the most famous inter-state experiment in cooperative ocean management at the regional level is the U.N. Regional Seas Programme developed by UNEP on the basis of an original Mediterranean prototype.[9] Throughout the 1980's this Programme earned widespread praise on the part of most academic and other observers to the extent it represented a serious and early attempt to promote the cause of systematic collaboration among regional littoral states for protection of the marine environment from threats of pollution.[10] Yet despite its quasi-sectoral orientation, the Regional Seas Programme, a globally conceived "system",[11] has (at least beyond the Mediterranean) fallen short of expectations that it would generate *operationally effective* sub-systems within the designated regional seas.

Mark J. Valencia (ed.), Maritime Regime Building, 73–86.

Several reasons for this disappointment might be suggested:

(i) the original model, designed more or less successfully for the Mediterranean, was too ambitious to be amenable to effective implementation in other, less well endowed regions;[12]
(ii) in most developing regions ocean management still has too low a national priority to justify the large-scale expenditure of scarce financial resources;[13]
(iii) most developing countries lack professional and technical expertise in ocean management on the scale required to sustain sophisticated regimes;[14]
(iv) permanent commitment to regime maintenance is unlikely in most developing regions as long as external funding sources are willing and able to support projects over a medium-length period of 5 to 10 years;[15]
(v) the regional scale of the UNEP initiative involved excessive dependency on the diplomacy of groupings of too many countries with differing interests, priorities and capabilities;[16]
(vi) the initiative was too statist in conception, overstretching the capacity of bureaucracies and discouraging "civil society" institutions from seeking a central role as catalyst and manager;[17] and
(vii) the original UNEP goal of pollution prevention and control has been transcended by the even more ambitious, multi-sectoral, multi-functional goals of "ocean management" and "integrated coastal management".[18]

Some of these arguments will be examined later in this paper as applied to the Southeast Asian and Northeast Asian contexts.

Regional Network-Building In Southeast Asia: The SEAPOL Experience

Arguably, effective regime-building depends less on formal diplomacy than on informal networking. There are, of course, different kinds of networks: inter-personal and inter-institutional; intra-sectoral and inter-sectoral; intra-governmental and inter-governmental; intra-regional and inter-regional; cross-societal and inter-societal; ideational and informational; physical (experiential) and virtual (cyberspatial); and so on. When the concept of the Southeast Asian Programme in Ocean Law, Policy and Management (SEAPOL) was first proposed to Canada's International Development Research Centre (IDRC) in 1981, it was envisaged as an experiment in regional network-building. With the modest resources made available, the initial purpose was simply to provide a non-governmental forum for government experts of the region to meet annually, "off the record", with one another, and with a smaller number of academic specialists, to discuss law-of-the-sea issues of common interest or concern under congenial non-governmental ("track two") auspices that permitted maximum freedom for frank exchange of ideas and information.

Over the years since then, especially since 1991 when the Canadian International Development Agency (CIDA) replaced IDRC as the principal source of support for SEAPOL, the Programme has grown into a network of several different kinds, indeed of virtually all the kinds described above except perhaps the inter-institutional. Now, between its *Newsletter* and its electronic websites, the full-time, professional SEAPOL Secretariat maintains contact with over 800 associates, both within and beyond the region. All of these individuals have participated in at least one of SEAPOL's 30 or more conferences, workshops, or other activities. Most have had two or three such contacts with other SEAPOL associates. And perhaps 200 to 300 have had regular physical contacts with the network, in many cases 10 to 15 times or more over the past 19 years.

It is difficult to guess how this record of physical contact compares with other regional networks generated by medium-sized projects such as SEAPOL. But this experience over a period of almost two decades may be sufficient to permit a number of observations.

First, the original model for SEAPOL was the Law of the Sea Institute, a global initiative dating back to 1966, established in the aftermath of the U.S. Stratton Commission on the Oceans (which provided a sophisticated, cross-disciplinary vision of ocean management requirements) and immediately before the late Ambassador Pardo's call for a global re-structuring of the law of the sea at UNCLOS III (which was to provide a sharp and sustained focus on contemporary ocean law-and-policy issues).[19] SEAPOL network-building started out with a primary emphasis on law-and-policy issues, at the end of the UNCLOS III period of global innovation over a wide variety of normative and institutional matters;[20] but by the end of its IDRC phase, SEAPOL had begun to reach out to the scientific community, when the region's need for greater sophistication in ocean management became apparent.[21]

It might be questioned whether regional network-building of this kind is more likely to be "effective" when it purports to encompass all domains: ocean science, ocean technology, ocean management operations, ocean law, and ocean policy. On the one hand, the network task of communication may be complicated by the need to transcend so many technical terminologies without losing all claim to intellectual clarity, although LSI, SEAPOL, and other similar networks ("epistemic communities") would argue that this task has proved to be realistic.[22] On the other hand, the holistic approach to networking is in tune with the current intellectual fashion favouring "integrated" ocean or coastal management, and may gain credibility in the perception of contemporary sophisticates.[23]

Second, the idea of "effective" networking begs the question whether network-building should have a purpose beyond the mere process of communication and exchange, such as the institutional task of regime-building. In what circumstances, if any, is successful ocean regime-building possible without being preceded by a successful and ongoing experiment in network-building? Or are the two kinds of initiatives "separate and entire unto themselves", sustained by different dynamics?

Any ambitions that SEAPOL might have had to move beyond network-building to regime-building in Southeast Asia have been held in check by a number of factors, not least ASEAN's low level of involvement in "ocean policy" issues as such, and its structural unsuitability to undertake a role in "ocean management" in any operational sense.[24] Moreover, until the mid-1990's SEAPOL thought of itself essentially as a "track two" initiative,[25] a network process rather than an institution.

Quite simply, funds would not have been provided by IDRC or CIDA to establish and maintain a regional institution, at least not without the prospect of matching or comparable financial contributions from indigenous (public or private) sources.[26] In short, the region itself would have had to make an important contribution if a bridge was to be built between the SEAPOL network and a regional regime.

Third, even if the goal of ocean regime-building had been politically attractive for the ASEAN region, it would have had to be kept on a "back burner" for many years until the organization's membership became coextensive with all ten countries that constitute the geographical region of Southeast Asia.[27] Now, for the first time, it becomes feasible to imagine an inter-state role in ocean regime-building for the "ASEAN seas" – most, but not all, of the South China Sea, plus adjacent marine areas such as the Gulf of Thailand and the Andaman Sea.[28] But it will still be necessary to address the problems associated with ASEAN's limited structure and mandate. Admittedly, ASEAN has begun to accept a role in "mediating" the conflict over the Spratly Islands, thanks to the promotional efforts of the Informal Working Group on the South China Sea, but apparently because of ASEAN's traditional responsibility for regional security rather than a new-found responsibility for integrated ocean policy and management.[29]

Fourth, it is surely true that the total volume of external funds provided to the ASEAN region for ocean-related purposes since the 1970's greatly exceeds the total funds contributed by the public and private sectors of Southeast Asia. In recent years some of the major external providers, such as CIDA, have begun to require, as a condition of new or renewed funding, that project organizers accept responsibility for securing "conversion" of the project into a "sustainable" institution or process through indigenous or alternative support. It remains to be seen whether this is an attainable goal.[30]

One might take the position that the expanded ASEAN is now too big, too clumsy, and too diverse a grouping to undertake a significant role in cooperative management in the vast ocean areas they encompass within their combined zones of national jurisdiction and in the high seas areas beyond. This pessimistic view may seem justified if we are all condemned to be constrained by our past. Admittedly a significant change in ASEAN priorities cannot be forthcoming without a strong leadership initiative on the part of two or three major member states, and no such trend in ocean affairs is currently discernible to this observer. Yet patient efforts are being made under UNEP auspices to design a politically acceptable ocean science programme for the South China Sea despite repeated failures to implement the original and updated Action Plans for the "East Asian Seas" designated by the Regional Seas Programme.[31]

So it is still possible, if not highly probable, that SEAPOL's networking with the ocean science community as well as the law-and-policy community may be seen as a contribution to the building of the elusive bridge between network and regime. Present indications suggest, however, that a regime-building success of this kind is more likely at the sub-regional level, as explained below.

Sub-Regional Institution-Building In The Gulf Of Thailand: The SEAPOL Experience

The SEAPOL IV program of the current 1996–2001 period of CIDA funding includes a Gulf of Thailand Project, with the purpose of facilitating the negotiation of an intergovernmental mechanism for promotion and implementation of cooperative management arrangements on the part of the four littoral States of these semi-enclosed waters: Cambodia, Malaysia, Thailand and Vietnam. The rationale in support of this Project is that global and macro-regional ("ocean-wide" or "sea-wide") institutions are generally too large, too clumsy, too expensive, and too politically divisive to be operationally effective even in single-sector ocean management, such as fishery management. In other, non-ocean contexts, more success in cooperative management has been achieved in *cross-border* settings involving only two, three or four neighboring countries. The Gulf of Thailand Project is, therefore, designed as an experiment in promoting cooperative management in a *sub-regional* sea.

In the case of the four littoral Sof the Gulf of Thailand, recent political developments have been favorable to the goal of sub-regional ocean management. The management-of-sub-regional-seas (MOSS) approach to cooperative ocean or coastal management may be an idea whose time has arrived. One reason for this kind of optimism is that the world community concept of integrated ocean management has become so complex and sophisticated – much more so than in the UNCLOS III era – that the national level is inadequate, at least for developing countries, and, on the other hand, the regional or macro-regional level introduces too many additional complications and unsustainable costs. So, by default, the best case for cooperative ocean management, and for ocean regime-building, exists at the sub-regional level.

At the time of writing, the MOSS approach to regime-building in the Gulf of Thailand appears to be progressing quite steadily. Perhaps it is not premature to offer a few observations based on SEAPOL's experiment in that sub-region.

First, political scientists will argue that progress in the Gulf of Thailand experiment can be explained by the recent political history of the sub-region. The tragic and destructive wars that ravished Indo-China for most of the 20th century have finally abated and given way to a period of relatively peaceful relations and potential prosperity for the four neighboring littoral States of the Gulf. The diplomatic community of this sub-region is more open than ever before to at least a modest experiment in cooperation, albeit reflecting a mood of pragmatic watchfulness rather than a totally trustful optimism.[32]

Second, although the political milieu of the Gulf of Thailand seems conducive to the establishment of a formal inter-governmental mechanism, say along the lines initially of a "coordinating body" or "joint committee", many questions will have to be addressed and negotiated before such a mechanism becomes operational: questions about size, purpose, structure, composition, functional authority, legal status, and financial provision.[33] At the present time (August 2000), it appears that at least three of the four national bureaucracies have reached consensus on the need to begin formal negotiations on these institutional issues, and one of these three is ready to take general recommendations on the need for such a mechanism to the Cabinet level.

Third, some of the government participants in the Gulf of Thailand Project point to the refurbished version of the Mekong River Commission (MRC) as a possible model for the kind of sub-regional regime that might be set up in the Gulf: a forum for consultations on current issues and for recommendations on proposed projects.[34] Because of cost concerns, especially on the part of Cambodia and Vietnam, the idea of such a mechanism is attractive only if it is likely to bring in large-scale external funding and technical assistance in the MRC manner. Given the difficulties experienced over the troubled waters of the Mekong for many years,[35] the MRC model may not seem a happy choice. But optimists ascribe the past dysfunctionality of the Mekong regime to basic political conflicts within and between the four Lower Mekong States (Cambodia, Laos, Thailand, and Vietnam) that have largely abated. They even point to recent evidence of improved relations with the two Upper Mekong riparian States (Myanmar and China), without which there will never be a fully functional regime for the Mekong Basin as a whole.[36] In the Gulf of Thailand there is no comparable history of institutional failure to overcome, and no other parties to pull in from the same "political ecosystem".

Fourth, to law-of-the-sea specialists in particular, the case for negotiated cooperative management arrangements for the Gulf of Thailand is especially compelling, since the geographical situation in question fits perfectly the definition of a "semi-enclosed sea" in Article 122 of the 1982 U.N. Convention on the Law of the Sea.[37] Under Article 123 the States bordering such waters "should cooperate with each other" in at least three sectors of ocean use: fishery management, protection of the marine environment, and scientific research.[38] It is not clear whether the mechanism suggested for the Gulf of Thailand would necessarily be limited to these three sectors: others have been advocated.[39]

Fifth, a more fundamental question about the MOSS approach to ocean regime-building has not had to be addressed so far under SEAPOL's Gulf of Thailand Project. At the outset it might be argued that the chosen grouping of littoral States for cooperative ocean management at the sub-regional level should, ideally, be those coastal states adjacent to the neighboring *large marine ecosystem* (LME) that would constitute the *optimal unit* of ocean management. But the Gulf of Thailand as a whole can be taken as a LME, even although ecologists may argue about its seaward limits, at least for certain migratory species that move beyond the geographical or legal mouth of the Gulf. Most participants so far have been willing to limit the spatial scope of the suggested regime to the waters within the "mouth", even though delineation may be arbitrary from an ecological perspective.

In other parts of the world, geography may not offer such a clear choice of spatial limits based on the geo-legal concept of enclosed or semi-enclosed waters. In these less clearly definable areas, the LME approach may make the best sense, so that sub-regional ocean regime-building would begin, not with a law-and-policy network as in the Gulf of Thailand, but with a major international scientific program devoted to studying in detail the structural and behavioral characteristics of the LME as a potentially optimal unit of management. A classic case of such an approach is the current, massively funded Meso-american Biological Corridor Programme (MBCP), which is predicated on the need to preserve the biodiversity of Central America by maintaining the integrity of the migration linkage of the South and North American fauna and flora through a network of protected areas.[40] Within this frame of reference, the Meso-american Barrier Reef Area has been designated tentatively as an ideal unit of sub-regional management under a regime that could be shared by the four neighboring littoral States of the Gulf of Honduras in the southern sector of the Caribbean Sea: Belize, Guatemala, Honduras and Mexico.

Yet many scientists concede the argument for a synthesis of the institutional and scientific approaches to the identification of an optimal grouping of littoral states for the purposes of cooperative ocean management. The contemporary LME perception of how coastal management should be designed takes into account not only the LME characteristics but also the human communities that border and utilize the resources which constitute the ecosystem. This systemic concept has been described as the *geo-political eco-system* (GPE). Accordingly, the new approach is to encourage sub-regional groupings of coastal States to work together within programs that integrate ocean scientists and specialists in ocean law-and-policy in a common effort to establish cooperative mechanisms whose management responsibilities would be framed around the shared GPE.

The Distinctiveness Of Northeast Asia

The difficulties experienced in promoting the need for ocean regimes in Northeast Asia may be due to the special, if not entirely unique, political characteristics of the region. Much might be made, for example, of the region's lack of any history or tradition of political cooperation. The Chinese, Japanese, Korean and Russian peoples who dominate the region have always been uneasy neighbors at best, and often bitter enemies. Even though there is less hostility now in the relationships among China, Taiwan, Japan, South Korea, North Korea and Russia – less perhaps than at any point since the mid-19th century – the cultivation of truly congenial relations at the inter-governmental level continues to tax the diplomatic skills of their most enlightened officials and politicians. Accordingly, the political milieu of Northeast Asia seems the least favorably inclined of all regions to support a formal initiative for inter-governmental regime-building. Almost any bold proposal by one of these countries would seem bound to provoke suspicions on the part of at least two of the others.

There is also a marked degree of distinctiveness in the marine geography of Northeast Asia. Whereas most other marine regions consist of countries that look out at a single sea or ocean that is perceived as a shared, and potentially unifying, environment – as an extension of their land-based economies – the countries of Northeast Asia look out either at the North Pacific, which is too vast to be perceived as their "shared dominion", or at a number of discrete seas (Yellow, East China, Japan and Okhotsk) in each of which strong "patrimonial" sentiment on the part of at least one littoral State tends to undermine the concept of shared authority. The geography of Northeast Asia seems unfriendly to the ideal of regional cooperation regarding the seas.

Moreover, half of these countries are too affluent for Northeast Asia to be eligible for UN designation as a developing marine region. Only China and North Korea clearly meet the traditional UN criteria for such treatment. Of the various seas of Northeast Asia perhaps only the Yellow Sea comes close to qualifying as a developing marine area, albeit with South Korea as one of the three littoral states. This anomaly, which prevented the inclusion of the seas of Northeast Asia in the "East Asian Seas" designated by UNEP, still makes it necessary for China to be treated as part of Southeast Asia for this purpose.

It must also be said that the cause of regional cooperation in Northeast Asia is complicated by having at its center a country with huge potential, limited capacity, an ancient tradition of cultural domination, and a continuing foreign policy that seems to reflect a basic reluctance to be part of a multilateral regional regime on an equal footing with lesser powers. With good reason, Chinese rhetoric for over 50 years has been obsessed with the threat of US hegemony in the North Pacific, but China's own posture in recent years has been widely perceived as equally hegemonic. Perhaps more than anything else, China's hunger for leadership status in Northeast Asia discourages bold efforts by its neighbors to embark on costly regime-building initiatives. Very clearly, the Chinese preference in the region is for bilateral arrangements within their control.

Lessons Learned From The SEAPOL Experience

It has become common in the academic literature to refer to networking of the SEAPOL kind as a "track-two" process. It may be agreed that the advantages of a "track-two" initiative are several:

(i) it is directed by organizers who are usually more or less free of political influence by governments;[41]
(ii) it offers a forum for government officials (and sometimes policy-makers) of different countries to meet one another, academic and scientific experts, and sometimes private sector representatives, to discuss current issues in an informal and congenial setting, freed from the constraints of official protocol;
(iii) it offers officials of one country an "off-the-record" ("back-channel") opportunity to meet privately with counterparts of another country to discuss *bilateral* issues that are proving difficult to resolve through formal inter-governmental diplomacy;
(iv) it creates incentives and provides the means for academic specialists of developing countries to develop a constructive and mutually beneficial relationship with officials of their own and neighbouring countries; and to facilitate their access to information that may not be otherwise available;
(v) it enables representatives of the least developed countries within a region to participate in international meetings and consultations that they could not otherwise afford to attend: and
(vi) it contributes to the establishment, maintenance or upgrading of publishable

academic/technical literature in developing regions deficient in high-quality research facilities.[42]

On the other hand, a "track-two" initiative also suffers from a number of disadvantages:

(i) it tends to be perceived either as "academic" in orientation (because of the participation of relatively "unconstrained" academic experts) or as potentially critical (because of the NGO status of the organizers);
(ii) because the organizers usually lack a strong political or personal connection with policy-makers, the practical influence of such an initiative on policy depends on the willingness and ability of the participating officials to take such a role upon themselves;[43]
(iii) usually the "track-two" initiative is taken within the framework of a medium-term project that is funded subject to a number of conditions, budgetary constraints, deadlines, and other administrative requirements imposed by the funding source that affect the scale, tempo, style and flexibility of the operation;[44] and
(iv) if the organizers assume a public information, public participation, or public advocacy role, they take the risk of alienating the policy-makers and thereby losing contact with their bureaucratic participants, who are the link with officialdom.

It was because of these disadvantages that SEAPOL, in the mid-1990's, began to move away, cautiously, from its traditional "track-two" role at the sub-regional level, where the risks of doing so were more acceptable than at the regional level. Under the Gulf of Thailand Project it seemed realistic that SEAPOL might be encouraged by the officials of that sub-region to facilitate the development of what might be described as a *dual regime-building process*. Four years later this is what appears to be emerging. While SEAPOL continues to serve as catalyst and coordinator under the Project, the key government officials (the "National Coordinators") at the "track-one" level will attempt to move their governments toward the first stage of regime-building through the establishment of an intergovernmental mechanism. It is assumed that for a short transitional period both inter-locked initiatives will proceed down their respective tracks.

The idea of a dualist approach to regime-building is surely less than radical to-day in the age of "civil society" ethos, but questions arise about its feasibility in a region as "difficult" as Northeast Asia.

First, because of the relative affluence of such countries as Japan, Taiwan and South Korea, it might be difficult to persuade a Western international development agency to undertake a major funding role in a dual regime-building experiment in Northeast Asia without matching or comparable contributions from the governments of the affluent countries. Realistically, such an experiment might have to begin, as in Southeast Asia, with a single-track, "track two" network-building" (or re-building) project along the lines of SEAPOL, including "National Coordinators" with some degree of influence within their bureaucracies who sustain the hope of converting the project eventually into a dual-track process of regime-building.

But are the government systems of Northeast Asia sufficiently flexible to permit key officials to participate "off the record" in a track-two network-building project that is known to have a regime-building purpose? Would the three affluent governments agree to cover the costs of participation of some or all of the other three (China, Russia, and North Korea), or would they have to be absorbed by the donor agency? Are the academic specialists or their institutions in Northeast Asia sufficiently motivated to accept the risks of failure associated with such a tricky challenge? Is the language barrier in that region insuperable? Since the suggested initiative could not be conducted in any one of the major languages of Northeast Asia (Chinese, Japanese, Korean and Russian), would the key participants be able to proceed entirely in English, knowing that they are all placed at more or less the same disadvantage? More fundamentally, is the risk of failure at the macro-regional level too great, forcing the experiment to begin at the sub-regional level, as in Southeast Asia? If so, which of the four discrete sub-regional seas is the best suited for a MOSS approach to sub-regional ocean regime-building? Which is the closest to the Gulf of Thailand in terms of factors conducive to inter-state cooperation? Or is each sub-region so "unique" that lessons learned from experience elsewhere are of little relevance to other areas?

In short, if the comparison of regional experiences is to be useful, perhaps we must all find a way of determining which factors are the most critical to success in ocean regime-building.

Notes

1. The voluminous literature on regime-building can be traced back to seminal works by Ernst Haas, Robert Keohane, Stephen D. Krasner, and others in the mid-1970's, emerging out of earlier empirical studies on European integration. Regime theory is a response to the need for a middle ground between sovereignty and world government. See generally, K.T. Litfin (ed.), *The Greening of Sovereignty in World Politics* (1998) for trends in environmental regime-building. Since the peaking of the regime theory literature, the concept of "global governance" has been advanced as another approach to development of the theoretical middle-ground between sovereignty and world government.
2. See for example, the early works of Oran Young: e.g., *Resource Management at the International Level: The Case of the North Pacific* (1977); *Resource Regimes: Natural Resources and Social Institutions* (1982); and *International Cooperation: Building Regimes for Natural Resources and the Environment* (1989).
3. *Ibid.*
4. Young, *Resource Management at the International Level, supra* n. 2, which, despite its sub-title, is concerned exclusively with the Western Arctic Ocean, or more precisely, "the marine areas to the north and to the south of the Bering Strait together with the associated coastal littorals of eastern Siberia and western North America" (termed "Beringia"). For a succinct and contemporary explanation of the "regime" concept, see Mark J. Valencia "Regional Maritime Regime-Building: Prospects in Northeast and Southeast Asia", *Ocean Development and International Law Journal* 31 (2000): 223.
5. During the Cold War era the only evidence of regime development was a degree of scientific cooperation for the conservation of polar bears. Anne Fikkan et al. "Polar Bears: The Importance of Simplicity", *in* Oran R. Young and Gail Osherenko (eds.), *Polar Politics: Creating Environmental Regimes* (1992): 96–151.

6. See for example, Mark J. Valencia (ed.), *International Conference on the Sea of Japan* (Honolulu: East–West Center, 1989); and Hyung Tack Huh, Chang Ik Zhang, and Mark J. Valencia (eds.), *Proceedings of the Internatioinal Conference on East Asian Seas: Cooperative Solutions to Transnational Issues* (Seoul: Korea Ocean Research and Development Institute, 1993).
7. The break-through in the (future) development of cooperative arrangements for the Arctic circumpolar region may be ascribed to three principal factors; (i) the end of the Cold War era, which endowed the Arctic Ocean with an extremely high degree of strategic sensitivity; (ii) the establishment of the 10–member Arctic Council, the first political arena available for consultations and decisions on critical issues affecting the circumpolar region as a whole; and (iii) recent concerns about the impact of an unprecedented rise in Arctic temperatures. All seem conducive to regime-building.
8. Several writers, including myself, have expressed discomfort with the over-use of the term "regime", which has acquired too many meanings to have a cutting edge. Even in the literature on the theory of international relations, each scholar tends to develop a slightly different definitional starting-point. In the law-of-the-sea literature, it may refer to the total outcome of conglomerate treaty-making such as UNCLOS III (e.g. Edward L. Miles "Ocean Policy Development in the 1990's: The Uses and Limitations of the Diplomatic Arena" in K Matics, T McDorman et al., (eds.), *Summary and Selected Papers of the SEAPOL Tri-Regional Conference* (1995): 32–60; and Robert L. Friedheim, *Negotiating the New Ocean Regime* (1993)); or to specific parts of the 1982 UNCLOS III Convention (e.g. Bing Bing Jia, *The Regime of Straits in International Law* (1998); or various kinds of sub-global cooperative arrangements in the context of ocean management. The over use of this admittedly convenient term might be reduced by distinguishing between "settlements" and "arrangements", between global and regional initiatives, and between prototypes and regional variations. For example, it might be useful to refer to most of the UNEP Regional Seas initiatives as "regional systems" based on the Mediterranean prototype, and the subsequent regional MOU arrangements on port state control as "regional systems" based on the Paris MOU prototype.
9. The prototype is a cluster of instruments consisting of the 1976 Barcelona Convention for the Protection of the Mediterranean Sea against Pollution (a "framework" convention) and two protocols: the Protocol for the Prevention of Pollution of the Mediterranean Sea by Dumping from Ships and Aircraft, and the Protocol Concerning Cooperation in Combatting Pollution of the Mediterranean Sea by Oil and Other Harmful Substances in Cases of Emergency.
10. See for example, Douglas M. Johnston and Lawrence M.G. Enomoto, "Regional Approaches to the Protection and Conservation of the Marine Environment" *in* Douglas Johnston (ed.), *Environmental Law of the Sea* (1981): 324–37.
11. See comment on terminology, *supra* n. 8.
12. Any rigorous regime entails substantial costs. It was always the hope of UNEP officials that the countries of each designated regional sea would eventually be able and willing to absorb a growing proportion of these costs, but given the nature of these instruments much of the funding required would have to go into training programs in science and technology, not just a relatively low-cost inspectorate as in the case of strictly regulatory regimes.
13. Environment in general still has a low priority in most developing countries, as measured by *per capita* expenditures, despite three decades of continuous global diplomacy to raise environmental standards led by the more affluent states. On environmental initiatives within Southeast Asia, see Douglas M. Johnston, "Environmental Law as 'Sacred Test': Western Values and Southeast Asian Prospects" *in* Douglas M. Johnston and Gerry Ferguson, *Asia-Pacific Legal Development* (1998): 405–465.
14. This difficulty is, of course, becoming less acute, as more and more students graduate from ocean-related programs. But most of these specialists are dependent on foreign universities in developed, mostly Western, countries.
15. So far as is known, no developing region has taken over full financial responsibility for the maintenance of a SEAPOL-type network in the field of ocean law, policy and management.
16. As argued below the solution to this problem might be to explore the possibility of sub-regional cooperative arrangements with smaller groupings of 3 to 5 neighboring littoral states, as in the Gulf of Thailand.

17. It is safe to say that if the UNEP Regional Seas Programme were being designed now, it would draw upon the resources and talents of "civil society" institutions on a scale that could never have been imagined in the mid-1970's.
18. The UNEP Regional Seas Programme, like UNCLOS III, was the product of the 1970's, when concern over pollution threats occupied center stage in the international arena. Today, in an age of greater sophistication, it is clear that the oceans are threatened by a much more complicated array of problems and deficiencies that call for an integrated approach to longer-term objectives of ocean management.
19. It might be recalled that the LSI was founded, at the University of Rhode Island, by a marine geologist, an oceanographer, and a political geographer, not by law-and-policy specialists, although the Board in subsequent years would become dominated by specialists with expertise in contemporary law-of-the-sea issues. In the early years the scientists had a major influence on the Institute's policy of broad cross-disciplinary thinking about the ocean, driven initially by the Krause-Knauss-Alexander troika, reinforced by Schaefer and Chapman. This "philosophy" attracted economists and political scientists and lawyers with a broad "policy", or even "policy science", orientation.
20. The first funding of SEAPOL, by IDRC, was devoted to the problems associated with the implementation of the 1982 UN Convention on the Law of the Sea in Southeast Asia.
21. The first determined effort to bring scientists into the SEAPOL network was in July 1993 at its Overview Workshop on the Gulf of Thailand, which was held in Kuala Lumpur and resulted in the adoption of recommendations for cooperation in oceanography and marine biology. See K.L. Matics and Ted. L. McDorman (eds.), *SEAPOL Overview Workshop on the Gulf of Thailand: Summary and Selected Papers* (1994): 79–81. As a result, scientists have been involved in all subsequent Meetings of Experts under the Gulf of Thailand Project, and special sessions for scientists were designed into the SEAPOL Tri-Regional Conference held at Bangkok in December 1994. See Matics, McDorman et al., *supra* n 8. Furthermore, SEAPOL since the mid-1990's has maintained close relations with the marine science community based in Bangkok through its contacts with Chulalongkorn and other Thai universities, with the WESTPAC program of IOC, and with COBSEA, the UNEP unit responsible for coordinating the Action Plan for the East Asian Seas. Indeed the SEAPOL Secretariat has participated in a number of WESTPAC and COBSEA meetings and workshops. So the prospects for an integrated approach to ocean management in the Gulf of Thailand seem favorable.
22. In my view, the early LSI conferences reflect a more or less shared optimism –albeit challenged by a few "political realists" – that UNCLOS III presented an unprecedented opportunity for the world community to re-structure the law of the sea in such a way as to permit the development of equitable and efficient uses of the ocean. It can be argued that to the extent UNCLOS III itself was fuelled by the same kind of idealism, it drew heavily upon the early LSI mind-set. Later, it is true, most LSI participants fixed more attention on the need for negotiated compromises on intractable North-South and other issues. SEAPOL was conceived 15 years later as a forum to promote the cause of cooperation at the regional level, in a region that seemed to have the inter-governmental apparatus to respond to such a challenge. In both cases the ideals and compromises involved have been discussed by an "epistemic community" noted for avoidance of narrow and technical discourse.
23. It would appear to be feasible to undertake a holistic approach to cooperative management in the Gulf of Thailand. See *supra* n. 21. Several recent projects associated with Chulalongkorn University, WESTPAC and COBSEA will involve a combination of scientists and non-scientists, such as economists, lawyers, and sociologists.
24. Even within the limits of its traditional mandate, ASEAN has lost much of its (always modest) international reputation as an "effective" political organization. During the region's financial crisis of 1997–98, it failed to provide support to the faltering economies of its principal members, and its response to other regional crises such as the recurrent "seasonal haze" problem has been only slightly less weak. Efforts by Thailand (chiefly) to modify the organization's policy of non-interference in the internal affairs of its members have been curbed by the traditionalists, even in the face of incremental disintegration of Indonesia, its largest member. *The Economist*, July 29–August 4, 2000: 20. After its Bangkok meeting in July 2000, the delegates were warned by Mr. Jayakumar, Singapore's Foreign Minister, that the "regional club must quickly get its act together to counter 'the perception of

ASEAN as ineffective and a sunset organization". *Ibid.*: 39. At Bangkok, ASEAN undertook a modest structural reform through the creation of a regional emergency-response troika, but this has failed to impress most observers. *Ibid.*: 39–40. Yet it cannot be said that ASEAN has failed to take any interest in ocean affairs. See, for example, Valencia, *supra* n. 4.

25. SEAPOL has always been designed and administered by a non-governmental group wholly detached from government agencies. In the early years it was financed principally by IDRC, a Canadian-based, publicly-funded, but non-governmental international organization. Since the early 1990's SEAPOL has been funded principally, and on a larger scale, by CIDA, which is Canada's official international development agency. Although more than 80% of SEAPOL's associates are government officials, SEAPOL has always been free of governmental influence, and, by avoiding controversy, it has never been treated as a confrontational NGO.
26. In Phase IV, SEAPOL has been pressed by CIDA to find a way of converting itself into a "track-one" process or institution, preferably through indigenous sources of support in Southeast Asia. But philanthropic assistance is notoriously elusive in this region, and ocean affairs have a low priority in ASEAN. Recently SEAPOL has become an accredited NGO observer with APEC, which conducts a number of ocean-related task forces over the wider Asia-Pacific macro-region, but APEC is still only a loosely conceived network of government institutions and is mostly focussed on economic issues.
27. SEAPOL now consists of the following member states: Brunei, Cambodia, Indonesia, Laos, Malaysia, Myanmar, the Philippines, Singapore, Thailand and Vietnam.
28. Previously the Andaman Sea might have been considered as falling outside the ASEAN region, or at least as peripheral, but now, with the admission of Myanmar, it is certainly one of the ASEAN marine areas, though geographically distinct from the South China Sea, and even more so than the Gulf of Thailand.
29. For a constructive and moderately optimistic analysis of the Spratly Island dispute, see Mark J. Valencia, Jon M. VanDyke, and Noel A. Ludwig, *Sharing the Resources of the South China Sea* (1997). For a more pessimistic view, see Bob Catlen and Makmur Keliat, *Spratlys: The Dispute on the South China Sea* (1997).
30. See *supra* n. 26. This might be seen as part of the toughening stance in favour of "conditionality" on the part of external funding agencies. *The Economist*, August 5–11, 2000: 43.
31. Difficulties in implementation are now attributed mainly to Chinese reluctance to participate in a multilateral program in certain sensitive sectors, such as fisheries, and reluctance to participate at all except on a bilateral basis. This policy of bilateral participation within the framework of a multilateral program has been pursued for many years by the members of SEAFDEC. Such a policy does not, of course, augur well for genuinely multilateral regime-building in the region.
32. It should be noted that Thailand's dominance in shipping, fishing, hydrocarbon production, scientific research, and other uses of the Gulf has contributed to an attitude of wariness on the part of its neighbors.
33. At least one of these countries appears to be willing to enter into treaty negotiations for the establishment of a formal, inter-state mechanism along the lines of an international commission, but the initial step is likely to be more tentative – perhaps just a "joint committee".
34. See Prathes Sutabutr, "Lessons Learned from the Political and Diplomatic History of the Mekong River Commission" *in* Douglas M. Johnston and Ankana Srivivatnanon, *Integrated Studies of the Gulf of Thailand*, 3 (2000): 49–80.
35. *Ibid.*: 53–62.
36. Myanmar has begun to send representatives to attend certain workshops in Indo-China, such as SEAPOL's workshop on the problems of landlockedness, which was held in Vientiane in February 2000, hosted by the Laotian Ministry of Foreign Affairs. At that meeting the Myanmar ambassador expressed his government's sympathetic interest in the problems of watershed management in the Lower Mekong Basin and conceded that the case for extending the regime to the Upper Mekong might be made.
37. The definition in Article 122 applies to "a gulf, basin or sea surrounded by two or more States and connected to another sea or ocean by a narrow outlet or consisting entirely or primarily of the territorial seas and exclusive economic zones of two or more coastal States".

38. Under Article 123 cooperation among the bordering states is urged for three principal purposes: "(a) to co-ordinate the management, conservation, exploration and exploitation of the living resources of the sea;
(b) to co-ordinate the implementation of their rights and duties with respect to the protection and preservation of the marine environment;
(c) to co-ordinate their scientific research policies and undertake where appropriate joint programmes of scientific research in the area ..."
39. Other problem areas suggested by some participants for inclusion in the mandate of the proposed mechanism include: exploration and exploitation of hydrocarbon resources in disputed areas; port development; dispute settlement procedures; piracy and other acts of violence; and community-based coastal management. But it is generally agreed that its mandate should not overlap with that of existing regional or sub-regional institutions.
40. The MBCP has received very substantial funding from GEF.
41. Only once in its 19 years has SEAPOL felt persuaded to postpone or alter a scheduled activity by reason of governmental concerns: a forward-looking workshop on "The Future of Islands" was postponed because of tensions over the Spratly Islands.
42. SEAPOL has published over 30 proceedings, compilations and studies since the mid-1980's, making up a fairly large part of the published English-language literature on ocean law, policy and management problems in Southeast Asia.
43. The willingness of the Gulf of Thailand officials to assume this role, particularly those who serve as "National Coordinators" under the Gulf of Thailand Project, is an important reason for its progress.
44. Like other medium-scale projects funded by international development agencies, SEAPOL is required to be accountable to CIDA, in a fairly detailed manner. Because of prior commitments, it is not always possible to respond at short notice to unexpected developments.

Hasjim Djalal

MANAGING POTENTIAL CONFLICTS IN THE SOUTH CHINA SEA: LESSONS LEARNED

There are both similarities and differences between the situations in the South China Sea and Northeast Asia. As in the South China Sea, there are many territorial and sovereignty issues between and among the countries in the region. However, the South China Sea territorial and sovereignty disputes are more multilateral than the territorial disputes in Northeast Asia, which are mostly bilateral.

The main territorial and sovereignty disputes in the South China Sea concern the Paracels and the Spratlys. In Northeast Asia they include the Diaoyutai (Senkaku) Islands between China/Taiwan and Japan, the Tokdo (Takeshima) islands between Korea and Japan and the four Northern Territories (Southern Kuriles) between Japan and the Russian Federation. As the result of these disputes over ownership of islands, difficulties have arisen with regard to the delimitation of maritime boundaries between the countries concerned.

In both the South China Sea and Northeast Asia there is the issue of divided states/countries regarding China and Korea. Indeed, the rivalry between China and Taiwan protrudes into the attempts to manage the potential conflicts in the area. The role of China is therefore very significant in both regions.

Attempts to formulate "joint development" have already produced an agreement between Japan and South Korea. But no hydrocarbons have been found in the area and the agreement is also opposed and protested by China. In the South China Sea, attempts to seek solution through joint development have produced successful results, particularly that between Malaysia and Thailand and that between Malaysia and Vietnam, both without involving China. Thailand, Malaysia and Vietnam have strong political will to seek solutions primarily because they are all members of ASEAN. While China has always professed to be willing to shelve territorial sovereignty disputes in favor of joint development in the South China Sea, in reality it has not been easy to understand what China really means by "joint development" and "shelving territorial sovereignty disputes".

Bilateral attempts to seek solutions to clearly bilateral problems such as the

Mark J. Valencia (ed.), Maritime Regime Building, 87–92.

Takeshima/Tokdo and the Northern Territories/southern Kuriles island disputes, have not resulted in any concrete agreement. Similarly, such attempts to settle the Spratlys disputes by bilateral negotiations between the parties concerned in the South China Sea have not yielded positive results.

In both cases, however, efforts to negotiate solutions to land boundaries have proven more successful than attempts to seek solutions to territorial and sovereignty disputes over islands. One of the reasons for this different result may be the possible consequences for maritime zones of settling these island sovereignty disputes.

There seems to be no specific format or forum to discuss the matter in Northeast Asia, while in the South China Sea various fora exist but with different degrees of success. The informal Track Two Workshop initiated by Indonesia has been one of the most active forums in developing dialogue, confidence building, and concrete cooperative efforts and networking in the South China Sea. Attempts to formally discuss the matters between China and ASEAN, without the participation of Chinese Taipei, have also made some progress, particularly in discussing a "code of conduct" and other relevant issues in the ASEAN-China dialogue. The attempt of the ASEAN Regional Forum (ARF) to deal with the South China Sea issues has been ineffective, particularly because the ARF involves many non-regional powers whose motives may be suspect.

The attempts by academics and think-tanks to better understand the issues of the South China Sea have been on the whole useful, although in some cases they have not obtained full cooperation from China. For example, China attempted to prevent an ASEAN-ISIS (Institute for Strategic and International Studies), and Philippines Institute for Strategic and Defense Studies conference on the South China Sea. There is no forum or format to discuss similar issues in Northeast Asia, except through the ARF which from time to time discusses the issues of the Korean Peninsula and the Taiwan Strait.

There are also geographic similarities between the South China Sea and the Seas of Northeast Asia in that they are "enclosed or semi-enclosed seas." Article 123 of UNCLOS 1982 requires that:

"States bordering an enclosed or semi-enclosed sea should co-operate with each other in the exercise of their rights and in the performance of their duties under this Convention. To this end they shall endeavour, directly or through an appropriate regional organization:

a. to co-ordinate the management, conservation, exploration and exploitation of the living resources of the sea;
b. to co-ordinate the implementation of their rights and duties with respect to the protection and preservation of the marine environment;
c. to co-ordinate their scientific research policies and undertake where appropriate joint programmes of scientific research in the area;
d. to invite, as appropriate, other interested States or international organizations to co-operate with them in furtherance of the provisions of this article."

Most of the countries bordering the South China Sea, except Taiwan, Thailand and Cambodia, have ratified UNCLOS 1982, as have all countries in the Northeast Asia except North Korea. Under UNCLOS 1982, all countries in Northeast Asia are obliged to cooperate and seek peaceful settlement to disputes. As in the South China Sea, Article 123 of UNCLOS 1982 could be used as a basis for co-operative initiatives in Northeast Asia.

When I took the initiative to launch the workshop process on Managing Potential Conflicts in the South China Sea in 1989, endorsed by the Indonesian Minister of Foreign Affairs and financially supported by Canada, Indonesia and I had no ulterior motive except to promote peace, stability and cooperation in the South China Sea. We saw this as important for the development of the region as a whole, including Indonesia. I was therefore motivated by the conviction that everyone in the region should be guided by the principle that the promotion of regional peace, stability and cooperation in the South China Sea is part of the national interest of the respective countries, and that cooperation is preferable and better than confrontation. My perception was largely shared by the countries in the region. Therefore the first lesson that can be learned regarding Northeast Asia is the need to find someone with similar perceptions, preferably someone from the region whose country is not directly involved in the territorial or sovereignty disputes. It may be difficult to find this personality in Northeast Asia. Nevertheless, it would be ideal if Northeast Asian countries could agree to have one or two of their prominent personalities take the initiative and for the initiative to be supported by disinterested countries, such as Canada or Norway, Sweden or Finland. This initiative should be assisted by other leading personalities from neighboring countries within the context of promoting wider regional peace, stability and cooperation.

The experience of the South China Sea countries is replete with conflicts and potential conflicts very similar to the experience in Northeast Asia. Yet, the spirit to promote cooperation and to avoid conflicts may be stronger in the South China Sea than in Northeast Asia due to historical and cultural differences. In taking the initiative in the South China Sea, Indonesia benefited greatly from the ASEAN experience in managing the conflicts in Indo-China, particularly in Cambodia, and by its own experience in managing and seeking a solution to the conflicts in the southern Philippines. There are perhaps lessons that could be drawn with regard to the potential conflicts in Northeast Asia, from the experience on the Korean Peninsula, and in the border conflicts between the then Soviet Union and China and between China and Vietnam. The Antarctic model is not appropriate to either region because it entails a moratorium on exploitation which no South China Sea or Northeast Asian country wants.

The attempts to manage potential conflicts in the South China Sea began with second track diplomacy and some agreements became formal intergovernmental positions. For example, the principles of cooperation agreed by the South China Sea Workshop in 1991 became in 1992 the formal ASEAN Declaration on the South China Sea. The Workshop attempts to study and promote a "code of conduct" in the South China Sea resulted in the current willingness of China and ASEAN to discuss a "code of conduct" in the formal ASEAN-China dialogue. The Workshop efforts also laid the groundwork for the formal bilateral "codes of conduct" between the Philippines and Vietnam. The Workshop's formulation of cooperative efforts in the fields of marine science, environmental protection, safety of navigation and others have similarly been initiated in the larger context by other formal fora, including the dialogues between ASEAN and China and in the ASEAN Regional Forum and the Council for Security Co-operation in the Asia-Pacific. The good lesson that can be learned from this process is that informal initiatives can be very useful in inducing formal cooperation, albeit in other fora.

In launching an informal initiative, it is important to take into account several basic principles.

1. Use an all inclusive approach and do not exclude any directly interested countries or parties. The South China Sea Workshop dialogue even included Laos as a land-locked country and it proved helpful in creating a sense of regional community regarding the issues.
2. Start with less sensitive issues which participants feel comfortable discussing without incurring the animosity of their respective governments or authorities. Our experience showed that oil and even marine scientific research proved to be too sensitive. Environmental protection is a more comfortable topic.
3. The participants should be senior or important personalities in their governments or authorities although they are participating in the process in their private capacities.
4. Do not institutionalize the structure of the process by creating a permanent or well-organized mechanism but keep the process as flexible as possible.
5. Differences should not be magnified and cooperation should be emphasized. Bringing "provocative international attention" to, or immediately internationalizing the process may be detrimental in the long run. China is particularly opposed to internationalization because it may mean involvement of the United States in the issues.
6. In view of the delicacy and sensitivity of some issues, it is wise to follow a step by step approach and take into account the principles of cost effectiveness. In Northeast Asia, it may be wise to start with the Sea of Japan (East Sea) which may be somewhat less controversial than the Yellow or East China Seas. China may wish to participate because of its fishing interests and access via the Tumen River but it would not be a dominant player.
7. It should be understood that the process of managing potential conflicts is a long-term continuing process where lack of immediate concrete results is not cause for despair and frustration.
8. Keep the objectives simple. The South China Sea Workshops have two objectives: to learn how to co-operate; and to implement co-operation. The goal is to build confidence through dialogue.
9. The roles of the initiator and the convener of the process as well as the roles of disinterested supporters and sponsors are very crucial. The initiator or the convenor must have patience and dedication as well as tenacity and sufficient knowledge of the delicate issues involved. At the same time, the convener must be able to retain the respect and the continued support and cooperation of all participants.

In managing the potential conflicts in the South China Sea over the last ten years, I have learned lessons that could be relevant to the Northeast Asian region. Some of those lessons follow:

1. More powerful countries in the region should be mindful of the views of their neighbors. In particular, the powerful countries should be careful that they are not perceived to be dominating or bullying their weaker neighbors.
2. Attempts should be made to broaden participation in cooperative programs and to deepen the areas of cooperation. The more the cooperative efforts are perceived as mutual benefits, the more likely the efforts are to be successful.
3. There should be an emphasis on regional and common interests. The countries of the region should learn how to pursue their national interests within their regional context; in fact they should perceive the pursuit of regional interests as part of their national interest. Thus, a "sense of community" should be developed among the participants.
4. There should be a gradual progression from the concept of national resilience to the concept of regional resilience and regional cohesion. ASEAN's positive experiences in this regard have been very instructive and could be useful for the countries of Northeast Asia.
5. The countries in the region should be less sensitive to the concept of national sovereignty, since issues which in the past might arguably be solely of a national character, are now increasingly becoming regional and have regional implications, including environmental issues, domestic political stability issues, and monetary and financial issues.
6. Within the true sense of Asian good neighborliness, the countries in the region should be helpful to their neighbors in need.
7. The countries in the region should also avoid an arms race and coordinate their defense needs, thus bolstering regional harmony and transparency.
8. Major external powers, wherever possible and practicable, should support the development of a constructive atmosphere for peace, stability and progress.
9. Countries in the region should exercise preventive diplomacy by preventing disputes from becoming open conflict and preventing conflict from spreading or intensifying.
10. Countries in the region should develop concrete cooperative programs or projects so that potential conflicts can be managed by converting them to cooperative efforts.
11. Countries in the region should develop various fora for dialogue – bilateral or multilateral, formal or informal. The more fora the better. The various fora for dialogue should eventually be able to produce an agreed code of conduct for the region.
12. Countries should pursue various avenues of peaceful settlement of disputes, either through bilateral negotiation, if the disputes are bilateral, or multilateral if the disputes are multilateral. For example, Vietnam wanted to include the Parcels in the Workshop discussions but it was pointed out that this was a purely bilateral issue between Vietnam and China. On the other hand, China wants to

resolve the Spratlys issues bilaterally but it cannot do so because the issues are multilateral in nature. The compromise is that China can discuss the issues bilaterally but a solution must be multilateral.

13. Third party mechanisms for dispute settlement should also be explored and utilized, such as good offices, mediation, arbitration, and if necessary, eventual adjudication through the International Court of Justice or the Law of the Sea Tribunal where China, Japan and South Korea are well-represented. The ASEAN Treaty of Amity and Cooperation (TAC) has already formulated mechanisms for dispute settlement among ASEAN countries. If mechanisms for dispute settlement in the Northeast Asian region do not exist or are not satisfactory, a new mechanism should be considered, by drawing from the TAC or other models.
14. The countries in the region should, wherever and whenever possible, attempt to settle their land, maritime and jurisdictional boundaries as soon as possible and respect the agreed boundaries. They should not settle boundary problems through unilateral enactment of national legislation, because enacting legislation tends to harden positions rather than enabling parties to seek a solution.
15. In some disputed areas, the application of the joint development concept may be useful as long as the zone of the dispute is or can be identified.
16. While encouraging Track One activities in Northeast Asia to be more responsive and imaginative in dealing with potential conflict, more discussion by the Track Two fora, including by academics and think tanks can be helpful.
17. The interests of non-regional countries should be taken into account and their potential contribution to conflict avoidance in the region should not be discounted.

To conclude, I would encourage the development of linkages and networking, not only among academics, experts and strategic think-tanks in Northeast Asian countries, but also linkages between and among various regional and sub-regional initiatives, particularly between Southeast Asia and Northeast Asia. Developing linkages and networks among the various Track-One and Track-Two activities and initiatives is essential. For this purpose, patience, persistence, consistency and prudence are necessary to overcome the many obstacles to peace.

Jon M. Van Dyke[1]

THE SOUTH PACIFIC: LESSONS LEARNED

INTRODUCTION

The Pacific is the world's largest ocean, and it contains many of the world's smallest countries. Most of these isolated islands of the Pacific were under colonial domination from the mid-nineteenth century (or earlier) until (usually) the 1970s, when most became independent. Some are still connected with, or integrated into, a larger metropolitan power (i.e., French Polynesia, New Caledonia, and Wallis & Futuna, are still connected to France, and Hawai'i, American Samoa, Guam, and the Northern Marianas are connected to the United States[2]). New Zealand (Aotearoa) and Australia participate in many Pacific regional organizations and activities; they are viewed as partners, but play separate and different, although still important, roles, because of their larger size and differences in culture and history. The regional organizations used to be titled "South Pacific ...." but increasingly the term "Pacific" is now used, because the Republic of the Marshall Islands, the Federated States of Micronesia, and the Republic of Palau (all situated north of the equator) have become active members of these organizations since they emerged from their colonial status in the late 1980s and early 1990s, and Guam and the Commonwealth of the Northern Mariana Islands also participate in some of them.

This chapter explores the origins and accomplishments of the South Pacific Commission (SPC)(now the Secretariat of the Pacific Community), the South Pacific Forum (SPF), the Forum Fisheries Agency (FFA), and the South Pacific Regional Environmental Programme (SPREP).[3]

The major treaties negotiated by these groups and their member nations include the Tuna Treaty, the South Pacific Nuclear Free Zone (SPNFZ) Treaty, the SPREP Treaty, and the Waigani Treaty. Particular focus is given to the work of SPREP, one of the most inclusive South Pacific regional organizations, with 26 members. The Pacific Island Development Program at the East-West Center in Honolulu should also be mentioned, because it has been an effective organization to identify research priorities and to coordinate academic work relevant to the region.

Mark J. Valencia (ed.), Maritime Regime Building, 93–103.

South Pacific Commission/Secretariat Of The Pacific Community

The South Pacific Commission (SPC) was formed in 1947 by four nations with colonies in the Pacific (France, Great Britain, the Netherlands, and the United States) in order to maintain the stability of the region and assist with education, health, and economic development in their colonies.[4] Most of the island colonies also became members of the organization, which was based in Noumea, New Caledonia, and its meetings featured a unique mix of representatives from both the metropolitan powers and the islands themselves. In the 1960s, as the movement toward decolonialization picked up momentum, a growing feeling that the colonial nations were interlopers in the area led to a revolution of sorts, and the island members worked to change the SPC's form and mission, moving to "replace trusteeship with collegial co-operation and technical expertise with direct financial assistance."[5] This revolution, as well as the rapid growth of independence in the South Pacific, led to the formation in 1965 of the first purely indigenous regional organization, the Pacific Island Producers Association (PIPA), followed soon by the Forum. Today the SPC is now longer viewed as the colonial body it once was. It now has 26 members (the same as SPREP), and has recently been renamed the Secretariat of the Pacific Community, to acknowledge its northern Pacific members and to move away from the colonialism implied in the word "commission."[6] This body has concentrated on technical assistance, and has focused, for instance, on the development of the tuna industry, providing important data through its tuna tagging projects.

The Forum

Largely to counter the big-power domination found in the SPC, the independent and self-governing island countries in the Pacific created the South Pacific Forum in 1971. This new organization has had a broad political agenda. It has always acted through an annual meeting attended by the heads of government of its members, and has a Secretariat based in Suva, Fiji.[7] The environment has been only one of the many issues it has addressed, but by unifying the South Pacific Island nations, it paved the way for organizations which could address the environmental concerns of the entire region. Each newly independent nation has been invited to join the Forum, and it now contains 16 members: Australia, the Cook Islands, the Federated States of Micronesia, Fiji, Kiribati, Marshall Islands, Nauru, New Zealand, Niue, Palau, Papua New Guinea, Samoa (formerly "Western Samoa"), Solomon Islands, Tonga, Tuvalu, and Vanuatu. The Forum created the important Forum Fisheries Agency, provided the venue to negotiate the South Pacific Nuclear Free Zone Treaty (SPNFZ), assisted with the development of the SPREP Treaty, has promoted the Ocean Resources Management Training Program,[8] has assisted in the development of the 1995 Treaty of Waigani (discussed below) on the movements of hazardous and radioactive wastes, and has issued important statements drawing attention to the inadequacies of the international regime governing the shipment of ultrahazardous radioactive cargoes by sea.

Pacific Island nations have vigorously protested these shipments since they began in the early 1990s.[9] At the meeting of the South Pacific Forum in October 1999, the Pacific Island leaders expressed their concern once again and called specifically for a compensation regime to be established that would indemnify the island communities for any economic losses that their tourism and fishing industries might suffer as a result of an accident "even if there is no actual environmental damage caused."[10] This communique also urged members to work within the International Maritime Organization (IMO) and the International Atomic Energy Agency (IAEA) to develop "a strong regime of prior notification to, and consultation with, coastal states on planned shipments of radioactive materials and MOX fuel (consistent with security requirements), the development of a regime for the preparation of Environmental Impact Statements and Emergency Response Plans."[11] New Zealand has taken a lead in protesting these shipments, arguing that they should not be permitted through New Zealand's EEZ because of the " 'precautionary principle' enshrined in the Rio Declaration," and that "there should be recognition in international law of the right of potentially affected coastal states to prior notification, and, ideally, prior informed consent for shipments of nuclear material."[12]

The Forum Fisheries Agency

In 1979, the 12 countries that were then members of the Forum established the Forum Fisheries Agency (FFA) to coordinate regional fishing concerns in light of the international recognition (in the drafts that eventually became the 1982 United Nations Law of the Sea Convention[13]) of the 200–nautical-mile exclusive economic zone (EEZ).[14] The FFA's members are now the same 16 countries that are members of the Forum, and its main functions are to set policy for fishing in the South Pacific Region and to negotiate agreements (through its staff, based in Honiara, Solomon Islands) with fishing companies that wish to fish in the EEZs of its members. Others functions include "accumulating detailed and up-to-date information on aspects of living marine resources in the region; evaluating and analyzing data to provide clear, timely, concise, complete and accurate advice to member countries; [and] developing and maintaining a communications network for the dissemination of information to member countries."[15] The FFA members outlawed fishing for tuna without a license within their EEZs, but until 1987 the U.S. refused to recognize these prohibitions with regard to tuna, a migratory fish that moves from zone to zone. Eventually, however, political developments led the U.S. to agree to meet with leaders of the Pacific Islands and to negotiate a Multilateral Fisheries Treaty.[16]

This treaty authorized up-to-50 U.S. vessels to fish in the EEZs of the 16 countries in the FFA. The treaty was originally to end in 1993, but the parties agreed to extend it for another ten years, granting an additional 5 licenses to the United States and increasing the price paid to the island countries for the licenses.[17] The FFA distributes the licensing funds to the individual states, monitors fishing in the EEZs, and provides observers for the boats.[18]

More recently, the FFA has coordinated the Pacific Islanders' role in the important multilateral negotiations designed to create a new fisheries organization for the Pacific combining distant-water fishing countries with the island and coastal countries of the region.[19] These high-level multilateral negotiations were designed to create the regional organization anticipated by Article 64 of the 1982 Law of the Sea Convention[20] and by the 1995 Straddling and Migratory Stocks Agreement.[21] The final negotiating session was held in Honolulu from August 30 to September 5, 2000, and a treaty was signed by most of the negotiating parties, but China, France, and Tonga abstained[22] and Japan and South Korea refused to sign the agreement.[23] The FFA members worked hard during the three-year negotiating period to ensure that the convention area would be as large as possible, that decisions could be made without unanimous agreement, that developing countries would receive financial assistance to carry out their obligations under the treaty, that the treaty could come into force even if the distant-water fishing nations did not ratify it, and that a vessel monitoring system would become mandatory for all vessels. Although not all the FFA positions were achieved to extent desired,[24] the final version of the treaty was signed in September 2000 by all the FFA members except Tonga.

The South Pacific Nuclear Free Zone Treaty (SPNFZ)

In 1985, under the auspices of the Forum, the nations of the South Pacific adopted the South Pacific Nuclear Free Zone Treaty,[25] creating a unique nuclear free zone in the Pacific. The parties to the Treaty agreed to prevent testing, stationing, manufacturing, and dumping of nuclear weapons and devices within their territories and to discourage the use of the region for nuclear testing and waste disposal.[26] The treaty permits, however, nuclear-powered vessels and ships carrying nuclear weapons to go through the waters covered by the treaty without restrictions, leading some to question the teeth of the treaty.[27] France continued to test nuclear weapons at Muroroa in French Polynesia for a number of years,[28] but finally ended that program in 1996. The SPNFZ treaty has been important as a symbolic statement issued by the Pacific Island community, and with the end of the Cold War and the easing of international tension, it may be possible to revisit the text and tighten the regime created by it.[29]

The South Pacific Regional Environmental Programme

The Early Days. The idea of a South Pacific Regional Environmental Programme was originally conceived at a nature conservation workshop in 1969, which led to a workshop in 1973, which in turn led to a program for the conservation of nature included within the SPC's agenda in 1973.[30] SPREP was finally formally established in 1982, as a joint initiative of the SPC and the Forum. In 1982, at the "Conference on the Human Environment in the South Pacific," the delegates decided to set up SPREP as a separate entity within the SPC. At this conference, SPREP's first "Action Plan for Managing the Natural Resources of the South Pacific Region" was produced. This document was revised in 1991 and 1997, and remains the focus of SPREP's activities.

During the early 1980s, the United Nations Environment Programme (UNEP) provided funds to permit the Pacific Island countries to negotiate a regional-seas treaty, which was completed in 1986.[31] This treaty is formally titled the Convention for the Protection of the Natural Resources and Environment of the South Pacific Region,[32] but it is usually informally called the "SPREP Treaty." The Treaty is designed to protect both the land and marine resources of the region, and contains two protocols – on waste dumping and combating pollution emergencies. The Treaty was particularly important in completely prohibiting the dumping of both high- and low-level nuclear waste in the area it covered.[33] Although the Mediterranean[34] and Baltic[35] Treaties also contained such a prohibition, the Pacific region is much larger and contains sites that were considered by many as appropriate for nuclear waste dumping. Nonetheless, in an important concession that led to the later ban on all nuclear waste dumping in the 1996 Protocol[36] to the London Convention, 1972,[37] the United States agreed to the prohibition. The SPREP Treaty also contains valuable provisions requiring environmental assessments with regard to any major activity affecting the SPREP Treaty area.[38]

After the SPREP Treaty was completed in 1986, bi-annual intergovernmental meetings began to be held, and after 1990, these meetings became annual events. Also in 1986, a five-member steering committee was established, consisting of representatives from Polynesia, Melanesia, Micronesia, the metropolitan powers (France/United Kingdom/USA), and Australia/New Zealand.

In 1991, the leaders of SPREP decided that the organization should become autonomous from SPC and the Forum. Samoa offered to host the organization's headquarters, and SPREP moved to Apia, Samoa in 1992. In 1993, SPREP's members signed the Agreement Establishing SPREP in order to formalize its new status as an independent intergovernmental organization. In 1995, Niue became the tenth nation to ratify this Agreement, and SPREP officially became autonomous.[39]

SPREP Today. SPREP follows the model utilized earlier by SPC which allows all political entities to participate in its activities, whether they are independent or not, and today, 26 such political entities nations participate in SPREP's policy-making decisions.[40] In its latest Action Plan (for 1997–2000), SPREP described its primary four-year goal as "To build national capacity to protect and improve the environment of the region for the benefit of Pacific island people now and in the future."[41] Its five current objectives are:

- To protect natural heritage through the conservation and sustainable use of biodiversity.
- To understand and respond to climate change, particularly through integrated coastal management.
- To minimise pollution and wastes, and improve preparedness for pollution emergencies.
- To plan, manage and regulate development in a manner that is environmentally sustainable.
- To strengthen environmental education, training, and information systems.

The staff of SPREP grew from fewer than ten in the 1980s to about 35 employees by the time the organization moved its headquarters to Apia in 1992. Today, SPREP has more than 60 full time employees, working throughout the Pacific Islands. SPREP's budget, almost entirely based on contributions, has also been steadily growing. In 1995, the total general budget was about 7.3 million dollars. The largest share came from the United Nations Development Programme (UNDP), which gave 29% of the total budget. The second largest donor was the Australian Agency for International Development (AusAID), which contributed 27% of SPREP's 1995 budget. New Zealand gave 8%, and a number of other donors gave similar amounts.[42]

In 1997, SPREP helped coordinate the adoption of a Strategic Action Programme for International Waters of the Pacific Region, to combat the degradation of water quality and associated critical habitats and the unsustainable use of resources.[43] Most of SPREP's activities are carried out with the assistance of international or national agencies. Its main current activities include the South Pacific Biodiversity Conservation Programme, the Pacific Islands Climate Change Assistance Programme, and the Programme of Capacity Building for Sustainable Development in the South Pacific, which are funded through the United Nations Development Programme; the Waste Management Education and Awareness Programme, funded by the European Union; the Climate Change and Environmental Education and Training Programmes, funded through the Australian Agency for International Development (AusAID); the Atmospheric and Radiation Measurements in the Tropical Western Pacific, funded by the U.S. Department of Energy; and meteorological services, in conjunction with the World Meteorological Organization.

For the future, SPREP will be focusing on protecting the biodiversity of the region, preparing for the impacts of climate change, promoting integrated coastal management, preventing pollution, managing wastes (and encouraging the ratification of the Treaty of Waigani,[44] discussed below), preparing for emergencies, and building capacity within each island community so that the environment can be understood and protected.[45]

The Wellington Driftnet Convention

One example of quick collective action taken by Pacific Islanders is their adoption in 1989 of the Convention for the Prohibition of Fishing with Long Driftnets in the South Pacific[46] (often called the Wellington Convention or the South Pacific Driftnet Convention). This treaty was negotiated swiftly because of the concern that large amounts of juvenile albacore tuna were being harvested through the high-seas driftnetting utilized by Japanese, Koreans, and Taiwanese. The treaty prohibited the landing or transshipment of driftnet catches in the ports of the contracting parties, the importation of any fish or fish product caught with a driftnet, and the possession of any driftnet on board any vessel within the fisheries jurisdiction of the contracting parties.[47] After adopting their own treaty, the Pacific Islanders worked effectively together to promote the adoption by the United Nations General Assembly later in 1989[48] and again in 1991[49] of resolutions supporting global restrictions and calling upon countries to ban the use of high seas driftnets entirely.

The Treaty Of Waigani

Another important initiative taken in the Pacific was the adoption in September 1995 of the Waigani Convention on the movement of hazardous and radioactive wastes.[50] The Waigani Convention, when it takes effect, will require contracting parties to prohibit the import of hazardous and radioactive wastes and establishes mandatory notification procedures for transboundary movements of nonradioactive hazardous waste. As of September 1999, Australia, the Federated States of Micronesia, Fiji, Papua New Guinea, and the Solomon Islands had ratified the Convention, and another five ratifications were needed before the treaty would take effect.[51]

Lessons Learned

It may be hard to translate lessons from the Pacific to other areas, because the Pacific is unique in its huge size and its small, scattered population. Most of the Pacific is not industrialized, and its pollution problems are modest compared to those of other areas.

But certain lessons are evident. When the benefits have been seen to be high, as with regard to the exploitation of the important fishery resources of the Pacific, a strong and coordinated cooperative body (the Forum Fisheries Agency (FFA)) has been established, with a skilled secretariat, and it has taken important initiatives and provided significant benefits for the region. This initiative has been taken, perhaps, because the small islands feel vulnerable when dealing with the industrialized distant-water fishing countries, similarly to the vulnerability found among the Caribbean islanders and the small island communities in the Indian Ocean. Although those countries (mostly in the Western Pacific) with greater fishing resources have coordinated their actions to some extent, they have been relatively generous toward those island countries with fewer fish in their waters, and the regime has maintained its cohesion through this sense of cooperation and sharing.

With regard to environmental protection, the countries of the region have adopted sound treaties, and established a small secretariat to coordinate environmental activities, but almost all the funding has come from outside the region, because most threats to the environment are distant and the priority for environmental protection is low. But when they perceive a regional threat, they do act effectively together. Pacific Islanders acted in a coordinated manner to demonstrate their abhorrence of nuclear testing by adopting the 1985 South Pacific Nuclear Free Zone Treaty, and they acted to ban driftnets through the adoption of the 1989 South Pacific Driftnet Convention and by working together to adopt strong U.N. General Assembly resolutions. More recently, they have expressed their strong concern about the movement of hazardous cargoes through their waters and about global warming and sea-level rise, but they have not yet been effective in stopping these shipments or in forcing an effective global response to global warming.

Pacific Islanders have created functioning regional organizations that have played important roles in allowing the small islands to speak with a more uniform and louder voice when talking to the larger powers. The island communities have a natural cultural affinity, and generally enjoy working and coordinating policy with each other.[52] But political conflicts within some of the countries (particularly Fiji and the Solomon Islands) have caused the regional organizations to be less effective than they might otherwise have been, and the fact that many countries in the region are dependent on outside aid makes them less able to criticize the activities of those countries (like Japan) that give them aid.

The SPREP Secretariat has established a sound agenda, but it has avoided the most controversial subjects, focusing on consensus- and capacity-building rather than confrontation. The global-warming/climate-change issue is another one where we see Pacific Islanders working together effectively in international forums to ensure that their voices are heard. Although such coordinated action may not be a "regime" in the legal sense, it does appear to be regime-like. To summarize, a good beginning has been made in the Pacific, but how effective these initiatives will be in the long run remains to be determined.

NOTES

1. The author gratefully acknowledges the assistance in the research and drafting of this paper provided by Sat Khalsa, member of the class of 2001, William S. Richardson School of Law, University of Hawai'i at Manoa.
2. Pitcairn is still governed by the United Kingdom and the Tokelau Islands are a political dependency of New Zealand. The Cook Islands and Nuie are "freely associated states" with New Zealand, and the Republic of the Marshall Islands, the Federated States of Micronesia, and the Republic of Palau are "freely associated states" with the United States, but they are now all viewed as essentially independent countries, with the right to conduct their own foreign affairs, and are all members of the Pacific's regional organizations in their own right.
3. Several other Pacific Island cooperative activities should also be mentioned. The Pacific Island nations have worked together since 1972 to coordinate research on deep seabed minerals through an organization first called the Committee for Coordination of Joint Prospecting for Mineral Resources in the South Pacific Offshore Areas (CCOP/SOPAC), and later called the South Pacific GeoSciences Commission (SOPAC).

   They also negotiated a treaty called the Convention on the Conservation of Nature in the South Pacific, which was adopted in Apia, Samoa, on June 12, 1976, and came into force in the 1990s (sometimes called the Apia Convention). The purpose of the Apia Convention was to take action for the conservation, utilization, creation, and development of natural resources of the region through careful planning and management. In particular, the parties are encouraged to create protected areas to safeguard natural ecosystems, superlative scenery, striking geographical formations, and areas of historic, cultural, aesthetic, or scientific value. See Florian Gubon, "Steps Taken by South Pacific Island States to Preserve and Protect Ocean Resources for Future Generations" *in* Jon M. Van Dyke, Durwood Zaelke, and Grant Hewison (eds.), *Freedom for the Seas in the 21st Century* 1993): 121, 124–125.
4. *See* Biliana Cicin–Sain and Robert W. Knecht, "The Emergence of a Regional Ocean Regime in the South Pacific", Ecology Law Quarterly (1989): 171, 179; Jon M. Van Dyke and Susan Heftel, "Tuna Management in the Pacific: An Analysis of the South Pacific Forum Fisheries Agency", Univ. Hawaii Law Review 9 (1981): 1, 4.
5. Cicin-Sain and Knecht, *ibid.* (citing Richard Herr, "Regionalism in the South Seas: The Impact of the South Pacific Commission, 1947–1974" (unpublished dissertation, Duke University, 1976)).
6. See Secretariat of the Pacific Community, SPC's History, <http://www.spc.org.nc/En/history.htm> (last visited August 19, 2000); "Flags of the World", *Pacific Community*, <http://fotw.digibel.be/flags/spc.html#desc> (last visited August 19, 2000).

7. The Secretariat was originally called the South Pacific Bureau for Economic Cooperation (SPEC), but now is called the South Pacific Forum Secretariat.
8. Cicin-Sain and Knecht, *supra* n. 3: 180–81, 184–85.
9. See listing of protests in Jon M. Van Dyke, "Applying the Precautionary Principle to Ocean Shipments of Radioactive Materials", Ocean Development and International Law Journal 27 (1996): 379, 386.
10. Thirteenth South Pacific Forum, Forum Communique, para. 31 (Koror, Palau, Oct. 3–5, 1999).
11. *Ibid.* para. 33.
12. Letter from Don McKinnon, New Zealand Minister of Foreign Affairs and Trade, to Michael Szabo, July 7, 1999. Legislation is now being examined by New Zealand's parliament that would further restrict vessels powered by or carrying nuclear materials from entering New Zealand's waters.
13. United Nations Convention on the Law of the Sea, Dec. 10, 1982, U.N. A/CONF.62/122; *I.L.M.* 21 (1982): 1261.
14. See generally Jon M. Van Dyke and Susan Heftel, "Tuna Management in the Pacific: An Analysis of the South Pacific Forum Fisheries Agency", Univ. Hawaii Law Review 3 (1981): 1.
15. Francis Bugotu, Peter Sitan and Teekabu Tikai, "A Review of the Achievements of the Forum Fisheries Agency in its First Decade of Operations", *in* Richard Herr (ed.), *The Forum Fisheries Agency: Achievements, Challenges and Prospects* (1990): 3.
16. Forum Fisheries Agency, Multilateral Treaty on Fisheries with the United States between the Governments of Certain Pacific Island States and the Government of the United States of America, *I.L.M.* 26 (1987): 1048 and <http://www.ffa.int/frame_index1.html> (last visited August 21, 2000). Two incidents that led to the U.S. willingness to negotiate were the seizing of a U.S. fishing vessel by the Solomon Islands, and the beginning of preliminary negotiations regarding access to fishing between Kiribati and Russia. *Ibid.* See generally Jon M. Van Dyke and Carolyn Nicol, "U.S. Tuna Policy: A Reluctant Acceptance of the International Norm" *in* David J. Doulman (ed.), *Tuna Issues and Perspectives in the Pacific Islands Region* (Honolulu: East-West Center, 1987): 105.
17. During the first five years of the original Treaty, the FFA countries were paid about $12 million per year by the U.S. government and the tuna fishing industry. After the extension the total payment went up to $18 million annually. The Treaty also requires the U.S. vessels to fund and carry FFA observers on board to monitor compliance and to do scientific data collection. See Forum Fisheries Agency, Multilateral Treaty on Fisheries with the United States between the Governments of Certain Pacific Island States and the Government of the United States of America, <http://www.ffa.int/frame_index1.html> (last visited August 21, 2000).
18. For additional information about the FFA, see Gracie Fong, "Governance and Stewardship of the Living Resources: The Work of the South Pacific Forum Fisheries Agency" *in* Jon M. Van Dyke, Durwood Zaelke and Grant Hewison (eds.), *Freedom for the Seas in the 21st Century* (1993): 131–141.
19. See Final Act of the Multilateral High Level Conference on the Conservation and Management of Highly Migratory Fish Stocks in the Western and Central Pacific, September 5, 2000.
20. See generally Van Dyke and Heftel, *supra* n. 14: 11–17.
21. Agreement for the Implementation of the Provisions of the United Nations Convention on the Law of the Sea of 10 December 1982 Relating to the Conservation and Management of Straddling Fish Stocks and Highly Migratory Fish Stocks (UN Doc. A/CONF.164/37, 8 September 1995), *I.L.M.* (1995): 1542; see generally Jon M. Van Dyke, The Straddling and Migratory Stocks Agreement and the Pacific, International Journal of Marine and Coastal Law 11 (1996): 406.
22. China abstained because of its concern about Taiwan's classification as a "fishing entity," with some rights to participate separately in decisionmaking, and France abstained because it wanted the French islands in the Pacific to have separate status in the Commission that is to be established.
23. Japan and South Korea stated that they view the treaty as too restrictive of their historic fishing practices in the high seas.
24. Among the many compromises, for instance, was the decisionmaking provision, which established "chambers" consisting of the FFA and the non-FFA members of the Commission, and provided that each chamber would need to support a decision by a three-fourths majority, with the proviso that no proposal could be defeated by fewer than three votes in either chamber.

25. South Pacific Nuclear Free Zone Treaty, Aug. 6, 1985, *I.L.M.* 24 (1985): 1440. The treaty came into force in 1986 when Australia became the 8th nation to ratify it. See generally Jon M. Van Dyke, Lewis Alexander, and Joseph Morgan (eds.), *International Navigation: Rocks and Shoals Ahead?* (1988): 352–372.
26. See Florian Gubon, *supra* n. 3: 125-26.
27. See, e.g., Michael Hamel-Green, *The South Pacific Nuclear Free Zone Treaty: A Critical Assessment* (1990); Ramesh Thakur, "The Treaty of Rarotonga: The South Pacific Nuclear-Free Zone" *in* David Pitt and Gordon Thompson (eds.), *Nuclear Free Zones* (1987); Greg Fry, "Regional Arms Control in the South Pacific" *in* David Pitt and Gordon Thompson (eds.), *Nuclear Free Zones* (1987); Peter Glebbeek, *The South Pacific Nuclear Free Zone Treaty: A Lost Battle Against the Superpowers?* (The Hague, Netherlands: Institute of Social Studies, Working Paper Series) 73 (January 1990): 10–11.
28. See generally Jon M. Van Dyke, Kirk R. Smith, and Suliana Siwatibau, "Nuclear Activities and Pacific Islanders", *Energy* 9 (1984): 733
29. Article 5(2) of the treaty allows each nation in the region to decide for itself if it wants to give port access and/or navigation rights to nuclear armed and/or propelled vessels. Glebbeek, *supra* n 27: 14–15.
30. For more on SPREP's history, see generally South Pacific Regional Environmental Programme, "What's SPREP", <http://www.sprep.org.ws/whatsprep_.htm> (last visited on Auguest 17, 2000); *see also* South Pacific Regional Environmental Programme, *SPREP Annual Report 1995/96* 9 (1996) (hereinafter cited as "Annual Report 1995/96"). Arthur Dahl, who had been with the Smithsonian Institute in Washington, D.C., and more recently has worked at the United Nations Environment Programme, is recognized as "SPREP's founding father," and was the sole Regional Ecological Advisor in the SPC in 1974. "V-Files – The Early Days of SPREP: A Roundtable with Arthur", SPREP's Environment Newsletter (December 1997): 9.
31. See Jon M. Van Dyke, "The United States and Japan in Relation to the Resources, the Environment, and the People of the Pacific Island Region", *Ecology Law Quarterly* 16 (1989): 217, 222–223.
32. Convention for the Protection of the Natural Resources and Environment of the South Pacific Region, Nov. 25, 1986, *I.L.M.* 26 (1987): 38 (hereafter cited as "SPREP Treaty").
33. *Ibid.* art. 10(1). Subseabed emplacement was also prohibited. *Ibid.*
34. Convention for the Protection of the Mediterranean Sea Against Pollution, Feb. 16, 1967, art. 4, 15 *I.L.M.*; *Ibid.* annex I(7) (1976): 290–291.
35. Convention on the Protection of the Marine Environment of the Baltic Sea Area, March 22, 1974, art. 9, *I.L.M.* 13 (1974): 544, 549.
36. See David Hunter, James Salzman, and Durwood Zaelke, *International Environmental Law and Policy* (1998): 767–770.
37. Convention on the Prevention of Marine Pollution by Dumping of Wastes and Other Matter, December 1972, *I.L.M.* 12: 129.
38. SPREP Treaty, art. 16.
39. For more on the SPREP Treaty, *supra* n. 32, see Mere Pulea, "The Unfinished Agenda for the Pacific to Protect the Ocean Environment" *in* Jon M. Van Dyke, Durwood Zaelke, and Grant Hewison (eds.), *Freedom for the Seas in the 21st Century* (1993): 103, 107–110, and A.V.S. Va'ai, "The Convention for the Protection of the Natural Resources and Environment of the South Pacific Region: Its Strengths and Weaknesses", in *Freedom for the Seas, Ibid.*: 113–20.
40. *Annual Report 1995/96 supra* n. 30: 7. These 26 political units are: American Samoa, Australia, Cook Islands, Federated States of Micronesia, Fiji, France, French Polynesia, Guam, Kiribati, Marshall Islands, Nauru, New Caledonia, New Zealand, Niue, Northern Mariana Islands, Palau, Papua New Guinea, Pitcairn, Samoa (formerly Western Samoa), Solomon Islands, Tokelau, Tonga, Tuvalu, United States, Vanuatu, and Wallis and Futuna.
41. South Pacific Regional Environmental Programme, *Action Plan for Managing the Environment of the South Pacific Region 1997–2000* (1997): 6 (hereinafter cited as "1997–2000 *Action Plan*").
42. *Annual Report 1995/96 supra* n. 30: 35. Some donors contribute to particular projects, as well as to the general budget.
43. "Strategic Action Programme for Waters of the Pacific", *SPREP's Environment Newsletter* (December 1997): 10.

44. Tamari'i Tutangata, "Signing on to Watching Waste", *Islands Business* (September 1999): 48.
45. *1997–2000 Action Plan.*
46. Convention for the Prohibition of Fishing with Long Driftnets in the South Pacific, *done* at Wellington, November 24, 1989, and Noumea, October 20, 1990, *I.L.M.* 29 (1990): 1449.
47. See generally Gubon, *supra* n. 3: 126–27.
48. "Large-Scale Pelagic Driftnet Fishing and Its Impact on the Living Marine Resources of the World's Oceans and Seas", G.A. Res. 44/225, U.N. GAOR Supp. (No. 49) (U.N.Doc. A/44/746/Add.7 1989), adopted by consensus Dec. 22, 1989, reprinted in Environmental Policy and Law 20 (1990): 36.
49. U.N.Doc. A/RES/46/215 (1991). See generally David Hunter, James Salzman, and Durwood Zaelke, *International Environmental Law and Policy* (1998): 721–731.
50. Convention to Ban the Importation into Forum Island Countries of Hazardous and Radioactive Wastes and to Control the Transboundary Movement and Management of Hazardous Wastes Within the South Pacific Region, Sept. 16, 1995 (commonly referred to as the Waigani Treaty or Convention, because it was opened for signature at the 1995 meeting of the Forum in Waigani, Papua New Guinea). This treaty is not yet in force.
51. Tutangata, *supra* n. 44. Only two Pacific Island countries (Federated States of Micronesia, and Papua New Guinea) have ratified the Basel Convention on the Control of Transboundary Movements of Hazardous Wastes and their Disposal, March 22, 1989 (UNEP Doc. T/BSL/000) *I.L.M.* 28 (1989): 657, which regulates the movement of hazardous wastes at the global level.
52. The Pacific Islands have not, however, made any governmental moves to create a regional human rights organization. See Jon M. Van Dyke, "Prospects for the Development of Intergovernmental Human Rights Bodies in Asia and the Pacific" *in* Ellen L. Lutz, Hurst Hannum, and Kathryn J. Burke (eds.), *New Directions in Human Rights* (1989): 51.

*Hiran W. Jayewardene**

THE INDIAN OCEAN: LESSONS LEARNED

INTRODUCTION

In the Indian Ocean region, the regional organization dedicated to co-operation in marine affairs is IOMAC – Indian Ocean Marine Affairs Co-operation. However, there are a number of other organizations in the region which deal with sub-regional, and specialized marine activities such as tuna fisheries and marine environmental management, as well as more general aspects such as trade and economic co-operation.

Essentially a pioneering developing country regional initiative, IOMAC is an organization that emerged from efforts of Indian Ocean countries to forge co-operation in ocean affairs following the conclusion of the Third Law of the Sea Conference and the adoption of the 1982 United Nations Law of the Sea Convention.

In the early 1980s, the idea of a wide-ranging framework for Indian Ocean co-operation was conceived. IOMAC developed from a process of consultations in the African-Asian Legal Consultative Committee (AALCC) commencing in 1981 for promoting co-operation, building ocean capabilities, and harmonizing approaches. IOMAC is supported by a Secretariat located in Colombo – Sri Lanka.

This Indian Ocean co-operation process has directly and indirectly, contributed to the emergence of a new Indian Ocean regime, triggering a range of regional activities and interest in the Indian Ocean. It has somewhat of a long history with examples that would perhaps find some application elsewhere, and lessons that may be learned against the backdrop of the complex geo-politics of the region and changing scenarios. The primary aim of this paper is to detail the IOMAC experience in the wider regional context, insofar as it may be a basis of comparison, or have some bearing on similar efforts in respect of other ocean regions.

---

* NOTE: The views expressed by the writer in this paper are his personal views and unless otherwise stated, do not in any way reflect the formal position of the organization for Indian Ocean Marine Affairs Co-operation (IOMAC) or the IOMAC Secretariat.

Mark J. Valencia (ed.), Maritime Regime Building, 105–130.

Co-operation In "Marine Affairs"

Although it may be said that co-operation in the field of marine affairs is a relatively new development, the idea of such co-operation in the Indian Ocean within a formal international framework was conceived nearly two decades ago. The concept of marine affairs as an integrated inter-disciplinary approach, or multi-dimensional one, perhaps owes a great deal to the development of the modern Law of the Sea. Just as much as it is preferred that development undertakings on land are integrated, recent ocean development approaches too have taken on this broader dimension. The text of the 1982 United Nations Convention on the Law of the Sea clearly shows the mixing of a multitude of other elements with international law. As in other areas, the 1992 United Nations Conference on Environment and Development (UNCED) and related developments have also underlined the multi-dimensional environmental under-pinnings for management of human activities. So too, in the Indian Ocean, in the aftermath of the Third United Nations Conference on the Law of the Sea, there emerged a consensus. There was recognition of the need for progressing to a range of national capabilities in dealing with newly extended, and generally recognised areas of national jurisdiction.

Consequently, these developments were accompanied by the emergence of a new imperative for international co-operation. The 1982 Law of the Sea Convention itself, laid emphasis on three important elements very relevant to the present discussion. These were: *firstly,* the notion of international co-operation to which there are numerous references in the text; s*econdly*, recognition of the important role of science and technology; and *thirdly,* the provision for institutional arrangements for co-operation.

For those who participated in the Third Conference, the closing stages provided opportunities for reflection on the historic character of the Conference and far-reaching provisions of the Convention they had helped bring forth. There was also appreciation of the wonderful experience of co-operation, of working together with so many colleagues from so many nations, and the wealth of experience and expertise that had been marshalled. Monumental as the Conference had been, like all good things, it would come to an end, and the processes and most of the close working relationships were soon to disperse. These were invaluable bonds as vehicles for co-operation. In the minds of many, there was the realisation that some of the experience and contacts that had been forged might continue to be harnessed for the benefit of their nations and the common good. If not more widely shared, certainly there was amongst the delegations of the region of the Indian Ocean, a growing feeling that though the Law of the Sea Convention had stood as a distant goal for several decades, the Convention, although then within reach, would only be a beginning – the beginning of a new era of ocean development that lay ahead. The challenge was to harness ocean resources; and to come to terms with the realities of managing large expanses of ocean – often at water-to-land ratios of much more than ten to one.

Many of these nations were developing countries. The Conference experience had frequently shown their strength in law and diplomacy, but often there was insufficient marine expertise. This was especially so in science and technology which is necessary to be able to deal effectively with substantive issues such as fisheries, continental shelf delimitation, deep-seabed mining, marine scientific research, archipelagic baselines and so many others. A study of the composition of UNCLOS delegations reveals the great disparities in the inclusion of supporting technical personnel.

This is recited in the Resolution on The Development of National Marine Science, Technology and Ocean Service Infrastructures adopted by the Conference, which sought to strengthen the relevant capabilities of these developing countries without which they could not realise the benefits of the new ocean regime.[1] It is useful to note another significant aspect of the approaches to co-operation of the time. It was the recognition that science and technology – which was the principal substantive focus of the Conference in promoting co-operation – would need to be supplemented by a wider competence encompassing such disciplines as policy analysis, law, economics, development, and management, as well as environmental concerns. They broadly covered the gamut of "oceanology" – for want of a term, and were understood to be generally reflected in a broad commitment to "marine affairs" co-operation.

It was also this appreciation of the need to develop wider national ocean capabilities and to promote international co-operation that led the African-Asian Legal Consultative Committee (AALCC), acting on a proposal by Sri Lanka at the 1981 Session in Colombo, to embark on a review of the state of co-operative international marine activities in the Indian Ocean. That was the initiative which led to the process of Indian Ocean Marine Affairs Co-operation (IOMAC).

The Indian Ocean

The Indian Ocean, ranging from Eastern Africa to Western Australia and bordered to the north by the Asian continent, is perhaps one of the world's most important seas – although it is described as the third largest ocean. It covers an area of approximately 73,600,000 square kilometers.

The Indian Ocean carries half of the world's container ships, one third of the bulk cargo traffic, and two thirds of the world's oil shipments. It is a lifeline of international trade and economy. On its rim live one third of the world's population – close to two billion people. The region is rich in hydrocarbon and hard mineral resources, and has valuable marine resources in the form of tuna and other fish species in the coastal and oceanic regions, and potential minerals in the continental shelves and deep ocean regions.

There are as many as 39 countries, including island states, which have participated in the IOMAC Conference. There are also a number of contiguous and landlocked countries in the hinterland of Asia and Africa which are very closely inter-linked with littoral states. They are regarded as constituting a part of the region of the Indian Ocean basin which along with its adjacent seas and gulfs, may be regarded as a whole for purposes of co-operation and rational management. In spite of its large extent and apparent diversity, it is said that the Indian Ocean as a region should be viewed as one general system composed of many different elements.

The Announcement of the First IOMAC Conference described the Indian Ocean scene of the 1980s as follows:

> "Surrounded by a majority of developing states of Asia and Africa, some of which are amongst the least developed, and whose populations represent the largest single concentration of the world's population, the Indian Ocean – one of the smaller oceans – but perhaps the most vital in terms of dependence for nutritional needs, transport, communications and security, has been the scene of increasing competition for access to resources and maritime activity. Limited national capabilities in marine affairs, particularly in marine science, technology and access to information, greatly hampers the realization of the benefits of the new regime and full potential of ocean resources through integration of the marine sphere in the development strategies of Indian Ocean states".[2]

RATIONALE AND GOALS

The inspiration and direction for a co-operative marine affairs effort in the Indian Ocean resulted from the emergent norms of the new ocean regime ushered in by UNCLOS on the one hand, and on the other – the expressed needs and aspirations of Indian Ocean States.

The New Ocean Regime:

The 1982 Law of the Sea Convention makes several references to international co-operation. Parts XIII and XIV of the Convention dealing with marine scientific research and marine technology are particularly relevant. Specifically –

Section 2 of Part VIII deals with International Co-operation. Article 242 provides for promotion of international co-operation. In paragraph 1 it is stated:

> States and competent international organizations shall, in accordance with the principle of respect for sovereignty and jurisdiction and on the basis of mutual benefit, promote international co-operation in marine scientific research for peaceful purposes.

Under Section 2 of Part XIV on Ways and Means of International Co-operation, Article 266 provides for promotion of the development and transfer of marine technology as follows:

1. States directly or through competent international organizations, shall co-operate in accordance with their capabilities to promote actively the development and transfer of marine technology on fair and reasonable terms and conditions.
2. States shall promote the transfer of marine scientific and technological capacity of States which may need and request technical assistance in this field particularly developing States, with regard to the exploration, exploitation, conservation and management of marine resources, the protection and preservation of the marine environment, marine scientific

research and other activities in the marine environment compatible with this Convention, with a view to accelerating the social and economic development of the developing States.

3. States shall endeavour to foster favourable economic and legal conditions necessary for the transfer of marine technology for the benefit of all parties concerned on an equitable basis.

As regards institutional arrangements for co-operation, Articles 275 and 276 of Section 3 of Part IX of the Convention stipulate the establishment and functions of National and Regional Marine Scientific and Technological Centres:

Article 276: Establishment of Regional Centres

States in co-ordination with the competent international organizations, the Authority and national marine scientific and technological research institutions, shall promote the establishment of regional marine scientific and technological research centers, particularly in developing States, in order to stimulate and advance the conduct of marine scientific research by developing States and foster the transfer of marine technology.

Article 277: The functions of such regional Centres shall include, inter alia

(a) training and educational programmes at all levels on various aspects of marine scientific and technological research, particularly marine biology, including conservation and management of living resources, oceanography, hydrography, engineering, geological exploration of the seabed, mining and desalination technologies:
(b) management studies
(c) study programmes related to the protection and preservation of the marine environment and the prevention, reduction and control of pollution;
(d) organization of regional conferences seminars and symposia;
(e) acquisition and processing of marine scientific and technological research in readily available publications;
(f) prompt dissemination of results of marine scientific and technological research in readily available publications;
(g) publicizing national policies with regard to the transfer of marine technology and systematic comparative study of those policies;
(h) compilation and systematization of information on the marketing of technology and on contracts and other arrangements concerning patents;
(i) technical co-operation with other states of the region.

Another significant development in the closing stages of the Law of the Sea Conference which is particularly relevant, is the Resolution adopted by the Conference on the Development of National Marine Scientific and Technological Infrastructures and referred to above. That Resolution was initiated by the indefatigable Dr. Mario Ruivo of Portugal, then Secretary of the Inter Governmental Oceanographic Commission (IOC). It was sponsored by a number of developing countries including Sri Lanka, and piloted through the Group of 77 for unanimous support, and later adopted by the Conference as a whole. It states in part:

> *Recognizing* that the Convention on the Law of the Sea is intended to establish a new regime for the seas and oceans which will contribute to the realization of a just and equitable international economic order through making provision for the peaceful use of ocean space, the equitable and efficient management of its resources, and the study, protection and preservation of the marine environment;
>
> *Bearing* in mind that the new regime must take into account, in particular, the special needs and interests of developing countries, whether coastal or land-locked, or geographically disadvantaged;
>
> *Aware* of the rapid advances being made in the field of marine science and technology, and the need for the developing countries, whether coastal, land-locked or geographically disadvantaged, to share in these achievements if the aforementioned goals are to be met;
>
> *Convinced* that unless urgent measures are taken, the marine scientific and technological gap between the developed and developing countries will widen further and thus endanger the foundations of the new regime;

The Resolution goes on to emphasize the importance of international action, the role of regional centers, and the inadequacy of efforts of the United Nations system in addressing the needs of the developing countries in this respect. It calls on the competent organizations and funding agencies to provide assistance for strengthening national ocean capabilities. The thesis has been advanced that these provisions of the Convention in particular, and related developments calling for international co-operation entails an "obligation to act".[3]

These provisions are relevant insofar as they provided formal inspiration for, if not the obligation for initiation of post-Conference co-operative efforts. Although contemplated in the formation, and central to the idea of IOMAC, its goals and functioning, the idea of a regional Centre or focal point as envisaged in Article 276 was avoided. This was done so as not to precipitate a potentially divisive scramble among the very nations IOMAC was trying to unite, in their likely bids to host such a Centre. Since its establishment, IOMAC has come to perform some of those functions. Further, the IOMAC Marine Affairs mandate went beyond the essential science and technology mandates given to the Centres.

Indian Ocean – The Move Towards Co-Operation

In the late 1960s and the early 1970s the Indian Ocean had become the scene of intense competition by the Big Powers – especially the United States and the Soviet Union. The British withdrawal of forces "East-of-Suez" following de-colonization, and the resultant lack of Western presence in the Indian Ocean is given as the reason for the subsequent increase in competition for dominance in the Indian Ocean. The real reasons may have lain more in the realm of deployment of the Undersea Long-range Missile Systems with increasing range and effectiveness. The Soviet Union perceived a threat of missile attack over the top of the Himalayas and across the vast southern reaches of the Asian continent to its soft underbelly. In a classic strategic geopolitical scenario, the secret battles of anti-submarine warfare were waged beneath the waves. Nuclear ballistic missile attack submarines and hunter-killers prowled the Indian Ocean. This conduct of the super powers was appropriately described as "a warlike presence in time of peace". The issue of military bases arose, followed by interference in local politics to obtain access to host facilities. This presence was in turn perceived as a threat to the security, domestic politics, and development of the nations of the Indian Ocean region. The military presence of the superpowers in the Indian Ocean thus became vital to their own security and survival in the context of nuclear deterrence. These powers were to remain in the region for some time. To this day, the United States maintains a presence at Diego Garcia in the Chagos Archipelago.

It was against this backdrop, that in 1971 the General Assembly of the United Nations, acting on an initiative taken by Sri Lanka, adopted at its 26th regular session, a Resolution on the declaration of the Indian Ocean as a Zone of Peace.(General Assembly Resolution A/RES/2832 (XXVI) of December 1971). This initiative was taken by Sri Lanka along with other Indian Ocean States in the context of the big-power politics of the time, with the aim of freeing the region from international tension and rivalry. At the time, this was considered as essential for bringing about an atmosphere of peace and tranquillity within which countries of the region could pursue their development. For over two decades, the Ad Hoc Committee of the General Assembly on the Indian Ocean Zone of Peace, (established by the General Assembly in 1972) met annually to review progress. When prospects for promoting co-operation in the Indian Ocean were considered in the early 1980s, leading to the Sri Lanka initiative in the AALCC in 1981, one of the obvious choices for an international Indian Ocean forum was the Ad Hoc Committee of the United Nations. Yet, being aware of the difficulties faced in the realization of the goals of the Indian Ocean Zone of Peace (IOPZ) especially in terms of US opposition, it was felt that the logical corollary to the Zone of Peace would be an initiative to concentrate on non-controversial areas where international co-operation of a practical nature might be achieved. The Peace Zone proposal though focusing primarily on the exclusion of big power rivalry and prohibition on non-peaceful uses, in its long term goals, it considered the eventual progression to a co-operative regime. In fact, in the final stages of the Ad Hoc Committee, in the latter part of the 1980s, there was also a trend towards economic co-operation.

Given the political sensitivities of the time, and to avoid the perception that there was a shift away from the Peace Zone, it was considered prudent to seek a separate forum for the new Sri Lankan initiative on co-operation in the non-peaceful uses of the Indian Ocean. For this reason, the 1981 Sri Lankan Indian Ocean Co-operation initiative, although seen as a logical corollary to Sri Lanka's 1971 Peace Zone initiative, was deliberately de-linked. The idea was that rather than be bound up in the prevailing controversies of the prohibitive approach toward "non-peaceful uses" of the Indian Ocean being pursued under the auspices of the IOPZ Ad Hoc Committee – a new forum should be found for promoting peaceful uses of the Indian Ocean. In proposing a focus on co-operation in respect of peaceful uses, the aim was to seek some progress in practical co-operation in the interim, thus supplementing the basic goals of the U.N.'s Peace Zone Resolution. In order to further allay brewing suspicions and to emphasize that the new initiative of 1981 was not a substitute for the Peace Zone, the terminology of the proposal was deliberately changed from "co-operation in the peaceful uses"-which was seen to evoke connotations of the security sphere – to co-operation in "economic, scientific and technical fields.

Following the conclusion of the preliminary studies and deliberations thereon in the AALCC, the First IOMAC Conference was convened in Colombo in 1985 under the long title "Economic, Scientific And Technical Co-Operation In The Indian Ocean In the Field of Marine Affairs In The Context Of The New Ocean Regime". The restriction of the broad scope for co-operation initially contemplated "Economic, Scientific And Technical" to the marine sector, reflected the origins of the initiative in the Law of the Sea Conference and close association with the U N Office for Ocean Affairs and the Law of the Sea in its organization. In fact, the Office of the Under Secretary General and Special Representative of the Secretary General of the United Nations and then incumbent Ambassador Satya N. Nandan, played a key role in bringing together and co-ordinating with the U N agencies that showed interest in supporting the new initiative, and in representing the United Nations at the Conference. It was thought initially, that being at sea with a focus on marine affairs activities would be less controversial and more productive than one which focused on terrestrial issues where activities were more intense and the potential for controversy was greater. Further, it was felt that the marine affairs bias might be shed after some progress in marine activities, and/or when it was considered opportune.

There was another parallel development through the United Nations Economic and Social Commission for the Asia and the Pacific (ESCAP). It was to replicate for the Indian Ocean under the auspices of the United Nations Development Programme (UNDP), the successful model of the Committees for Co-ordination of Offshore Prospecting for Mineral Resources (CCOP) that had been sponsored earlier for East Asia and the South Pacific. Two *ad hoc* Expert meetings in Bangkok in the early 1980s established the feasibility and desirability of a co-operative mechanism for offshore prospecting for mineral resources. The second meeting also went on to adopt terms of reference for creation of COMINDEX or Committee for Indian Ocean Exploration – as proposed by one of the experts – the late Dr. Siddique, then Director of the National Institute of Oceanography (NIO) of India. The new body was to have a wider mandate for science and technology than the CCOPs. However, the lack of awareness and interest in ocean activity in most Indian Ocean countries resulted in the failure of the proposed organization to get off the ground. That failure was to condition the framing of the first objective of IOMAC. It was a commitment "to promote awareness" in the region of the resource potential of the Indian Ocean. It also gave the impetus to go beyond the narrow concept of mineral resource prospecting of the CCOPs, through "exploration" envisaged by COMINDEX, to the multi-disciplinary "marine affairs" mandate of IOMAC.

Over a decade later, the initial focus on marine affairs promulgated by the pioneers of Indian Ocean co-operation through IOMAC, was vindicated. In a re-awakening of the region to the prospects for regional co-operation, the 1995 Australian sponsored International Forum on the Indian Ocean Region (IFIOR) – affirmed that the marine affairs sector "represented one of the building blocks for wider Indian Ocean co-operation".[4]

The First Conference set out its justification as follows:

> "The high cost of ocean activities, limited experience of developing states, especially in marine, scientific and technological applications as well as the essential multi-disciplinary and modern integrated ocean management approaches, also seriously limits the capacity of these states for independent individual advancement. A broader framework for pursuing such advancement offers the prospect of access to greater resources, technical co-operation and sharing of facilities and experience within the region and from outside. By comparison, the Pacific and East-Asian regions demonstrate remarkable progress in certain marine activities, such as offshore prospecting, where broad-based co-operative activity initially supported by UNDP and the UN system, in association with technologically advanced states, has benefited less developed states of these regions.
>
> Co-operation in marine affairs within an international framework for the region, affords the prospect of accelerated development of national capabilities and rational integrated management of this vital ocean, in the interest of long-term productivity, optimum use and equal opportunities for participation and access to resources."

Accordingly, the First Indian Ocean Co-operation Conference (IOMAC-I) had the following objectives:

a) Creating an awareness regarding the Indian Ocean, its resources and potential for the development of the States of the region, and furthering co-operation among them, as well as with other States active in the region, bearing in mind the new ocean regime embodied in the 1982 United Nation Convention on the Law of the Sea;
b) Providing a forum where Indian Ocean States and other interested nations could review the state of the economic uses of the Indian Ocean and its resources and related activities, including those undertaken within the framework of intergovernmental organizations, and identifying fields in which they would benefit from enhanced international co-operation, co-ordination, and concerted actions; and
c) Adopting a strategy for enhancing the national development of the Indian Ocean States through the integration of ocean-related activities in their

> respective development process, and a policy of integrated ocean management through a regular and continuing dialogue and co-operative international/regional action with particular emphasis on technical co-operation among developing countries.

As Prime Minister Joseph Warioba of Tanzania recalled in 1990:

> "IOMAC began in 1981 as part of measures aimed at giving practical effect to the emerging new ocean regime embodied in the UN Convention on the Law of the Sea in which all of us have a stake.
>
> IOMAC was born out of a realization that though the UN Convention on the Law of the Sea, confers rights and duties to coastal and hinterland states, to explore and exploit the resources of the ocean, these rights did not, in actual fact, translate into tangible benefits for most of the developing nations of the Indian Ocean region.
>
> ... there is today, a broad realization that marine development is only possible if efficiently co-ordinated in its various components, even where some of them are not complementary. In the absence of such a framework, there is a lot of unnecessary duplication of work, inadequate assessment of ocean development in the management of marine resources and the development of marine affairs and the failure to develop an inter-sectoral approach to the development of marine methodologies as well as lack of a proper forum for expressing innovative ideas relating to the effective and integrated management of the marine sector".[5]

Gearing For Co-Operation

History of IOMAC

The African-Asian Legal Consultative Committee (AALCC), International Indian Ocean Expedition, the Indian Ocean Zone of Peace (IOPZ), the concept of a Committee for Indian Ocean Co-operation (COMINDEX) or Indian Ocean CCOP – Committee for Co-operation in Offshore Prospecting for Mineral Resources, and the Indian Ocean Fishery Commission (IOFC), are but some of the better known precursors of more recent efforts to forge international Indian Ocean co-operation.

As indicated earlier, the concept of IOMAC originally grew out of the deliberations at the Asian African Legal Consultative Committee (AALCC) held in Colombo, Sri Lanka. On 29 May 1981 at its Twenty Second Session, the AALCC acting on a proposal made by Sri Lanka, and calling for a "comprehensive study of international co-operative activities in the Indian Ocean", decided to initiate a study on the "Economic, Scientific and Technical Co- operation in the use of the Indian Ocean" and to include the item on the Agenda of that Committee's Twenty Third Session. The AALCC Secretariat's study presented in 1983, at the subsequent Tokyo Session, gave a useful overview of the state of inter-governmental agency activities in the region. At the request of States, this was supplemented with additional information presented to the Committee during its 1985 session in Kathmandu, Nepal. At this session, and recognizing the importance of the item, it was then resolved in a proposal by the AALCC's long-serving and able Secretary General Dr. B Sen, that to ensure the information from the States in the region be made available for examination of both national and regional priorities, the subject warranted a separate forum. Accordingly, Sri Lanka, supported by a core group of countries and the AALCC Secretariat, was requested to convene a special Conference on Marine Affairs Co-operation in the Indian Ocean. Consequently, it was resolved that the Government of Sri Lanka with the encouragement and support of a number of African and Asian countries, would convene an Indian Ocean Co-operation Conference. These were the developments that marked the beginning of the process of Indian Ocean Marine Affairs Co-operation.

There were two major landmarks in the development of IOMAC:

IOMAC-I, Colombo-Sri Lanka 1985–87

In 1985 following consultations with competent UN organizations and agencies in Geneva in May that year, and a Preparatory Meeting of Indian Ocean States in Colombo in June 1985 that identified areas and issues for co-operation, the First Conference on Economic, Scientific and Technical Co-operation in the Field of Marine Affairs in the Context of the New Ocean Regime (IOMAC-I), was convened in Colombo in two phases – a Consultative Phase in July 1985 and Ministerial Level Final Phase in January 1987. The Final Phase of the Conference at Ministerial Level considered and adopted in the form of a declaration (although not in express words)[6] three important instruments that set the framework for the organization and its work, as well as its decisions on implementation arrangements:

1) the IOMAC Framework and Principles of Co-operation;
2) the Programme of Co-operation;
3) the Plan of Action; and
4) Implementation Arrangements

A Work Plan was also distilled from the Plan of Action.

A Secretariat was established in Colombo under the implementation arrangements.[7]

These measures helped set in motion a process of practical co-operation in a number of fields. The organization then commenced implementing a number of co-operative activities principally with the financial and technical support of the United Nations system.

IOMAC-II Arusha, Tanzania 1990

In keeping with the decision to have periodic conferences, in 1990, the Second Indian Ocean Conference: IOMAC-II, was convened in Arusha under the Chairmanship of Tanzania. Thirty countries and fourteen organizations participated.

IOMAC-II adopted the Arusha Agreement on the Organization for Indian Ocean Marine Affairs Co-operation which sought to provide a more formal basis for the IOMAC framework of co-operation established in 1987. IOMAC-II also adopted inter alia, the resolution on the participation of other States active in the Indian Ocean and the Technical Co-operation Group (TCG) which facilitated their participation.[8]

Participation

From its inception, IOMAC has sought to be an open forum to secure the widest possible participation of States and organizations with a legitimate interest in the Indian Ocean, and in co-operation. In convening of the First Conference, guidance was sought on the practice of the United Nations. The closest parallel was the Ad Hoc committee for the IOPZ. Participation in IOMAC therefore closely followed the system of membership in the IOPZ, and was structured as follows:

1) Indian Ocean States
   a – littoral States
   b – hinterland States; and
2) Major Maritime Users – including the Big Five as well as those States with large registered tonnage afloat

Littoral States includes both continental/mainland and island states. As regards, hinterland States, IOMAC has used as a rule of thumb the determination that a land-locked State that is immediately adjacent to or touches/shares a border with) a coastal State of the Indian Ocean is deemed to be an Indian Ocean Hinterland State.

As regards the Big Powers – i.e. the Permanent Members of the Security Council of the United Nations, they are included in the Major Maritime User (MMU) category. The UK and France however subsequently took the position in IOMAC that they were in fact Indian Ocean States by virtue of their possessions in the Indian Ocean. While the UK did not sustain this position, France was able to gain qualified acceptance within IOMAC as a functional non-political determination for purposes of co-operation. There has also been agreement to widen the major maritime users group to include those active in conducting marine scientific research and extensive fishing activities, since the tonnage criterion only applies to the shipping aspect of the "marine affairs" mandate. This means that South Korea, Portugal and Spain are likely to qualify.

In terms of membership of IOMAC – in the words of IOMAC Standing Committee Chairman Ambassador Hasjim Djalal of Indonesia "IOMAC is not against anybody. Its doors are open to all". That is the essence of the spirit of international co-operation which IOMAC has sought to foster for the region.

Principles and Framework

The First Indian Ocean Conference on Economic, Scientific and Technical Co-operation in the Field of Marine Affairs conducted in Colombo, Sri Lanka, on 27 January 1987, represented an unique undertaking and opportunity for States to assess, identify prospects and devise a framework for maritime co-operation in respect of the ocean as a whole. It is perhaps without precedent.

The Conference recognized eleven basic principles that should be incorporated by the Governments in taking economic, scientific and co-operative action in the context of the New Ocean Regime, which are summarized as follows:

1. Take measures to integrate the marine sector into development strategies.
2. Give due regard to the rights and needs of the landlocked and geographically disadvantaged states.
3. Take measures to establish a system to acquire and disseminate marine affairs information.
4. Make, harmonize or strengthen adjustments in implementing co-operation with other states in the region.
5. Formulate and establish marine affairs policies and co-ordinate them at the national and international level.
6. Develop and maintain safe and efficient maritime transport services.
7. Support and strengthen existing marine affairs institutions. and, where necessary, establish new ones.
8. Influence international organizations to accord greater emphasis in marine affairs.
9. States should co-operate with each other's initiatives.
10. Convene plenary meetings of the Conference on Indian Ocean Marine Affairs Co-operation at least every two years.
11. Take measures that will effect action in accordance with the above-mentioned principles.

Statutory Framework

IOMAC functions under a framework of instruments adopted by the Ministerial phase of the First Conference in 1987. An attempt to formalize this arrangement in terms of a treaty adopted by the Second Conference has so far not attracted the requisite ratifications.

The Framework and Instruments of 1987

In 1987, IOMAC-I adopted the complex of constituent instruments providing a Framework For Co-operation, Programme Of Co-operation, Plan Of Action, Work Programmes And Implementation Arrangements. Since then, IOMAC has functioned under this framework to implement the programs and activities in keeping with its objectives.

The Arusha Agreement

Driven partly by the formal requirements for securing requisite financial support, in terms of a formally structured organization, IOMAC embarked on the process of further consolidating the basic institutional framework of the 1987 Ministerial Phase. The resultant Agreement of 1990 was signed and or ratified by nine Indian Ocean countries, *viz.*: Indonesia, Iran, Kenya, Mozambique, Sri Lanka, Mauritius, Nepal, Pakistan and Tanzania. The agreement has not yet entered into force due to insufficient ratifications.

Organization: Insititutional Arrangements

The institutional framework of IOMAC is made up of the following elements: the Conference as plenary body; the Standing Committee which functions as the executive body; the Technical Co-operation Group (TCG) which provides for co-operation with extra-regional States; and the Secretariat which is responsible for the day-to-day administrative functions on behalf of the executive body.

Although two major Indian Ocean conferences were held as IOMAC-I and IOMAC-II, the latter mainly focused on the adoption of the Arusha Agreement. The Chairmanship passes with the hosting of the Conference.

The Standing Committee has been a popular and active body attracting good participation and productive deliberations. The Secretariat as initially envisaged is a modest entity supported by the host government at its seat in Colombo. The Secretariat headed by the Secretary General is responsible for convening of meetings, co-ordinating co-operative activities and implementation of programs. It is essentially the administrative unit which draws on special expertise on an *ad hoc* basis from institutions of the host country or from participating States and specialized international organizations and other entities.

IOMAC has also established a regional Network of National Focal Points, focal points in co-operating countries active in the region, and at intergovernmental organizations. This Network facilitates regular contact. Guidelines have been developed for the designation and functioning of focal points. Provision has been made for "national technical focal points" to supplement the National Focal Points where needed to expeditiously reach relevant marine line agencies.

Scope of Marine Affairs Activities

The following fields are regarded as the principal areas of marine affairs activity within the purview of IOMAC:

- marine sciences, and ocean services;
- marine technology; including remote-sensing and satellite applications;
- living resources;
- non-living resources;
- ocean law, policy and management;
- marine transport and communications; and
- marine environment.

Programs and Activities

Program of Co-operation

Working on the basis of the list of subjects and issues for co-operation compiled at the Preparatory Meeting of Indian Ocean States, the Consultative Phase of the First Conference (IOMAC-I) laid down the Programme of Co-operation spelling out the specific activities for each of the principal areas of co-operation. This was reviewed by the Second Conference (IOMAC-II) and supplementary guidelines have been laid down for future activities

Plan of Action and Work Program

In the Plan of Action derived from the Programme of Co-operation, activities are prioritized for implementation as Short Term, Medium Term and Long Term. However, it was formulated essentially as a guide. It is open to the participants to return at any time to the Programme and select from it, for early elaboration, some subject not currently included in the Plan of Action.[9] Based on the Plan of Action and Programme of Co-operation, the Secretariat maintains a list of ongoing activities in the form of a Work Programme presented to the Standing Committee for review[10].

Participation and Membership

Up to thirty-five countries have participated in IOMAC. Usually between fifteen and twenty-two countries attend the regular Standing Committee Meetings. Over thirty organizations have registered their participation with attendance varying depending on the respective mandates and the particular agenda. The 1990 Agreement requires a total of eight ratification's to bring it into force. But only six were secured.[11] Considering the complexities of national procedures for ratification, and in an effort to move away from the difficulties of ratification, IOMAC at its Session of the Standing Committee in 1998, re-emphasized a fall back to the instruments of the Ministerial Conference of 1987 as its constituent instruments, which had been the basis of its work for ten years. Thus participation, rather than formal membership seems to determine the commitment of States to co-operate.

Non-Indian Ocean States: Although in essence a developing country initiative – having been conceived and developed within the region – IOMAC has also provided for co-operation with major users of the Indian Ocean. A two-tier system that protects Indian Ocean States' priorities and interests, yet facilitates co-operation through a consultative body, is the Technical Co-operation Group (TCG). The model is based on the very successful UNDP experience in East Asia and the South Pacific in the CCOP and SOPAC. This forum for collaboration with developed countries active in the region has helped to promote understanding, and drawn support for co-operative activities, exchanges and expert input.

Substantive Areas And Achievements – Introduction

IOMAC is involved in the following activities:

1. Marine Science, Ocean Services and Marine Technology;
2. Living Resources;
3. Non-living Resources;

4. Ocean Law, Policy and Management;
5. Maritime Transport and Communications;
6. Marine Environment;
7. Interests and Needs of Land-locked States;
8. Training, Information and other fields relevant to co-operation in Marine Affairs.

In discharging its mandate, IOMAC has moved steadily to systematically work through groups of experts from the region and outside, to first identify ongoing activities, national needs, and prospects for co-operation. While preparing for long-term co-operation, IOMAC has also undertaken a number of activities in the region designed to address more immediate needs such as training, exploration and strengthening of capabilities. So far, the following achievements have been recorded as part of a long-term systematic approach to forging international organization and co-operation.

Marine Science and Ocean Services and Marine Technology

As early as 1986, even while IOMAC was being formed, the process inspired the UN-IOMAC Regional Meeting of Experts on Space Technology Applications in the Indian Ocean, in Colombo. This was followed by the UN-IOMAC Workshop on Oceanographic Space Information Systems in Karachi, Pakistan. Space technology received some impetus in IOMAC because it afforded *inter alia* the prospect for countries of the region to retrieve archived data and in the words Arthur C. Clarke "leap-frog into the future". A manual on remote sensing applications produced by IOMAC for the region has also inspired similar publications for other regions. The United States supported the sector workshop – First Indian Ocean Workshop on Co-operation in Marine Science in 1992 organised jointly by IOMAC, the IOC and the US State Department, in Colombo.

Living Resources

Perhaps one of the far-reaching contributions of IOMAC has been in relation to the most important commercial species of the Indian Ocean – tuna. As early as 1985, IOMAC anticipated and called for regulation of the tuna fishery and continued to monitor and promote the establishment of an Indian Ocean Tuna Commission to suit the needs of countries of the region. The 1989 IOMAC Meeting of Legal and Technical Experts, in Jakarta, Indonesia, brought a regional perspective to this subject. It had far reaching implications regarding the structuring of the Indian Ocean Tuna Commission. IOMAC and FAO maintained close links in this respect. That process took nearly ten years. Presently, IOMAC is focusing on other commercially important marine living resources such as sharks, holothurians and cephalopods and has been in consultation with FAO.

Non Living Resources

The 1986 IOMAC Technical Group on Offshore Prospecting for Mineral Resources in the Indian Ocean, in Karachi, produced the mandate and programs that the proposed Indian Ocean CCOP–COMINDEX had failed to deliver earlier in the decade. It explored the linkages and activities required in this region on the basis of priorities. A training program on offshore non-living resource exploration aboard the vessel Behr Paima was completed in Pakistan in co-operation with the IOC.

Ocean Law, Policy and Management

IOMAC has undertaken the preparation of marine affairs country profiles of selected countries under a Canadian funded project through the ACT Programme (Advice, Co-operation and Training). IOMAC has also undertaken the promotion of national ocean policies and deliberations on the delimitation of the continental margin through the UN Commission on the Limits of the Continental Shelf.

Marine Transport and Communications

The principal sectoral meeting was the IOMAC Experts Meeting on Co-operation in Shipping and Port Development, held in Mombassa, Kenya in 1990. On the recommendations of the meeting, the IOMAC Association of Shipping and Ports Authorities (ASPA) was formed. ASPA recently undertook a series of missions to countries of the region to promote co-operation.

Marine Environment

Significant achievements in this area are the Declaration of the Indian Ocean as a Sanctuary for Whales for All Time (1990) and extension to All Marine Mammals (1993). In 1995, under a program supported by the State Department, IOMAC established the Indian Ocean Conservation Association Network (IOCAN) following the Indian Ocean Conservation Meeting in Mombassa, to link scientists and institutions in the region. A tri-partite co-operative arrangement was established with the New England Aquarium in Boston, with IOMAC and Fauna International. It provides for exchanges among scientists and promotion of co-operative activities.

Interests and needs of land-locked countries

The two aspects of interest to land-locked countries in the Law of the Sea Conference were rights in respect of access to and from the sea[12], and access to the living resources of the adjacent Exclusive Economic Zones[13]. They were doggedly fought for through the Group on Land-locked and Geographically Disadvantaged States. In the early stages of IOMAC, Nepal and Uganda took joint chairmanship of a working group to study the regional implications. Although Nepal has sustained interest in IOMAC, no serious attempt was made to pursue the issue, perhaps partly because of bi-lateral tensions and opposition of adjacent coastal and transit States to discussion in a wider forum. With rapid expansion of coastal State fishing effort, the relevant "surplus"[14] would have been used up, thus limiting the prospect of land-locked country access.

Training and Information

IOMAC Marine Affairs Training Programmes have been held in Arusha (1987); Port Louis (1988): Cairo (1989) and Kuala Lumpur (1990). A training Workshop on Offshore Minerals was held in Pakistan with Support from Germany and IOC in 1994. A number of training programs have been conducted in the region in collaboration with the International Ocean Institute. Also, an Indian Ocean Marine Affairs and Aquatic Resources Information System (IO-MAARIS) was establised.

OTHER ORGANIZATIONS

Although IOMAC is the only dedicated marine affairs organization in the Indian Ocean region, there are a number of other organizations which are active in the marine affairs sphere. They deal with sub-regional and specialized marine activities such as tuna fisheries and marine environmental management, as well as more general aspects such as trade and economic co-operation. The organizations and recent initiatives bearing on marine affairs co-operation are briefly summarized here.

International Forum on the Indian Ocean Region (IFIOR)

This meeting convened by Australia was held in Perth from 11–13 June 1995 as a manifestation of its "Look West" policy, and as a "second-track" exercise. The specific aims were to develop a community among the countries of the Indian Ocean region; to identify and explore opportunities for closer trade and investment and prospects for enhanced regional co-operation in a wide range of areas; and to explore interest in the development of networks among business and academics of the region. The forum was non-governmental in nature and brought together 122 participants from 23 Indian Ocean countries in their individual capacities. The forum sought to complement and provide ideas for the Mauritius Government's inter-governmental Indian Ocean Rim Initiative.

Important outcomes were the establishment of a number of working groups, and creation of an academic network and a business forum. There were a number of provisions relevant to IOMAC. Regarding practical co-operation, the Report of the Chairman noted: "explore ways and means of maritime co-operation drawing on existing structures, especially IOMAC. IOMAC was asked to co-ordinate the maritime affairs working group – one of five such groups. The groups were to work "inter-sessionally"[15] suggesting a follow-up to IFIOR, which has not materialized. With the change of government in Australia shortly after IFIOR, support for the Indian Ocean initiative has generally declined. Some of the more ambitious programs have either not progressed or have dissolved. The venture into marine affairs has also not proceeded.

IORARC

The Indian Ocean Rim process emerging from the Mauritius initiative focuses primarily on trade and economic co-operation, and does not specifically include marine affairs – being only relevant in terms of more general, economic, trade, and social mandates, or other general areas of co-operation.[16] The two processes are seen as complementary: IORARC – dealing with *rim* inter-country trade and other linkages and IOMAC dealing with international activities in respect of the *ocean* itself. In this respect, guidelines for harmonizing approaches in possible areas of overlap were adopted by the IOMAC Standing Committee at its 12th Meeting in Jakarta in 1996. Six countries – Indonesia, Kenya, Mozambique, Sri Lanka, Mauritius and Tanzania, parties to the 1990 IOMAC Agreement adopted in Arusha, are also among the fourteen parties to the IORARC Charter adopted in Mauritius in March 1997.

Indian Ocean Commission (IOC)

The Indian Ocean Commission was formed in December 1982 by Mauritius. Madagascar, the Seychelles, and the Comoros. The French territory – Reunion – joined subsequently. The Commission is a union to promote economic trade and related activities among member countries. Political and military issues have been left out. Membership is open to any Indian Ocean island nation. The Secretariat is at Port Louis, Mauritius. High level meetings take place every two years. One result is that trade barriers among member countries have been removed.

Indian Ocean Tuna Commission (IOTC) and the FAO

Following the IOMAC initiative of 1985 to establish a regulatory body for Indian Ocean Tuna referred to above, it took over ten years for a regulatory body – Indian Ocean Tuna Commission (IOTC) – to be established in the Seychelles under the auspices of the Food and Agriculture Organization (FAO). This delay resulted in virtually uncontrolled tuna fishing for nearly fifteen years by distant-water fleets from countries of the European Union. Presently the Commission is moving towards controls on effort in respect of Big Eye Tuna, purse seine net sets on floating objects, and restrictions on vessels sailing under flags of convenience.[17] The FAO's Indo-Pacific Fisheries Commission (IPFC) and Indian Ocean Fisheries Commission (IOFC) were regional fora that were active in the past.

Intergovernmental Oceanographic Commission (IOC)

The IOC operates through two sub-regional committees for the Western and Central Indian Ocean regions known respectively as IO-CINDIO and IO-CINCWIO. IOC and IOMAC have enjoyed a close working relationship and have concluded a Memorandum of Understanding.

The Experience Of Regionalism In The Indian Ocean

Being one of the initial marine affairs initiatives springing from the expectations and enthusiasm of the Third Law of the Sea Conference, the overall experience of IOMAC which now spans two decades may have lessons relevant to other regions, and it may have elements that have provided guidance to other efforts in the region and can do so in the coming years. This is useful given the present interest of reviewing regional approaches in the context of prospective approaches to marine affairs for Northeast Asia.

Geo-political Setting

Intraregional Power Balances: Since the time when Indian Ocean marine affairs co-operation was conceived, the geopolitical relationships and balances in the Indian Ocean have undergone considerable transformation. Until the mid-nineties, India was essentially the dominant Indian Ocean entity. The other potential major Indian Ocean players in the power politics of the region – Indonesia, Australia, Pakistan, Iran, and South Africa were largely distance from the regional scene. The Peace Zone initiative brought a focus on regional security issues, with the principal adversaries being the superpowers. Thus IOMAC at its inception had to frame as its *first* objective the creation of an awareness regarding the Indian Ocean, its resources and their potential contribution to the development of the States of the region. Its *second* objective was to provide a forum where Indian Ocean States and other interested nations could review the state of the economic uses of the Indian Ocean and its resources and related activities. Its *third* objective was to adopt a strategy for enhancing the national development of the Indian Ocean State through the integration of ocean-related activities in their respective development process, and a policy of integrated ocean management, reflected the prevailing apathy of these nations towards the ocean and its relevance to development and security.

The most powerful regional country, India, had a strained bi-lateral relationship with IOMAC's sponsor Sri Lanka on security issues that lasted through the 1980s. At inception, IOMAC was intensely opposed by India for a variety of reasons that were not particularly cogent. This was despite the fact that Sri Lanka had sought to give India center stage at the First Conference. Thus it was not surprising that ten years later, Mauritius, another smaller island nation, was chosen by India to carry forth India's own Indian Ocean "Rim" or IORARC initiative. The Indian initiative had a similar mandate covering "economic, scientific and technical fields" but without IOMAC's initial focus on "marine affairs".

It was not until the mid-nineties that Australia[18] was to suddenly awaken from its slumber, and a new South Africa was to emerge as a major player. These changes coincided with a stirring of interest in the Indian Ocean in India, echoing a budding co-operative sentiment in South Africa. Australia initially sought to advance an idea of a "triangle" of co-operation linking itself with India and South Africa. It has subsequently become an advocate of the "inclusive" approach under the Indian inspired IORARC initiative, opposing the Indian insistence on selectivity of admission on a "seven by seven" formula. Both Australia and South Africa have since essentially ceased to be major players in a more broad-based Indian Ocean Rim Association that is still exclusive in membership in keeping with specific Indian concerns.

The moral here is that if the exercise is to be in an intergovernmental context, then the role of major regional players becomes important. Whatever initiative is taken, whatever the rationale, the dominant regional powers can play a fouling role if there is a perception of any negative ramifications, no matter how logical or well intentioned.

Extra-Regional States: In the Indian Ocean region, collaboration with advanced countries has drawn some criticism – notably from India. However, it provides a pragmatic underpinning for advancing co-operation in a region where a majority of countries are developing countries desperately struggling with their immediate terrestrial problems. With the exception of perhaps Australia, India and South Africa are anachronistic in that they have very advanced capabilities in science and technology, but are not able as yet to shoulder additional financial responsibilities on behalf of the region, like Australia and New Zealand have done in the South Pacific. For that matter Australia can only be expected to muster limited resources to address the balancing of a two-ocean policy – which itself is too dependent on the vagaries of internal politics. Such dependence too can bring its own concerns. Thus, if external resources are to be found, then a broader basis of co-operation as envisaged by IOMAC's TCG and its precursors in East Asia and the South Pacific would perhaps be worthy of attention. In this context, it is also important to note the shift in international aid away from multilateral frameworks. However, if the ideology of regional isolation were to prevail in an age of globalization, regional co-operation – at least in the Indian Ocean – would remain largely in the realm of moral exhortation and rhetoric. This would be more so in the area of marine affairs co-operation where the necessity of ocean-going platforms and equipment can often make costs of co-operation much higher.

A further consideration is that under the Law of the Sea, large areas of the Indian Ocean remain beyond the limits of national jurisdiction under the realm of the high seas. The presence of States with rights in the Indian Ocean is legitimate. Since a *mare clausum* is not contemplated, the presence of extra-regional States must not be seen as extending legitimacy to an intrusion into the region. The prospect of their participation should also be seen as beneficial – if not essential – in the regional context, just as it is accepted on a day-to-day basis in bi-lateral relations. It is a reality that must dawn as countries of the region move from ideology and policy to the practicalities of day-to-day co-operation. Indeed, it is a reality which new organizations in the region such as IORARC have come to experience. The Indian Ocean is bordered by some of the poorest nations. As much as technical co-operation between developing countries efforts are laudable, infusion of resources is a *sine qua non* for promoting effective international co-operation.

Statutory Framework and Institutional Aspects

Since its launch by the Ministerial meeting of IOMAC in 1987, IOMAC has continued to function under the complex of instruments adopted in the form of a declaration, although not specifically in those words.[19] During the early days of APEC, a comment on its progress was carried in the box on the back page of the International Herald Tribune where the writer questioned whether the day of the International Treaty as a formal vehicle for international co-operation was over. He may very well have been correct. Indeed, our experience has shown that in the evolution of the more recent processes of international co-operation, there has been a shift away from formal treaties and international agreements to less formal institutional arrangements. For instance, both in IOMAC and in the more recent Indian Ocean endeavour – IORARC the "Framework" and "Charter" were adopted at ministerial level. The pit-falls of formal ratification are best avoided.

IOMAC was formed in the period of global political transition and reflects a mix of the formal and informal approaches. It is the constituent instruments of IOMAC-I -the "Framework" adopted at Ministerial level in 1987 – by which the organization has functioned to this day. It was the further effort to crystallize that framework and early IOMAC practice, in the form of a Treaty that proved abortive. The treaty – the Arusha Agreement of IOMAC-II in 1990 – has fallen short of the requisite ratifications for entry into force. The record of participation in IOMAC has shown that States, although reluctant to go through the formalities of a treaty commitment, do show enthusiasm for participation in co-operative activities even in less formal arrangements. In IOMAC, this has been the case – where some of the smaller as well as bigger nations including the United States – have been active participants, with the United States even sponsoring a number of key activities, without any debate on the formalities of membership.

Scope of Activities and Functions

Each organization must define for itself the scope of marine affairs to be embraced, as IOMAC has done in defining its "Principal Sectors of Activity". In a field such as marine affairs, where multiple disciplines are involved, broad inter-disciplinary mandates could be perceived as duplicating, or could in fact cut across specific regional mandates of other organizations. In the framing of the Law of the Sea Convention, the roles of the respective organizations, notably those of the United Nations system were jealously guarded and are preserved in frequent references to "competent international organizations". There are no competent international organizations possessing broad marine affairs mandates. How then does a regional grouping forge an integrated approach, without raising concern regarding encroachment on the mandate of an organization with a specific marine sectoral competence? The issue is not peculiar to the international arena and it is more acute in the municipal context. On many occasions, raising the question as to which national agency was responsible for co-ordination of marine affairs has provoked internal controversy. One way of rationalising this issue whether at national or regional level is to see a central marine affairs role as encompassing *leadership, supportive* and *catalytic* functions.[20]

Firstly, where there is no pre-existing mandate, a new marine affairs entity may play a leading, unchallenged role. For instance, this is the case with regard to mineral resources in the Indian Ocean.

Secondly, where pre-existing mandates operate partially or fully in respect of a particular activity or program, the central marine affairs entity could play a collaborative or supporting role such as jointly organizing and hosting meetings and other activities in accordance with their regional priorities and programs. It is common to see the names of a number of organizations jointly hosting a meeting or co-operative activity.

Thirdly, whether mandates exist or not, a regional marine affairs organization could play a catalytic role in focusing attention on new areas or regional priorities to ensure a response to needs of the region. A good example is the role played by IOMAC in maintaining pressure over the years in securing a management regime for Indian Ocean tuna.

In regions where there are ongoing co-operative international activities, a regional marine affairs organization could focus on management, policy, and monitoring of regional marine affairs activities. It is a function that may not overlap with those of other organizations and can be undertaken in collaboration with sectoral organizations.

In IOMAC, a comprehensive, structured program and sectors of activity were adopted. However, this was tempered by the flexibility given the Standing Committee Secretariat to select areas and activities where implementation was feasible. Formal prioritisation of activities has been avoided by the Standing Committee in the face of the difficulties of systematic implementation. In the same manner, an organization could have a broad mandate under which activities are undertaken on an *ad hoc* basis – primarily on the basis of availability of resources.

Other Organizations

Definition of the scope of activities and functions has a significant bearing on the relationship with other organizations having competence in marine affairs in the region. However, in practice the importance to be assigned to the regional marine affairs effort and other organizations, especially "competent" sectoral organizations may be relative. Importance is perhaps inversely proportional to the geopolitical strength of participants and support for the regional initiative, on the one hand, and on the other, the regional presence and relationships of the respective sectoral organizations. In establishing the tuna management body for the Indian Ocean, the FAO was intensely involved in ensuring a measure of control over the proposed regulatory body as one of statutory competence. However, in other oceans such as the Pacific and the Atlantic, FAOs role in international tuna management was marginal.

A large number of organizations – over thirty (including NGOs) – are registered with IOMAC and have varying degrees of co-operation which fluctuates with time and interest. However, some of the UN entities and specialized agencies that work regularly with IOMAC with reference to specific areas of IOMAC activity are as follows.

In the area of marine sciences, IOMAC and IOC have a long-standing and close working relationship backed by a Memorandum of Understanding.

Regarding living resources, following the establishment of the Tuna Commission, the two organizations maintain contact in reviewing developments. With regard to FAO, on the initiative of IOMAC, a collaborative programme for holothurian conservation in the region is under consideration. IOMAC has also highlighted the plight of sharks increasingly targeted in the Indian Ocean, and has also called for a review of the squid fishery.

IOMAC works closely with ESCAP under a long-standing co-operative relationship. More recently, IOMAC has established co-operation with the CCOP with regard to marine mineral resources. A joint program for review of the Bay of Bengal Fan, its mineral resource potential and policy implications is planned for the near future.

The area of ocean law, policy, and management has seen significant co-operation with the UN Office for Ocean Affairs and the Law of the Sea which supported IOMAC at its inception.

In marine transport and communications, ESCAP and IMO have worked in close co-operation with IOMAC, especially in creating the regional entity for shipping and ports activities – ASPA.

In the area of environment, IOMAC concerns itself with specific projects and ocean wide issues. The United Nations Environment Programme (UNEP) gives priority to activities through a network of Regional Seas Programmes. With regard to whales and marine mammal conservation, the regional commitment to conservation expressed in IOMAC's 1990 Declaration is dependent on progress on global issues in the competent body – the International Whaling Commission (IWC) which is divided between conservation and commercial whaling.

With regard to training, in the past, IOMAC worked very effectively with the International Ocean Institute to run popular marine affairs management courses across the region to put in place well over one hundred people exposed to integrated ocean management approaches. There is now a call for a revival of these programs in the region to create a new generation of ocean managers.

At the last meeting of the IOMAC Standing Committee hosted by Indonesia, IOMAC settled on a basis for inter-action with IORARC. A number of countries in IOMAC are also active participants in IORARC. In time, a basis for closer co-operation must be found. A focus on complementarities rather than duplication of efforts will help the region produce good synergy. IOMAC and the Indian Ocean Commission have also exchanged information and visits.

Effectiveness

As detailed, IOMAC has triggered a number of specific developments for the Indian Ocean region. Most significant have been the realization of its primary goal of creating an awareness, and bringing about a recognition of the need for co-operation, which may be a signal contribution to the region. IOMAC has also provided the forum envisaged for deliberations on the integration of marine resources in national development and for forging the common strategies and co-operative activities further envisaged under its goals.

The creation of a dedicated marine affairs regime which provides a policy framework, an institutional nucleus, definition of programs, and identification and implementation of activities could make a marked improvement in a region where none has been in place, as has been the case in the Indian Ocean. Over the years, through a careful and systematic approach, IOMAC has steadily progressed to provide this region with a framework for international co-operation. Its value can best be assessed by reference to what was in place, or rather, that hardly anything was in place when we began[21]

NOTES

1. See Annex–IV of the Final Act of the Third United Nations Conference on the Law of the Sea, Official Records, (New York: United Nations, 1983).
2. Official Records of IOMAC.
3. M.C.W. Pinto, "Economic, Scientific and Technical Co-operation in the Indian Ocean" *in* Jean Carros Memorial Volume: 204.
4. Records of the International Forum on the Indian Ocean Region, Perth 11–13 June 1995.
5. Inaugural Address at the Second Indian Ocean Conference (IOMAC-II), Arusha, Tanzania, September 1990.
6. See M.C.W. Pinto, *supra* n. 3: 200.
7. See Official Records of IOMAC: Record of the First Conference IOMAC-I ("Blue Book").
8. See Offcial Records of IOMAC: Record of the Second Conference IOMAC-II.
9. Pinto, *supra* n. 3: 203. For the content of the Plan, see IOMAC "Blue Book": 10–29.
10. See IOMAC "Blue Book": 30–38.
11. The Agreement of 1990 was signed and or ratified by nine Indian Ocean countries, *viz*.: Indonesia, Iran, Kenya, Mozambique, Sri Lanka, Mauritius, Nepal, Pakistan and Tanzania. Following its IORARC initiative, Mauritius withdrew from IOMAC.
12. Part X of the 1982 U.N.Law of the Sea Convention.
13. Article 62, 69 and 70, *ibid.*
14. *Ibid.*
15. Australian Report to the Mauritius Working Group on the proceedings of the International Forum on the Indian Ocean Region, Perth, 11–13 June 1995.
16. See India in IOR-ARC: Towards a New Partnership in the Indian Ocean Rim.
17. See url. www.seychelles.net/iotc.
18. Even as late as the mid 1980s, during consultations with Australia, an inquiry regarding the second limb of the two-ocean policy of Australia declared by former Premier Hawke brought the response that "there was nothing in the file since then".
19. Pinto *supra* n. 3: 203.
20. H. Jayewardene, "Institutional Arrangements for Marine Affairs Mangement" (OETB/UN-DTCD, circa 1983).
21. Eleventh Meeting of the IOMAC Standing Committee, IOMAC Technical Cooperation Group (TCG) and Association of Ports and Shipping Authorities (IOMAC-ASPA), 12–18 October, 1995, Colombo, Sri Lanka. Welcome Address by the Secretary General., Official Records of IOMAC.

Mark J. Valencia

RELEVANCE OF LESSONS LEARNED TO NORTHEAST ASIA

INTRODUCTION

Reasonably successful and comprehensive multilateral regimes have been created for the Baltic,[1] the North[2] and the Mediterranean[3] Seas. In stark contrast, no comprehensive, multilateral maritime regime has been initiated in the Japan (East), Yellow and East China Seas. Yet, there are similarities between the regions in physical and ecological parameters, in the disparity of economic development of the regions' littoral countries, and in the diversity of ideological and political systems. And both regions' semienclosed seas have transnational multiple use conflicts that require international responses.

Why has maritime regime building been successful in Europe and unsuccessful in Northeast Asia? And are lessons learned in the European context applicable in Northeast Asia? To answer these questions, I explore the relevant similarities and differences between the two regions, critique the facile application of lessons learned in Europe to Northeast Asia, and delineate the status and constraints to maritime regime formation in Northeast Asia.

WESTERN EUROPE AND NORTHEAST ASIA: SIMILARITIES AND DIFFERENCES RELEVANT TO MARITIME REGIME FORMATION

Similarities

Although Western Europe and Northeast Asia have obvious fundamental differences, they are sufficiently similar as regions to be compared. Indeed, there are broad geographic, oceanographic, economic and political similarities between the semi-enclosed seas of Western Europe and Northeast Asia. For example, the Sea of Japan is physically similar to the Mediterranean in its great depths and narrow connections to its main oceanic water body.[4] The Yellow Sea is similar to the Baltic in its shallowness, heavy pollution, low flushing rates, overfishing of transnational

Mark J. Valencia (ed.), Maritime Regime Building, 131–148.

Table 1. Participants in Maritime Regimes

Baltic:		
	Gdansk Convention (1973)	
	Helsinki Convention (1974)	
	Original:	Denmark, Finland, East Germany, West Germany, Poland, Soviet Union, Sweden
	Present:	Estonia, the European community, Lithuania, Poland, Russia (St. Petersburg and Kaliningrad regions)
North Sea:		Belgium, Denmark, (France?), Germany, Netherlands, Norway, Sweden, United Kingdom
Mediterranean:		Albania, Algeria, Bosnia-Herzegovina, Croatia, Cyprus, Egypt, France, Greece, Israel, Italy, Lebanon, Malta, Monaco, Morocco (plus the Spanish territories of Mellilla and Ceuta), Syria
Northeast Asia:		China, Japan, North Korea, South Korea, Taiwan, Russia

stocks and conflicting multiple uses. And the East China Sea and the North Sea are similar in that they are underlain primarily by continental shelf, have high hydrocarbon potential, and have wide connections to the main ocean.[5] Ecologically, the Japan Sea is similar to the Baltic, the Yellow Sea to the North Sea, and the East China Sea, at least in its southern part, to the Mediterranean.

More important in terms of maritime regime initiation are the similarities in economic and political diversity of the nations bordering and enclosing these seas. The Baltic and the Mediterranean are bordered by both developed and developing countries. For the Baltic, this juxtaposes Denmark, Germany, Sweden, Poland and Russia. For the Mediterranean, France, Italy and Spain are contrasted with Algeria, Libya, Morocco and Tunisia. This economic diversity is also characteristic of the Japan Sea rim (Japan and South Korea vs. Russia); the Yellow Sea rim (South Korea vs. China and North Korea); and the East China Sea rim (Japan, South Korea and Taiwan vs. China).

Indeed, the differences between the two regions are not as obvious as they may superficially seem. For those who would point to a united and politically integrated Europe as the fundamental reason for the relative success of maritime regimes there, it must be remembered that when the 1973 Gdansk[6] and 1974 Helsinki Conventions[7] were signed to protect the environment of the Baltic, the signatories included the Soviet Union, Poland and both East and West Germany.

One might suggest that the divided states and ideological polarization in Northeast Asia distinguishes it from Europe and explains the lack of regime formation there. But the initial Baltic regime included East and West Germany, as well as communist and western quasi-capitalist states such as the Soviet Union and Poland vs. Denmark and Sweden. And the Mediterranean regime was initiated and implemented by a group which included Israel, Libya, and Syria. And now that

Russia has abandoned its communist ideology and the Cold War has all but ended in Northeast Asia, why haven't maritime regimes been initiated?

One might point to the relatively similar levels of economic development in Europe as a major factor in avoiding North-South divisions over the trade off between development and environmental protection. While this may be valid for the North Sea countries, it was not so for the Baltic states when the regime was first initiated, and it was and remains invalid for the Mediterranean states on its southern rim.

One might suggest that the bitter sovereignty disputes over islands such as Tok Do/Takeshima and the Senkakus/Diaoyutai and their attendant maritime space are the constraint to maritime regime initiation in Northeast Asia. But Greece and Turkey were able to join and co-operate in the Mediterranean regime despite their sometimes violent dispute over islands in the Aegean. And in 1975–1976 prior to the initiation of the North Sea regime, England and Iceland engaged in the infamous, "Cod Wars,"[8] which involved vessel collisions and shooting incidents.

Theory based on the European experience is also not very helpful. There seems to be a general premise in the literature that lessons learned in one region are transferable to another.[9] For example, Haas has analyzed the prospects for effective maritime environmental governance in Northeast Asia and has concluded that the main reasons for the failure to initiate maritime regimes are weak international institutions; weak organization of knowledge; the lack of willing regional environmental leadership; and most important, the lack of an epistemic community to pressure governments.[10]

There are several difficulties with this analysis and its conclusions. First, Haas focuses only on initiation of regimes for marine environmental protection whereas the regimes for the Baltic and North Seas cover a broad range of marine resource uses and are best termed sea use management regimes. Thus his analysis misses some of the factors and complexities of the origin of such multiple use regimes. Second, Haas categorizes the Baltic and the post-1987 North Sea regimes as effective because of the development of strong international institutions even though, he asserts, they lack transnational scientific involvement. This observation would appear to diminish the importance of epistemic communities in regime initiation, implementation and evolution. Yet Haas maintains that such communities are the most important factor in regime creation. Moreover, I would argue that such an epistemic community does exist in the region involving national and international networks of actors and NGOs particularly in Japan, South Korea and Russia.[11] While one might debate the effectiveness of their transnational linkages, they do exist. Indeed, environmental concern in the region is strong and growing,[12] and there is relatively high capacity for formulating environmental policy.[13] Yet, maritime regimes have not been initiated.

Third, the region has certainly not lacked catalytic marine pollution[14] or resource management incidents which meet Haas' criterion of "offering opportunities for ambitious national environmental ministers to submit vigorous new proposals for collective action." For example, in January 1997, the Russian tanker Nakhodka broke in two in the Sea of Japan spilling much of its 19,000 tonnes of fuel oil which then blanketed the southwestern coast of Honshu, causing severe environmental damage preliminarily estimated at 7 billion yen. And the news that the Soviet and Russian Navy had dumped 18 decommissioned nuclear reactors and 13,150 containers of radioactive waste from 1978 to 1993, most of it in the Sea of Japan, caused an uproar in the world environmental community. It jolted nuclear-sensitive Japan and South Korea, and even drew adverse comment from North Korea. Yet these severe incidents did not prompt the creation of a regime.

Fourth, regarding a lack of regional leadership on marine environmental protection, it is true that the country with the most capacity in this sector – Japan – has shied away from such leadership. But for internal and historical reasons[15] South Korea has been very active in the international and regional environmental area and appears able and willing to take the lead. However, there have been no followers.

And finally, the region does not lack international institutional leadership and support in this arena. UNEP's Northwest Pacific Action Plan has existed since 1994 and has been working to improve the contractual environment, enhance national capacity, and build national concern. The support of UNEP has led to multilateral maritime regime initiation in nine regional seas despite the absence of a regional environmental institutional authority – but not in Northeast Asia.

We thus return to our original questions: are all lessons learned in the European context applicable to Northeast Asia, and if not, which are, and what are the reasons that maritime regime initiation, implementation and evolution have been unsuccessful there?[16] To answer the first question we must undertake a re-analysis of the factors favoring success in Europe.

First of all, on closer examination, the fundamental factors favoring regime initiation, evolution and implementation in Europe[17] are unique to that region. Comparability is not the same as transferability. The Baltic region in particular can be considered a "special case." There is only one physical maritime exit and the western Soviet Union needed to use this exit for access to the open sea. Thus the communist Soviet Union had considerable incentive to co-operate with its western-oriented neighbors in the management of the Baltic. And East Germany simply followed the Soviet lead. Moreover, there was a long history of co-operation between the littoral nations of the Baltic ranging from the medieval Hanseatic League[18] to the International Council for the Exploration of the Sea founded in Copenhagen in 1902.[19]

Second, the ideological divide between East and West Germany although superficially similar to that between North and South Korea, was never as bitter or stark. Indeed, communication between the two Germanies continued throughout the Cold War and the border was semi-porous unlike the hermetically sealed border between North and South Korea.

Third, Sweden acted as an honest broker and go between for NATO and the Soviet Union. Its opinion was considered objective by both sides. And Sweden was a world leader in environmental concerns, hosting the 1972 Stockholm Conference. If Sweden said there were serious problems with the Baltic environment that required co-operative management, it was likely to be taken at face value.

Finally, the 1975 CSCE[20] was being negotiated as the overarching security conference in Europe at the time of the formation of the Baltic regime. Although its main topics of discussion were security and economics, environment was also on the agenda. In this case, the confrontation between NATO and the Eastern bloc in the Baltic region actually helped encourage a co-operative management regime there – because the parties could agree on so little else. And West and East Germany followed their respective mentors in CSCE matters.

Regime formation in the North Sea was also a response to a unique combination of factors. North Sea regime initiation was favored by the similar economic status of the littoral countries; the concert of leadership of the United Kingdom, the Netherlands and Norway; and the connectivity between the scientific community and policy-makers in these three countries. This connectivity and the common interest in tourism may well have been the driving factors in the co-operative attempt to clean-up the Mediterranean. None of these factors are present in Northeast Asia.

Finally, and perhaps most important, the importance of epistemic communities in regime formation assumes a bottom-up origin of regimes. This is certainly one source of regimes – but not the only one. In fact, if a regime is initiated in Northeast Asia it is likely to originate from the top down rather than from any "bottom-up" pressure by an epistemic community.

Another problem with a blanket application of the criteria for "success" in Western Europe to Northeast Asia is that maritime regimes in Europe have had rather mixed results and "success" is a very relative term and difficult to measure. Although the Baltic countries have made great strides towards regional co-operation in marine policy, co-operation did not come easily and was only instituted after several aborted attempts. In the end, regime initiation was due to a general improvement in relations between the communist and Western European nations, combined with recognition of the Baltic as a common resource, and genuine concern for its living resources, particularly its fisheries. Also, the Marine Environment Protection Committee of the International Maritime Organization provided a forum for the first joint action of the Baltic Sea states to further their co-operative interest in environmental protection. The co-operative effort was effective in that it helped retard the environmental degradation of the Baltic.

UNEP's strategy of a convention followed by protocols, and concurrent assessment and regulatory activities was first developed for the Mediterranean Sea. Regional co-operation there began with a concern about ship-generated marine pollution; evolved into a concern about the effect of pollution on living resources; and eventually developed into a more general concern about the impact on the environment of a range of human uses and the general pattern of economic development.

However, the Mediterranean regime has not been fully effective. Ratification of the 1976 Barcelona Convention for the Prevention of the Mediterranean Sea Against Pollution and its protocols, especially the third protocol on land-based sources, was slow and implementation has been even slower. Control of land-based pollution requires fundamental and politically unpopular decisions in agricultural and industrial policies and practices. There is also growing resistance from those who are concerned that "co-operation" may erode national sovereignty. Eighty-three per cent of the contributions for the Mediterranean Action Plan (MAP) come from only three countries, and those contributions are inevitably late, causing the postponement and even cancellation of activities. Without the support of the European Union and the World Bank the MAP would have been even less effective. One of the MAP's priority subprograms, the Blue Plan, has also been plagued by organizational difficulties, lack of well-defined goals, problems with the host state, slow responses from the other governments, and financial shortages. Other programs have had similar difficulties, and suffer as well from the non-participation of key states and competing claims to ocean space. There is also a general concern that there are too many overlapping programs and activities.

A former co-ordinator of the MAP ventured some frank criticism of its implementation from his particularly pertinent perspective.[21] He felt that the program concentrated overly on marine pollution and was basically an amalgam of somewhat disparate activities. This is especially and increasingly a problem for the developing nations on the southern rim of the Sea. On the other hand, the developed Mediterranean countries are afraid of being subjected to a pan-Mediterrenean "tribunal" that might be dominated by the "South," and thus they do not support a legal committee to supplement the scientific component of the Plan. Another fundamental problem is that UNEP headquarters in Nairobi attempted to run the Plan from there, often disregarding the suggestions and wishes of the co-ordinator's office and, more importantly, those of the Contracting Parties to the Convention which they established. Since 1990, the program has been gradually refocused on integrated coastal management based on the concept of sustainable development. The MAP Coastal Areas Management Programme, implemented in a number of selected coastal areas, is the practical expression of that refocusing.[22] The MAP is now sharpening its objectives, reducing its priorities, and establishing better links with other initiatives.

Despite its shortcomings, the Mediterranean Plan process has yielded important general lessons for future attempts to form international marine environmental protection regimes.[23] Although pollution in the Mediterranean might have been worse than it is today if the Plan had not been instituted, this is partially due to factors other than the Plan itself. It was basically a political success but a substantive failure, in that co-operation resulted in a comprehensive legal and institutional Plan to clean up the Mediterranean, but the environmental condition of the Sea did not appreciably improve. The Plan was politically successful because the motives of participating countries for joining were mostly not environment-related. In particular, UNEP bore most of the initial financial burden and provided financial, technical and educational aid to strengthen the marine scientific capacity of the Lesser Developed Countries (LDCs). The Plan also provided opportunity for traditionally hostile countries to establish diplomatic ties. Moreover, signing conventions and protocols was initially inexpensive. But subsequent compliance was expensive and this explains why the Program stalled in its later stages.

In the beginning there was high uncertainty, high complexity, and a perception that pollution and its prevention were common problems. There were also different incentives due to perceived asymmetry in the abatement costs and effects of pollution. LDCs feared that developed countries were trying to exploit them by making them pay for pollution that the developed countries had caused. They also worried that prevention would make them less competitive and divert resources from their economic development. This generally describes China's present perception of environmental protection.

UNEP's contributions corrected the initial asymmetrical incentives. Moreover, the participation by LDC scientists reduced uncertainty regarding the distribution and effects of pollution, and therefore changed the perception of the problem. In particular, studies conducted under the direction of the secretariat supported neither the hypothesis that the Mediterranean was on the verge of "collapse" nor the assumption of extensive transmission of pollution across national boundaries. But such studies did indicate that cleaning up the Mediterranean would be very costly. Indeed, identifying land-based pollutants and rivers as the major sources of pollution meant that participating states would have to take measures which covered their entire territories. Since pollution was largely localized and the developed countries were the main polluters, it became apparent that they would have to bear the highest costs. The low pollution exchange and the consequent minor interdependence between North and South also meant that no single actor had real power over others. So reduction in ecological uncertainty led to reduction of economic and political uncertainty. France and, to a lesser extent, Italy were the major polluters of the Mediterranean and their participation was necessary to clean it up. France emerged as the scientific leader, and the developed countries had the scientific upper hand. But the false perception that the Plan was a response to a truly collective problem was used by the South to stall its implementation if the Plan did not satisfy their interests.

Maritime management regimes have supposedly reached their pinnacle in the North Sea where comprehensive sea-use planning has been ongoing since the early 1970s. The international goal of the North Sea regime is the development of a balanced and effective battery of instruments for both national and international administration and management. The general economic objective is the safe and efficient use of the various opportunities offered by the sea, both now and in the future. There are five specific plans: for offshore oil and gas development, for fisheries management, for water quality, for shipping routes, and for special sea uses. The North Sea regime also combines infrastructure facilities and furthers multiple or shared use of particular areas. An important feature is its small but efficient joint secretariat which facilitates co-ordination between two different conventions. The commissions established to implement the conventions are supported by technical working groups and a joint monitoring group.

Despite its accomplishments, formation of an effective action-oriented regime took a rather long time. Few direct measures to reduce the level of pollution in the North Sea were agreed upon during the first decade of regional effort. And due to lack of knowledge about the level and effect of pollutants, monitoring and information gathering constituted the most important work for that initial decade.

A third problem with learning lessons from Europe is a misunderstanding of the reasons for the emergence of environmental concerns and co-operation. It is often assumed that initiation, implementation and evolution of regimes for environmental protection in Europe are natural byproducts of the European Union and its predecessor, the European Economic Community, (now European Community [EC]) formed in 1957. However, in Europe, the expansion from economic to social and environmental issues was rather slow and tortuous. Initially, the primary impetus to introduce environmental protection was economic.[24] Environmental protection was included in EC directives in the early 1970s because differences in the environmental laws of the European states were viewed as barriers to trade.

The first United Nations Conference on the Human Environment in Stockholm in 1972 stimulated changes in values in many European countries which were translated into environmental laws, as well as the formation of the first EC Environmental Action Program in 1973. The emergence of acid rain problems within Europe in the late 1970s and early 1980s accelerated EC environmental institution building and legislation. Particularly important was the transformation of Germany's position on many environmental issues. The threat to German forests posed by acid rain heightened environmental awareness in that state. Also important was the formation of Green parties. Pressures mounted within the EC to create common environmental standards within the member states in order to deal with regional environmental problems.

In 1987, the EC gained competence over environmental protection matters when the Treaty of Rome was amended by the Single European Act. With the formation of the Act, the EC gained powers to negotiate internally on environmental matters and to formulate environmental laws that superseded those of member states. In 1993, this institution-building process was pushed forward by the Maastricht Treaty when member states agreed to work towards greater political and monetary union and established the European Union. Also critical to the process of environmental institution building in Europe was the leadership of powerful states, in particular Germany and the Netherlands. Indeed, it was not until Germany became more "green" domestically that European environmental co-operation on a large number of issues made significant progress.

Lessons Learned And Their Applicability To Northeast Asia

From these and other examples, it is possible to deduce some general factors that favor or retard multilateral maritime regime formation. These factors may or may not be applicable in Northeast Asia.

First of all, the parties must share norms of behavior.[25] This is important because norm-guided behavior is the minimum requirement for regime existence[26] and norms affect the values placed by participants on actions and strategies independently of their consequences. They also affect perceptions of policy options including the tendency to take advantage of opportunities. Clearly, the member countries must perceive that the benefits of participation in a co-operative arrangement outweigh costs. Benefit/cost considerations include direct benefits, such as better use of marine resources, as well as indirect benefits, such as the advancement of a state's aspirations for regional leadership. In the initial stages of co-operation, the costs should be kept as low as possible.

Also relevant in benefit-cost considerations are the objectives and functions of the arrangement. Multiple use regimes have found it difficult to overcome the often contrary factors that create their need.[27] Multiple use approaches lack a vigorous political constituency because this usually forms around a single use. By their very nature, multiple use regimes partition opportunity among interest groups and thus create a more complex political milieu. They must also overcome segmented entrenched interests, which feel comfortable with single use regimes. These interests include agencies within governments, which tend to resent allocation of funds, personnel, and authority to international endeavors.

It appears, then, that sector-specific approaches have a greater chance of success than some supranational or multipurpose system that seeks to perform a multitude of functions within the framework of a single authority. This conclusion is a political reality despite the logic and apparent need in some areas for an integrated management system. A corollary is that success is encouraged by the recognition and promotion of subregional efforts rather than by an overemphasis on comprehensive regionalization. To minimize controversy and politicization in co-operative efforts, perhaps priority should be placed on innocuous sectors and combined with decentralized decision making authority.

Positive perceptions of co-operation are also necessary for successful regional efforts. Clearly, public and private institutions must establish regional links, and there must be a cadre of powerful persons committed to the regional concepts, and a regional goal. For example, the ASEAN countries have consistently opposed a formal treaty on environmental protection as being too rigid and potentially divisive. And the Northeast Asian countries are clearly divided on this issue. In order to maintain momentum, expectations of progress must be reasonable but they must be satisfied. Conversely, if no progress is made within a reasonable time, the movement toward co-operation is weakened or its objectives are altered.

Several regional seas programs were only initiated after scientific revelations of regional pollution or a well-publicized environmental disaster. This is because governments tend to be forced into action only when significant political constituencies insist on it. In Europe the transition in relevant knowledge, perceptions, and values as they relate to the world's oceans produced a groundswell. The present generation views ocean space differently from previous generations. Although ocean ecosystems will probably never be completely understood, their complicated nature is slowly being revealed, and Europeans are becoming increasingly aware of their capacity to damage the ocean environment, with both immediate and long-term practical effects readily understandable to those without training in ocean science. For example, the loss of income to businesses dependent upon beachgoers and the loss of the opportunity to bathe in the ocean during a hot summer owing to the presence of assorted waste products in coastal waters generate enormous pressures on policy makers to "do something."

But the prerequisites of an effective public policy debate, such as clear statements of risk and the identification of costs and benefits, do not mesh well with the slowness, deliberateness, and uncertainty of the scientific process.[28] And in Northeast Asia, there is a general disconnect between public concern and policymakers, and little or no public policy debate in most countries of the region.

Disagreements stemming from uncertainty can be overcome by agreement on the precautionary principle, i.e., agreeing to take action even when cause and effect are only suspected rather than proven. Indeed, as pollution increases and becomes a publicly perceived problem, ocean management moves closer to center stage as a significant public policy concern meriting attention. The combination of a thorough planning process, public pressure and high-level political conferences were key factors in the formation of maritime regimes in Europe. These perceptions and processes are not strong or widespread in Northeast Asia. Clearly, regime formation is fundamentally dependent on who the participants are; changing perceptions of benefits and costs of a regime; and the level, quality and types of information available.[29]

There are both obvious and subtle reasons why regimes do not form. These include limited management authority, a lack of effective enforcement power, disagreement among member states, shortages of funds, and shortage of trained personnel or equipment. More subtle problems can include limited information and/or the ability to use it, jurisdictional limitations, differing time horizons, and "freedom" costs.[30] All of these constraints are present in Northeast Asia.

A lack of information regarding scientific knowledge relevant to effective ocean management can cause disagreements between governments and inhibit the generation of sound national and international policy. Boundary disputes or uncertainties retard the implementation of jurisdictional control, without which co-operation is made more difficult. Furthermore, existing jurisdiction may not encompass the entire ecosystem so that some critical elements requiring management are beyond state control. Ironically, although segmented or sectoral approaches to co-operative ocean management are much more likely to gain the political support necessary to progress, they may ultimately be unsuccessful in resolving the problem at hand, particularly if conflicting uses/users are involved. These constraints pertain in Northeast Asia.

There is obviously a time gap between the average length in political office of ministers and the tens of years required to implement and sustain successful regimes. Yet policymakers need to show results in the short term. This dilemma favors multiple short-term programs which may be insufficient for the achievement of long-term results. This is a constraint in Northeast Asian countries like Japan, South Korea and Russia where there are frequent changes in relevant officials and their tenure is short and uncertain.

"Freedom" costs at both the individual and state levels may ultimately block successful regime initiation as well. Individuals and states will have to surrender their absolute "freedom of the sea," that is, their absolute rights to use the ocean environment at any time, for any purpose and without regard for the interest and well-being of anyone else. Such freedoms will be surrendered with considerable reluctance in the absence of anything less than a clear, overwhelming, and immediate need. In Europe, formal sovereignty was perceived to be different from operational sovereignty – the legal freedom of action. The latter was eroded in the interest of effective collective action. Indeed, environmental interdependence and related international negotiations reinforced formal sovereignty while resulting in the self-limitation of operational sovereignty.[31] Traditional and rigid concepts of sovereignty in Asia prevent regime formation there.

Incipient Maritime Regime Formation In Northeast Asia

I contend that multilateral maritime regimes are on the verge of forming in Northeast Asia. This is primarily due to the lowering of political tension in the region which is in turn allowing increased communication and connectivity between and among maritime officials and actors in the region. Analysts need to pay more attention to informal networks to understand how Asian states work together.[32] Indeed, it can be argued that an easing of security tensions, the building of informal and formal economic ties, growing environmental awareness at the domestic level, and international pressures are stimulating the emergence of international co-operation in environmental protection.[33]

In January 1999, the Environment Ministers of China, Japan and South Korea met in Seoul, in the first in a series of planned annual meetings.[34] The Ministers expressed concern about environmental degradation in Northeast Asia and recognized the importance of close co-operation among the three countries. The priority areas for such co-operation are raising public awareness; information exchange and dissemination; research; environmental industry and technology; preventing air pollution; and protecting the marine environment. The Ministers also agreed to make use of the existing frameworks where possible and to form working groups or designate contact points where no framework exists. They also agreed on exchange of personnel and enhancement of communication and – most significant in terms of building an international epistemic community – on exchanges and co-operation between their NGOs and research institutes. At their February 2000 meeting in Beijing, the three Ministers agreed to undertake a project on environmental protection in western China.[35] The Ministers met PRC Premier Zhu Rongji who expressed support for co-operation among the three countries in this field, as well as hope that such co-operation would become a model for the region.[36]

China and South Korea also have ongoing co-operation supported by the Global Environment Facility (GEF) to protect the Yellow Sea marine ecosystem. The project began in 1991 and has nearly completed its second stage; it expects GEF funding for its third stage. The GEF is now also supporting a DPRK project on "Saving the Ecosystem of the Yellow Sea" through 2004.[37] Given the rapid political rapprochement on the Korean Peninsula, it should not be difficult to link the two efforts into a trilateral project which could be the basis for a management regime for the Yellow Sea.

There are stirrings on the domestic level as well. Ever so slowly, Japan's government is providing greater opportunities for citizen participation in environmental affairs.[38] More government money than ever is available to NGOs because, in part, the weak Environment Agency is discovering that NGOs can enhance its strength *vis a vis* powerful ministries and thus help further its bureaucratic objectives. However, government agencies may simply be more adept at co-opting NGOs and using them to enhance the international visibility of Japan's efforts rather than considering their input to policy decisions. But it is a "foot in the door" for NGOs and offers at least the possibility of influencing such decisions.

In China, environmental activists have for the first time been allowed to form associations and campaign publicly as long as they do not attack government policies.[39] The groups believe government officials realize that they can be helpful to their objectives. Russia has launched a new Integrated Coastal Zone Management Project within the framework of the Russian National Marine Research Program of the Ministry of Science and Technology.[40] And a special campaign to protect the environment of the DMZ on the Korean Peninsula is being launched by a group of Asian international experts.[41]

Most important, a regional NGO – the Northeast Asia and North Pacific Environmental Forum – has held six meetings in Northeast Asia. The forum was initiated in 1992 by the ROK Ministry of the Environment with assistance from the UNDP and nurturing by the Asia Foundation. Participants from NGOs, government, business and academia from Canada, China, DPRK, Japan, Mongolia, ROK, Russia and the United States focus discussion on transboundary environmental protection and pollution issues.

Nevertheless, compared with Europe, the process of regional environmental dialogue in Asia is still very young. It only began in the 1980s with initial scientific exchanges and limited inter-state dialogue. Since the 1990s, the pace of network building has grown substantially. Indeed, there has been a virtual explosion of activity in the region at least when compared to the situation a decade ago. There are now growing networks among non-governmental organizations, scientists, and environment agencies. Financial and technology transfer mechanisms are being established and environmental management capacity is being built up in areas where it was very weak.

There are several specific reasons for these positive developments. The growing severity of pollution has forced many states in the region to take environmental protection more seriously. Pollution that threatens human health and economic progress can no longer be ignored. These developments are also facilitated by increased wealth, and a keener interest in the quality of life.

Japan in particular has several good reasons to promote environmental protection in the region. It is becoming increasingly concerned about the adverse transnational environmental consequences of China's economic development and apparently realizes that building environmental protection capacity in its neighbors is in its long-term interest. Consequently, official development assistance has focused increasingly in this area. Financial and technology transfer mechanisms are being established and environmental management capacity is being built in areas where it was very weak. Moreover Japan is being constantly prodded by the United States to assume more of a leadership role in the region. And indeed, ever so tentatively, Japan is exploring its options to do so and environmental protection seems an innocuous, win-win arena.

Obstacles To Be Overcome

Why then, if such fundamental factors as an epistemic community, willing leadership, and increasingly obvious pollution problems exist, has a maritime regime not formed? For a regime to be effective it must meet the minimal conditions of states which exercise basic game power and offer benefits greater than what they can attain on their own.[42] Thus there cannot be an effective maritime regime in Northeast Asia without the full participation of China and Japan. But China is preoccupied with internal matters and in addition has placed most of its ocean attention on the South China Sea. And even there it has been most reluctant to co-operate. Indeed, China is generally opposed to any and all multilateral co-operation that could constrain its options, preferring bilateral co-operation which it can dominate and control. Moreover, with tension over Taiwan ratcheting up, China is reluctant to enter any discussions that might include it indirectly or otherwise.

As for Japan, it simply lacks the political will and credibility to lead the formation of a multilateral regime in Northeast Asia. South Korea could assume a key role, perhaps by offering to host and chair meetings, and thereby enabling the major powers to avoid appearing too dominant or assertive. But it may not be able to lead, and if it did lead, China and Japan might not follow.

Finally, the strong resurgence of the traditional concept of sovereignty prevails in Northeast Asia – with clear and manifest reasons. Here the uncertainty and weakness of States are obstacles to co-operation. Identity formation and exclusion are maximized at the State level preventing a rival process of identity to evolve at the regional level.[43] This concept must become more flexible before a formal multilateral maritime regime can form.

Equally important are honest, deeply rooted differences in priorities among the countries. China, in particular refuses to bear environmental responsibilities which are not commensurate with its social and economic development priorities and points to the Rio Declaration which states: "in view of the different contributions to global environmental degradation, states have common but differentiated responsibilities."[44]

Consequently, the parties cannot agree on such basics as financial burden sharing, institution building and leadership. The deliberations within NOWPAP are particularly revealing in this regard. Targeting potential "free riders" like China and North Korea, South Korea insists that all parties should contribute equal base amounts to the NOWPAP Trust Fund in addition to a second contribution based on a "capacity to pay."[45] Japan for its part has offered to host the Regional Co-ordinating Unit (RCU)[46] but South Korea feels that the RCU should only be established when sufficient NOWPAP funds are available. In other words, it has blocked Japan's attempt at leadership.[47] On the other hand, the ROK does support the notion of NOWPAP evolving into a legally binding agreement,[48] which Japan opposes.

The Chinese delegate to the 1999 NOWPAP meeting succinctly summarizes the situation as follows:

It is the fact that the implementation of NOWPAP is going slowly and we have to face this reality and need to sit down to seek reasons in a practical way. There exist indeed different views with regard to the arrangements for the Trust Fund of NOWPAP. The fundamental reason behind these differences is that we have not achieved a consensus in understanding of the national reality of our States in this region. All the wishes, even though they are all very good, will be difficult to become reality in practice if the basic aspects are not considered.

Three conditions favor the implementation of NOWPAP and are an important basis for our cooperation in this region:

(i) governments of the four member States all recognize the importance of marine environmental protection of the Northwest Pacific and have demonstrated willingness to cooperate in this area;
(ii) the number of the member States involved is small, and they do not have profound political, national and religious clashes; and
(iii) cooperation in this region has the support and active participation of UNEP and other international organizations.

Marine environmental protection can be undertaken in two stages. In the first stage, a State can concentrate its efforts on control of land-based sources of pollution, which is a major threat to the marine environment; and in the second stage when land-based pollution has abated, a State can participate in regional and international cooperation. In this latter stage, overfishing, marine oil spills, damage of coastal wetlands and beaches, and marine biodiversity conservation are likely areas of focus. However, we think the work in the first stage is prerequisite to the work in the second stage.

(i) The conditions which are not in favor of the implementation of NOWPAP are the main reasons for slow progress.

The four member States in this region are in different stages of marine environmental protection. Japan and the Republic of Korea are now in the second stage. It is hard to determine whether Russia is in the second stage even though great progress has been made. China is still in the first stage. In the years ahead, China will make large investments to control pollution of rivers and lakes.

There are several models of cooperation in marine environmental protection.

(ii) a) The first model is cooperation between developing countries. A weakness of this cooperation is the lack of financial resources. However, this is also an advantage in that these countries can take immediate action once such financial resources are made available.

b) The second model is cooperation between developed countries. The strength of such cooperation is the more readily available financial resources for co-operative activities. As long as the relevant countries reach a consensus on concerted action, practical results will be achieved.

c) The third model is cooperation between developing and developed countries. Cooperation of this kind is characterized by differences in capacity and financial resources and by the different bases for co-operation. Additionally, it is relatively difficult to obtain financial resources from outside for such regional cooperation because developed countries are involved. In such regional cooperation the developed countries do not want to have a disproportionately larger share of the obligations while the developing countries have great difficulty in fulfilling their obligations. This is the real reason for the slow implementation of NOWPAP.

Conclusions

In Northeast Asia there is still considerable resistance to the initiation of a multilateral management regime. The preference is still for "loose" co-operation from which participants can defect without penalty. There is a long list of domestic institutional problems regarding protection of the environment in the region. These include lack of lateral coordination within and between environment and resource management agencies; lack of integration between economic and environmental policies and planning processes; inadequate authority and budget for environment agencies to ensure sufficient weight in decision making processes; lack of environmental information; undeveloped managerial and administrative resources at all levels of government; low levels of public awareness and underfunded and understaffed environmental education programs; short time horizons which drive political and organizational decisions; outdated provisions in existing environmental laws and gaps on key issues such as solid hazardous wastes and radioactive pollution; slow enactment of domestic legislation to implement international treaty commitments; and inefficient markets, prices that do not fully reflect environmental costs and benefits, and uncertain ownership or control of natural resources. Moreover, in Asia, there are still great differences among states regarding environmental priorities and means for solving problems.

Perhaps the most important inducement for a multilateral regime would be the evening up of the levels of marine environmental technology and expertise throughout the region. The overall objective of the arrangement would be to manage the marine environment of Northeast Asian seas. But the most important spin off would be the provision of greater equity: equity in the sense of increased national responsibility to control pollution with potential transnational effects, and equity in the sense of a transfer of technology and knowledge from the more advanced for the benefit of all. In short, the major trade-off would be the benefit to Japan and South Korea of adherence by China, North Korea, and Russia to a predictable regime with common minimum standards of discharge, in exchange for training and technical assistance from Japan and South Korea. Until elites in Japan and South Korea realize that it is in their long-term interest to enhance their partners' capacity, regime formation will be difficult.

It is therefore not surprising that there still are very few international or regional environmental agreements in Asia. Instead, an Asian form of loose environmental cooperation is likely to continue well into the future. This loose cooperation will focus on establishing stronger networks among governments and non-governmental actors in the region and promoting common understanding of what the goals and priorities of action should be. In many ways the kind of cooperation that must emerge in Northeast

Asia is similar to that which developed between the European Union and the former East bloc states. There one of the greatest stimulants for improving environmental regimes was the promise of greater economic and social cooperation and integration. Finally, outside powers can help multilateral maritime regime initiation in Northeast Asia by keeping the protagonists apart and by helping to raise their capacity, thus buying time for the region to evolve its own process, means, and commitment to cooperation.

NOTES

1. For background, analysis and proposals for co-operation in the Baltic Sea, see Mathew Auer, "Prospects for environmental cooperation in the Yellow Sea," *Emory International Law Review* 5 (1991): 163–208; Ton Ijlstra, "Development of Resource Jurisdiction in the EC's Regional Seas: National EEZ policies of EC Member States in the Northeast Atlantic, the Mediterranean Sea, and the Baltic Sea," *Ocean Development and International Law* 23, 2–3 (1992); Baruch Boxer, "Mediterranean Action Plan: an Interim Evaluation," *Science* 202 (10 November 1978): 585–90; Gunnar Kullenberg, "Long-term Changes in the Baltic Ecosystem" *in* Kenneth Sherman and Lewis M. Alexander (eds.), *Variability and Management of Large Marine Ecosystems*, AAAS Selected Symposium 99 (Boulder: Westview Press, Inc., 1986); B.I. Bybern and S.H. Fonselius, "Pollution in the Baltic Sea" *in* Aoano Voipio (ed.), Elsevier Oceanography Series 30 (Amsterdam: Elsevier Scientific Publishing Company, 1986): 351–82; ICES, *Assessment of the Marine Environment of the Baltic. Cooperative Research Report XX* (Copenhagen, 1986); F.B. Pedersen, "The sensitivity of the Baltic Sea to natural and man-made impact" *in* J.C.J. Nihoul (ed.), *Hydrodynamics of Semienclosed Seas,* Elsevier Oceanography Series 24 (Amsterdam: Elsevier Scientific Publishing Company, 1982): 385–99; Aoano Viopio, *The Baltic Sea*, Elsevier Oceanographic Series (Amsterdam: Elsevier Scientific Publishing Company, 1981).
2. For background analysis and proposals for co-operation in the North Sea, see Sven Andersen and Brit Flostad, "Sea Use Planning in Norwegian Waters: National and International Dimensions," *Coastal Management* 16 (1988): 183–200; H. Carison, "Quality Status of the North Sea. International Conference on the Protection of the North Sea" *in* John King Gamble (ed.), *Law of the Sea: Neglected Issues*, Proceedings of the Law of the Sea Institute Twelfth Annual Conference held at The Hague, The Netherlands 23–6 October 1978; Gerard Peet, "Techniques and Methods for Sea Use Planning and Management in Selected Areas", Report of a literature study commissioned by Directie Noordzee, Rijkswaterstaat, 1986, Second Chamber of the State General, The Netherlands, Harmonization of Netherlands North Sea Policy 1989–1992, 44–5, SDU uigevergij; A.J. Smith, Elizabeth Kennet and M.B.F. Ranken, *Britain and the Sea; Further Dependence – Further Opportunities* (Edinburgh: Scottish Academic Press Limited, 1984); H.D. Smith and C.S. Lalawani, *The North Sea: Sea Use Management and Planning* (Cardiff: University of Wales Institute of Science and Technology, 1984); Elizabeth Young and Peter H. Fricke (eds.), *Sea Use Planning* (London: Fabian Society, 1975); Steinar Andresen, "The Environmental North Sea Regime: A Successful Regional Approach" *in* Elisabeth Mann Borgese, Norton S. Ginsburg, and Joseph R. Morgan (eds.), *Ocean Yearbook 7* (Chicago: the University of Chicago Press, 1989): 378–401; Steinar Andresen. "The 'Effectiveness' of Regional Environmental Co-operation in the Northern Seas," Paper presented at the Annual Meeting of the International Studies Association, Chicago 23–25 February 1995.
3. For background, analysis and proposals for co-operation in the Mediterranean Sea, see Aldo Chircop, "The Mediterranean Sea and the Quest for Sustainable Development," *Ocean Development and International Law Journal*, 23 (1992): 17–30; Norton Ginsburg, Sidney Holt and William Murdoch, *The Mediterranean Action Plan and the Maritime Development of a Region, Pacem in Maribus 111*, Proceedings of a Conference, Split, Yugoslavia, April 28–30, 1972 (The Royal University of Malta Press, 1974); Adalberto Vallega, *A Human Geographical Approach to Semienclosed Seas: The Mediterranean Case in Regional Development* (Chicago: The University of

Chicago Press, 1988); S.J. Holt, "Mediterranean: International Cooperation for a Sick Sea," *Environment*, 16 (1974): 29–3; United Nations Environment Programme, "Activities for the Protection and Development of the Mediterranean" *in Ocean Yearbook 1* (Chicago: The University of Chicago Press, 1978): 584–97; United Nations Environment Programme, "Recommendation for the Future Development of the Mediterranean Action Plan" *in Ocean Yearbook 2* (Chicago: The University of Chicago Press, 1980): 547–54; "Protocol for the Protection of the Mediterranean Sea against Pollution from Land-based Sources" *in Ocean Yearbook 3* (Chicago: The University of Chicago Press, 1982): 489–96; "MARPOL 73/78: The International Convention Concerning Pollution and the Mediterranean" *in Ocean Yearbook 6* (Chicago: The University of Chicago Press, 1986): 572–73; United Nations Environment Programme, "The Mediterranean Action Plan: Retrospect and Prospect," presented at the fourth Ordinary Meeting of the Contracting Parties to the Convention for the Protection of the Mediterranean Sea Against Pollution and its Related Protocols, Genoa 9–13 September 1985. Published as Document UNEP/IG.56/4, 26 June 1985.

4. Mark J. Valencia. *A Maritime Regime for Northeast Asia*. (Hong Kong: Oxford University Press, 1996).
5. *Ibid.*
6. About the Gdansk Convention, *wysiwyg://477/http://wwwibsfc.org/about/WS-1-1.htm*, 15 October 1999.
7. Helsinki Commission, *http://www.helcom.fi/oldhc.html*
8. Iceland. *Encyclopedia Brittanica.*
9. Robert O. Keohane, Peter M. Haas and Marc A. Levy, "The Effectiveness of International Environmental Institutions" *in* Peter M. Haas, Robert Keohane and Marc A. Levy (eds.), *Institutions for the Earth: Sources of Effective International Environmental Protection* (Cambridge: The MIT Press, 1993): 19–20.
10. Peter M. Haas, "Prospects for Effective Maritime Governance in the NW Pacific Region." *Marine Policy*, 24, 4 (2000): 341–8; Mark J. Valencia, "Comment on Prospects for Effective Marine Governance in the Northwest Pacific Region", *Marine Policy*, 24, 15: 439–440..
11. *Ibid.*
12. Mark Baker, Libby Bassett and Athleen Ellington, *The World Environmental Handbook* (New York: World Environment Center 1985); Hyon-Jin Kim 1999. "International Environmental Co-operation in Northeast Asia". Paper presented at the 40th International Studies Association Annual Convention, Washington D.C., 16–20 February 1999.
13. *Ibid.*
14. Mark J. Valencia, *supra* n.4: 101–102.
15. *Ibid.*; Samuel Leu, Korea, U.S. to Sign Pact on Ocean Resources. *Korea Herald*, 15 September 1999.
16. Peter Sand (ed.), *The Effectiveness of International Environmental Agreements. A Survey of Existing Legal Instruments* (Cambridge: Grotius Publications, Ltd, 1992).
17. Martin List and Volker Rithberger, "The Role of Intergovernmental Organizations in the Formation and Evolution of International Environmental Regimes" *in* Arild Underdahl, (ed.), *The Politics of International Environmental Management* (Boston; KluwEr Academic Publishers): 67–81.
18. Hanseatic League, *Encyclopedia Britanica*, *wysiwyg://425/http://www.britannica.com/...article/printable/7/0,5722,39977,00html, 1999–2000.*
19. ICES, *wysiwg://445/http://www.ices.dk/informat/about.htm,2000.*
20. The Commision on Security and Cooperation in Europe, *http://www.house.gov/csce/aboutcsce.htm.*
21. Salvino Busuttil, "The Governance of the Mediterranean," Paper presented at Pacem in Maribus XXI, Takaoka, Japan, September 1993.
22. Arsen Pavasovic. "Regional Co-operation and its Role in Integrated Coastal Management – Experience of the Mediterranean Action Plan", UNEP Coastal Zone Canada 94 (Coastal Zone Canada Association 94): 165–180.
23. Jon Birger Skjaerseth, "The 'Effectiveness' of the Mediterranean Action Plan," *International Environmental Affairs*, 5, 4 (1993): 313–34.
24. Miranda Schreurs. "Environmental and Energy Security and Co-operation in Northeast Asia". Paper presented at ESENA Conference, Nautilus Institute, Berkeley 1999.

25. Edward L. Miles. "The New Ocean Regime: Facilitating Implementation, Compliance and Evolution" *in* David Wilson and Richard Sherwood (eds.), *Ocean Governance and Maritime Strategy* (Sydney: Allen and Unwin, 2000).
26. List and Rithberger, *supra* n. 17.
27. Lawrence Juda and R.H. Burroughs, "The Prospects for Comprehensive Ocean Management," *Marine Policy* (1990): 34.
28. Gary Bryner, "Constructing International Institutions to Ensure Effective Implementation of Global Agreements." Paper presented at the Annual Meeting of the International Studies Association, Chicago, 23–25 February 1995: 7.
29. Miles, *supra* n. 25.
30. Juda and Burroughs, *supra* n. 27.
31. Keohane, Haas and Levy, *supra* n. 9: 416.
32. Peter J. Katzenstein. "Regionalism in Comparative Perspective". *Co-operation and Conflict* 31 (1996): 123–160.
33. Schreurs, *supra* n. 24.
34. China-Japan-Korea Tripartite Environment Ministers Meet (TEMM) 13 January 1999, Seoul, ROK.
35. Ding Wei, "China, Japan and ROK Sign Joint Communiqué on Environmental Protection", *People's Daily* (28 February 2000): 5.
36. "Premier Meets Minister," *China Daily* (28 February 2000): 1.
37. "GEF Supports NK Ecosystem Research," *Joongang Ilbo* (13 January 2000).
38. Robert J. Mason, "Whither Japan's Environmental Movement: an Assessment of Problems and Prospects at the National Level," *Pacific Affairs*: 187–207.
39. John Leicester, Building Environmental Movement is Planting Seeds of a "Green" China". *AP* 72, 2 (1999) (20 December 1998); Elizabeth Rosenthal. "Pollution Victims Start to Fight Back in China", *New York Times* (16 May 2000).
40. Y.G. Mikhaylichenko and N. A. Aibulatov, "ICZM Development in Russia." Paper presented at PACON 1999, Moscow, Russian Academy of Sciences.
41. DMZ Forum, ESSENA, Nautilus Institute, 29 January 1999.
42. Miles, *supra* n. 25.
43. Olav Knudsen, "What Promise for Regional Co-operative Security? A Comparison of the Baltic Sea Region and Northeast Asia." *Pacific Focus*, XIV 2 (1999): 5–42.
44. Statement by the Head of the Chinese Delegation at the Fourth Intergovernmental Meeting on the Northwest Action Plan (NOWPAP), UNEP (WATER)/NOWPAP IG. 4/7 Annex II.
45. Hwang Soon-Teik. "Opening Statement at the Fourth Intergovernmental Meeting on NOWPAP", UNEP (WATER)/NOWPAP IG. 4/7 Annex II.
46. Nobuyuki Sugimoto. "Opening Statement at the Fourth Intergovernmental Meeting on NOWPAP", UNEP (WATER)/NOWPAP IG. 4/7 Annex II.
47. Hwang, *supra* n. 45.
48. Chun Yung-Woo. "Opening Statement on NOWPAP", UNEP (WATER)/NOWPAP IG. 3/7 Annex II.

Mark J. Valencia

CONCLUSIONS AND LESSONS LEARNED

Introduction

The past few decades have witnessed the emergence of a vast array of regional arrangements and institutions dealing with all aspects of ocean management. The level of cooperation ranges from minimal dispute avoidance to relatively comprehensive ocean governance at the regional level. For the analyst, the regional level provides a convenient means of organizing the world into manageable units for which information can be collected and digested in an intelligible manner, and through which patterns of behavior may be discernible which are not evident at the global level.[1] Indeed, although many ocean resources are inherently transboundary in nature, few are functionally manageable at a global level.[2] Beyond the descriptive advantage of the regional approach, it may also be possible to identify regional characteristics which condition national responses to ocean management issues. More significant than the analytical advantages, however, is the fact that States have frequently resorted to regional action in the international dimension of their ocean management efforts. The practical successes achieved have also encouraged the prescriptive application of the regional approach by analysts, governments, non-governmental organizations, and global multilateral agreements including the 1982 United Nations Convention on the Law of the Sea (UNCLOS 1982).[3]

However, there often seem to be more examples of the *appearance* of such co-operative action than its *reality*.[4] There is a significant difference between representatives attending conferences, presenting papers, and participating in working groups, and governments seriously "investing" in joint activities involving the expenditure of funds, long-term commitments, and the cession of decision-making rights to a multinational organization. This is particularly so with respect to international fisheries authorities, regional seas action plan administrations, or international dispute settlement bodies. Outside of Europe, the record of the past two decades indicates a scarcity of such "investments." Nevertheless, reasonably successful and comprehensive regional regimes have been created for the Baltic,[5] the North[6] and the Mediterranean[7] Seas, as well as the South Pacific Ocean. And

Mark J. Valencia (ed.), Maritime Regime Building, 149–171.

regional or subregional regimes are being initiated in the South China Sea, the Gulf of Thailand, and the Indian Ocean. However no regional maritime regime has been created in Northeast Asia.

The papers in this volume describe and explain existing or incipient regional maritime regimes in an unusually broad comparative context, and extract lessons learned that may be applicable elsewhere. Moreover, the papers raise and address questions of relevance to policy-making. Why has maritime regime building been successful in Europe and unsuccessful in Asia? And are lessons learned in the European context applicable in Asia? More generally, what are the *conditions* that make possible the development of durable regional ocean management regimes? Are there particular modes of cooperation and institutional options which have a better chance of success? If no one mode is necessarily preferable, is it possible to suggest criteria by which the choice may be made in such a way as to increase effectiveness?

Are there particular types of issues, or even identifiable sectors, which are more amenable to regime development? Does regime development enhance conflict avoidance and dispute resolution? Has regime development at the regional level defined and enhanced emerging global regimes? To what extent have global patterns been altered by regional developments, especially as new global arrangements and institutions have continued to emerge, often with regional groupings as important players in negotiations?

Most relevant to the theme of this volume, is it really possible to "build" a regime at all in a conscious way? Were multi-purpose regimes really planned in their entirety, or just identified *ex post facto*? And has the regional experience to date validated the predicted contribution of epistemic communities to regime creation, or has their role in this process been overestimated?

These fundamental questions have long been a concern of theorists and practitioners.[8] But they are extraordinarily difficult to answer in any definitive manner, because of the *sui generis* nature of each regional experience and the virtual impossibility of showing direct causal links in the development of such complex systems. Nevertheless, these queries are addressed here based on a comparative review of experiences in seven regions.

Relevant Concepts[9]

The focus of the papers in this volume is on the development of international ocean management *regimes* at the regional level. The concept of the international regime first emerged as an approach to describing and explaining complex sets of international arrangements dealing with the same or closely connected issue areas, and with a particular concern for the cumulative effect of the various arrangements.[10] The notion of a regime has been most broadly defined by Krasner as clusters of

> ... implicit or explicit principles, norms, rules, and decision-making procedures around which actors' expectations converge in a given area of international relations. Principles are beliefs of fact, causation, and rectitude. Norms are standards of behaviour defined in terms of rights and obligations. Rules are

specific prescriptions or proscriptions for action. Decision-making procedures are prevailing practices for making and implementing collective choice.[11]

The content of a regime has obvious legal implications, given its concern with norms and rules, but the concept extends to non-binding or "soft law" instruments,[12] and to institutional and social elements and non-governmental actors. The concept also underscores the significance of knowledge to the effective creation and maintenance of regimes, as well as the potential role in regime creation played by epistemic communities, i.e., "specific communities of experts sharing a belief in a common set of cause-and-effect relationships as well as the common values to which policies governing these relationships will be applied."[13] In short, regime theory offers the most inclusive approach to what might be considered a regional system of ocean management, and as such can elucidate many elements of interest to policy analysts.

The "transformational approach" to regime formation argues for regimes to be designed to "generate increasingly greater commitment and deeper cooperation through a process of iterative, state-to-state negotiation that promotes identity convergence."[14] This approach is significant in circumstances where the possibility of widespread compliance with an extensive set of obligations is unlikely. "Transformationalism" argues for the "softening" of the regime in exchange for broader membership, in the belief that the functioning of the regime will, over time, increase the convergence of interests:

> To maximize this process [of promoting convergence] Transformationalism prescribes that regimes be highly inclusive, minimize the stringency of obligations, deemphasize enforcement, and utilize decision-making rules requiring near unanimity. ... According to Transformationalists, it is the weak convention that is most likely to beget the strong regime.[15]

While one of the most important advantages of regime theory is its flexibility and adaptability, this comes with its own *caveats*, in that an overly broad definition of what constitutes a regime may lead to a lack of precision and attempts to cluster unrelated elements together in the creation of regimes by hindsight.

Given that unilateral approaches were an alternative for the management of the vast new ocean areas that were brought under national control, why has the regional level of organization been adopted so widely, albeit unevenly, with respect to the oceans? And why did the trend seem to at least initially accelerate as states expanded their maritime jurisdiction in the last three decades of the 20th century? First of all, many ocean resources and uses such as fish and fishing, sealanes and shipping, environmental quality and pollution are inherently transboundary in nature. Second, many of these resources and uses are not functionally manageable at a global level.[16]

The generality of global arrangements is further enhanced by the practical difficulty of defining detailed approaches which are appropriate to all possible situations, given the phenomenal diversity of uses, management challenges and national implementation capacities throughout the world. The global approach serves an indispensable function in creating frameworks or blueprints for action, and in defining general principles. But the breadth of the global approach is sometimes achieved at the expense of depth. Indeed, the nature of obligations to global agreements tends towards the lowest common denominator in order to ensure that the largest possible number of parties might be included. This has led to some "commitments" being effectively unenforceable, either because they are legally non-binding,[17] or because their imprecision is such that the ultimate effect is the same.[18] This difficulty is most clear in the case of ambitious multi-sectoral law-making efforts such as the *UNCLOS 1982*.[19]

In contrast, the region can provide an important mediating level between the generalities of global regimes and the specifics of national implementation. If a region contains a smaller number of states with more congruent interests and similar management concerns,[20] there is a better chance of achieving more specific and more robust agreements than within a larger grouping. Further definition and hardening of global frameworks can thus be achieved through regional regime formation. This potential role for regions is explicitly recognized in the call for further regional action in the global multilateral agreements which provide the basic architecture of the international law of the sea, as well as other documents which contribute to the definition of international ocean management.

The definition of region, whether for analytical or operational purposes, offers the same flexibility as does the definition of regimes. A region might be defined around existing patterns of cooperation (regardless of whether that cooperation is marine-related), a management problem shared by all members of the region; geographic proximity and the presence of transboundary issues (as with some enclosed and semi-enclosed seas); cultural homogeneity; military alliances; and even *ad hoc* groupings intended to reflect a common position on a specific issue of special concern.[21] Thus states might be members of a number of overlapping "regions" defined for different purposes and according to different criteria.[22] The definition of region can be critical because it can determine the cost and durability of regional cooperation efforts.

Of particular relevance to developing states is that the regional level of co-operation offers the possibility of improved collective capacity and of capacity-building. Modern multilateral treaties such as the *UNCLOS 1982* and the UNCED-related conventions contain a wide range of positive obligations which will require a complex and expensive process of implementation before they can be fulfilled. This in turn presupposes the availability of significant scientific, managerial and enforcement capabilities, which may or may not be present.[23] Regional cooperation has been used as a means of addressing this general problem in at least three ways: pooling and more efficient use of scarce resources; attracting assistance in capacity building from regional agencies; and the presentation of a unified "regional front" allowing states to increase their "leverage," whether in direct confrontations with external powers[24] or in the context of highly factionalized global negotiations.[25]

Choices

Regional cooperation and regime formation clearly involve choices which are critical to the success of the regime. Analysts may obscure reality by imposing an artificial and distorted regional template on patterns of behavior that are actually defined at the global or bilateral level, or within the context of another region than the one used for the purposes of the regime.[26] For practitioners, this raises a more critical question – how to define the appropriate region for purposes of cooperation, given the possibility that there may be more than one option available.

Funding and agenda setting may become problematic at the regional level. It is usual to seek foreign aid to support regional efforts. But over-reliance on donor support for regional institutions opens up the possibility of pressure, whether implicit or explicit, to avoid policies and programs which challenge the interests of funders.[27] At the very least, it is likely that the need to satisfy the priorities of funding agencies will influence the general direction of activities, possibly in ways which would not have been the first choice of member states.[28] Also, the capacity building function of development agencies may be state-centric, neglecting the function of regime creation and regional co-operation. The problem of funding and other support for regional programs and institutions should be addressed early in the process of regime development, and not left to be dealt with once commitments are in place. In addition, the potential impact of the funding option on the content and direction of a program dictates that it should be considered at least in part as a substantive question, and not merely as the neutral means by which other objectives are met.

The decision to cooperate at a regional level on a particular issue area presupposes the identification of some potential benefit to be gained beyond what could be accomplished at the national or global levels. But there should also be a clear understanding of the *priority* assigned to the problem, the particular advantage sought by regional action, and at least a preliminary assessment that the benefits justify the inevitable costs.[29]

The scope of membership and participation in regional arrangements and institutions is also a significant choice, and one which may need to be revisited from time to time as interests or levels of commitment change.[30] The notion of "membership" may also be variable across issues, as with the development of sub-regional arrangements or additional obligations which only attract some of the members of the broader grouping. The scope of involvement of non-regional actors may be a particularly sensitive issue, especially where external access to regional resources is a concern.

The appropriate mode of cooperation is also a matter of choice: consultative mechanisms; task forces; cooperative research plans; establishment of coordinated management priorities; framework conventions; and/or creation of a permanent management commission?[31] The potential range of options is limited only by the creativity of the parties. These different approaches can exist on a continuum, with incremental movements up the scale of regional integration being possible as confidence and experience grows. And the variety of modes of cooperation speaks to the need for explicit consideration of all likely options, no matter how minimalist, before regional cooperative measures are rejected as unrealistic.

There are also numerous choices regarding institutions and obligations. Is a new institution required, and is it realistic to believe that states will agree to its creation?

If there are existing institutions covering the relevant region, can their functions be enhanced or adapted to assume the planned role? How will the new (or enhanced) agency interact and possibly overlap with the functions of other regional institutions and arrangements?[32] Which functions of an institution are appropriate, not only to the region, but for the particular institution? These questions will recur as interests and issues change over time, and regional institutions in particular must be prepared to address and justify their continued involvement in any given sector or program.[33]

Regarding obligations, is there a need and basis for formal and binding commitments through international agreements, or is the issue area more appropriately addressed through a "softer" document or arrangement? Resort to something other than a traditional binding agreement should not be considered a "failure," for what matters to management is what actually happens in practice, and that is not necessarily dependent on the presence of formal obligations.[34]

Lessons Learned

This volume contains papers on the experience of regime creation and evolution in the Baltic Sea,[35] the Mediterranean Sea,[36] the North Sea,[37] the South China Sea,[38] the Gulf of Thailand,[39] the South Pacific Ocean,[40] and the Indian Ocean.[41] This section integrates the "lessons learned" from these case studies.

Regime Initiation

Informal initiatives or "Track-Two" diplomacy can be very useful in inducing formal cooperation and intergovernmental statements, albeit in other fora. For example, the principles of cooperation developed by the South China Workshop in 1991 were the basis for a more formal ASEAN Declaration on the South China Sea in 1992.

The advantages of such "Track-Two" initiatives are many:

- they are usually co-ordinated by organizers who are more or less free of political influence by governments;
- they offer a forum for government officials and policy-makers of different countries to meet one another, academic and scientific experts, and sometimes private sector representatives, to discuss current issues in an informal and congenial setting, supposedly free from the constraints of official protocol;
- they offer officials an "off-the-record" ("back-channel") opportunity to meet privately with counterparts to discuss bilateral issues that are proving difficult to resolve through formal inter-governmental diplomacy;
- they create incentives and provide the means for specialists to form a constructive and mutually beneficial relationship with officials of their own and neighboring countries, and to access information that may not otherwise be available;
- they enable representatives of the least developed countries within a region to participate in international meetings and consultations that they could not otherwise afford to attend; and

- they contribute to the establishment, maintenance or upgrading of publishable academic/technical literature in regions deficient in high-quality research facilities.

However "Track-Two" initiatives also have a number of disadvantages:

- they tend to be perceived either as too "academic" or as potentially critical of current political processes;
- their practical influence on policy depends on the willingness and ability of the participating officials to take a leading and dynamic role;
- they are usually taken within the framework of a medium-term project whose funding is subject to a number of conditions, budgetary constraints, deadlines, and other administrative requirements imposed by the funding source that affect the scale, tempo, style and flexibility of the operation; and
- if the organizers assume a public information, public participation, or public advocacy role, they risk alienating policy-makers and thereby losing contact with their bureaucratic participants who are the link with officialdom.

The most successful approach seems to be subregional and dual track, i.e., while the "Track Two" forum serves as a catalyst, the "Track One" level attempts to form an intergovernmental mechanism – a regime. The birth of the Mediterranean Action Plan (MAP) was possible not only because of political will at the "Track One" level, but also because of the "Track Two" groundwork that preceded it. Indeed, the preliminary scientific groundwork enabled a convergence of perceptions of the problems and fostered a common interest in addressing them at the political level.

In launching such informal initiatives, the process should have the following characteristics:

- *inclusivity:* do not exclude any directly interested countries or parties;
- *sensitivity:* start with less sensitive issues which participants are comfortable discussing without fearing the disapproval of their respective governments or authorities;
- *senior participation:* the participants should be senior or rising personalities in their respective governments;
- *flexibility:* it is important not to prematurely institutionalize the structure of the process, e.g., by creating a permanent mechanism over the objections of any participant;
- *ad hoc and incrementalist:* the process should be *ad hoc* and step by step while taking into account cost effectiveness; it is important to begin with a manageable subregion like the North Sea or the Gulf of Thailand and expand to peripheral areas like the Northeast Atlantic or the South China Sea;
- *gradually broadening and deepening:* regime participation should begin with those states which are most heavily affected, contribute most to the problem and have the largest capacity to deal with it; the co-operation should slowly be broadened and deepened while promoting benefits for the regional states.
- *patience:* managing potential conflicts is a long-term affair in which the lack of immediate concrete results should not be cause for despair and frustration.

Leadership

The roles of the initiator, the convener and the sponsor of the process are critical. The ideal is a person from the region who is perceived as neutral and whose country is not directly involved in any territorial or sovereignty disputes. The initiator and the convener – often the same person – must have patience, dedication, tenacity and sufficient knowledge of the delicate issues involved. At the same time the convener must be able to maintain the respect and the continued support and cooperation of all participants to keep the process moving forward. The roles of initiator and convener are clearly very delicate and require extremely skilled diplomats.

In the Mediterranean example, UN agencies provided the necessary leadership to a region that was ready to accept it. Both the General Fisheries Commission for the Mediterranean (GFCM) at the beginning, and UNEP eventually, were highly respected by regional states, and other supporting international organizations. It appears to be essential for the lead organization to coordinate closely with other organizations and be responsive to the collective regional will. Because of their multilateral and non-partisan character, UN agencies have the merit of enabling states in conflict to sit at the same table.

Regime Evolution

Positive regime evolution can be enhanced by an increase in problem solving capacity and a dual strategic approach, i.e., a combined "soft" political and "hard" legal approach. Also contributing to positive evolution are the level of maturity of the regime, contextual factors such as public opinion, and a membership comprised of fairly equal and fairly wealthy nations. Another important positive factor is a combination of a high level political component and strong state and individual leadership, together with a more low key commission approach. Compliance should be elicited through a judicious application of mild pressure, convincing arguments, and exposure, as well as through elaborate reporting procedures. The regime should be highly transparent and include various sub-national actors. A strong knowledge base and external shocks help increase public awareness which in turn spurs the regime forward.

Building effective regimes takes time. There are various stages of regime formation and development. Although a regime may initially and for some time be a "travel club," it may still eventually become highly effective. Also, factors that may be very important in initiating regimes may not be so important during the implementation stage. For example, building a solid knowledge base and the role of epistemic communities and entrepreneurial leadership may be particularly important in the initial phase. But over time, the significance of such factors tends to diminish.

Effectiveness in a narrow sense may not be a full and fair measure of a regime. For example, although the Mediterranean Sea is not cleaner today than it was 25 years ago, and objectives and standards of MAP have frequently not been met or postponed, the process of cooperation has attained value *per se*. The existing regime provides principal and subsidiary fora in which regional States can address common issues with discrete negotiations. Regime members continue to be active and to periodically renew vows of regional solidarity, stake claims to benefits generated, commit resources, and more recently, allow more civil society participation both regionally and domestically.

This achievement of regime sustainability is a result of maintaining a focus on common interests amid diversity. Indeed, the cultural diversity of the Mediterranean is considered a regional heritage to be protected and fostered. This shared cultural value provides people and public institutions with a strong sense of regional identity. Diversity of political and economic systems and of capacity broadens issues, provides greater prospects for trade-offs, and stimulates pooling of knowledge and skills. And the need to co-operate and to reach consensus softens political and economic differences and moderates nationalist perspectives.

Structure

Powerful national focal points. National focal points must be powerful and not sectoral or marginalized. Unless regime participation is at the highest level of decision making or the responsibility of powerful cross sectoral agencies such as economic planning, participation will be perceived as weak – and so will the regime.

Challenge of integration. The true integrated approach has an inevitable and troublesome by-product: complexity, which increases as knowledge grows. This may lead to difficult decisions on "boundaries" in an otherwise unwieldy management process. Ecosystem-based integrated coastal area management requires a re-examination of regime boundaries and participation, including extra-regional participation.

Regime financing. To reinforce ownership and accountability, regime-building costs and core costs should be perceived to be borne equitably by regime participants. The UN Scale of Assessments, which was developed on a global scale, might not be equitable at a regional level, where there are fewer State actors. Also, if the majority of contributions come from only a few States, these States are likely to have the primary influence on regime development.

Regime control. It is essential that regional States perceive ownership of their regime in their region and perceive extra-regional or international organization support as facilitative only. Thus the central decision-making process in a regional regime concerned with environment and development must be controlled by a forum of regional States, although the process may have a broad range of input from intergovernmental and non-governmental organizations which can influence the decision.

Outside Aid. Outside assistance to regimes often has subtle or not-so-subtle side effects. In the South Pacific, for example, the fact that many countries in the region are dependent on outside aid makes them less able to criticize the activities of those countries (like Japan) that assist them financially. The SPREP Secretariat has established a sound agenda, but has avoided controversial subjects such as French testing at Muroroa, and has focused on consensus-and capacity-building rather than confrontation. Also, to appease the nuclear powers, the South Pacific Nuclear Free Zone Treaty permits nuclear-powered vessels and ships carrying nuclear weapons to go through the Treaty waters without restrictions.

Regime Functions

Treaty-making. A formal treaty is often the stated (or unstated) goal of a regime. But treaty-making is a slow process that may delay regime-building and give the impression of inefficiency. The process of convening groups of experts to conduct preparatory work, negotiate and adopt a treaty in a diplomatic forum, securing the necessary number of ratifications to bring it into force, and implementing it can take many years. Moreover, there is always the danger, as was the case in the Mediterranean, of different states adhering to different legal regimes regarding the same issue. There is no question that a legal framework to govern expectations in a multilateral context has great long-term value. But a regime must first assist member states in anticipating formal commitments through a gradual process of preparation and capacity-building.

Regime accountability. Accountability through reporting can be crucial to regime adherence. For example, under MAP Phase I there was a generic national reporting requirement in the Unamended Barcelona Convention. This was tightened and elaborated in the Amended Barcelona Convention. The legal obligation to report on national implementation action in the biennium has certainly promoted accountability vis-à-vis other regime participants, including civil society.

Public information and participation. A regime that does not provide for public participation at regional and national levels risks remaining a "travel" club with little accountability or effectiveness. Civil society participation has an important multiplier effect in broadening the popular support base. Commitment to public participation is important for increasing support for the regime, especially as it becomes more ambitious, e.g., in implementing integrated coastal area management.

Knowledge-building. Knowledge-building activities are at the heart of the regime. They serve to inform participation, develop common conceptions and perceptions, and ultimately steer the regime. These activities give a regime a dynamic quality and are critical for the setting of standards and timelines.

Capacity-building. In a regime where there are great disparities in critical knowledge and skills, capacity-building is as important as effective communication in problem-solving. The ability to convert common intent into effective concerted action requires a reasonably similar capacity level. The principle of common but differentiated responsibilities should be accepted only with the understanding that capacity to undertake regime commitments must be built.

Process

For the process of regime formation to be successful, the political environment must be supportive. A delicate balance must be struck between the "stronger" and "weaker" countries. If more powerful countries dominate the less powerful countries, the latter may not participate. But if the weaker countries are "uncooperative," a powerful country can kill an initiative by simply being unsupportive, because this sends a negative signal to other participants and potential donors. Major external powers, wherever possible and practicable, should support the development of a constructive atmosphere in the region for peace, stability and progress. The interests of powerful non-regional countries should be taken into account and their potential contribution to conflict avoidance should not be ignored. However, if a major regional power objects to their involvement, they should be perceived as outside supporters of the dialogue, not as participants or decision-makers.

Moreover the countries in a region must share political concepts. For example, a sense of "community" must develop among the participants. And there must be a gradual progression in the region from the concept of national resilience and absolute sovereignty to the concept of regional resilience, regional cohesion, and regional identity. For example, the Pacific Island communities have a natural cultural affinity, and generally enjoy working and co-ordinating policy with each other.[42]

More pragmatically, countries in the region must be willing to develop concrete cooperative efforts and programs or projects so that the potential conflicts can be managed by converting them to actual cooperation. And the countries must be willing to support various fora for dialogue in co-operation – bilateral or multilateral, formal or informal. These dialogues should aim initially at producing an agreed code of conduct for the region. Linkages and networking among academics, experts and think-tanks are important particularly in the preliminary and initial stages, as are linkages between and among various regional and sub-regional initiatives. Discussion by "Track Two" fora can be helpful in encouraging "Track One" activities to be more responsive and imaginative in dealing with potential conflict. And previous state experience in attempts at conflict resolution should be utilized. For example, in taking the initiative in the South China Sea, Indonesia's effort benefited from ASEAN's experience in attempting to manage the conflicts in Indo-China, particularly in Cambodia, and by its own experience in managing and seeking a solution to the conflicts in the southern Philippines.

The countries should be willing to explore third party mechanisms for dispute settlement and if appropriate, utilize them, including good offices, mediation, arbitration, and adjudication by the International Court of Justice or the Law of the Sea Tribunal. And the countries should, wherever and whenever possible, attempt to settle their land, maritime and jurisdictional boundaries though negotiations, and respect the agreed boundaries. For some disputed areas, the application of the joint development concept can build trust and confidence.

Finally, and most important, to be sustained, the regime must yield benefits that could not otherwise be obtained. For example, Pacific islanders have created functioning regional organizations that have played important roles in allowing the small islands to speak with a more uniform and louder voice when negotiating with the larger powers. The Forum Fishing Agency has been particularly effective in that regard.

Applicability Of Lessons Learned

General lessons can be drawn from these case studies that may be applicable elsewhere.

Contributing Factors to Regime Formation

Contributing factors to maritime regime formation include:

- pre-existing habits of cooperation and institutional development, whether in the same sector or more generally, including the presence of relevant functioning institutions;
- national and regional leadership;
- clearly defined benefits to be gained through regional cooperation, which may be based on the presence of significant management challenges with clear regional dimensions;
- the need for capacity-building, whether at the national level or through regional sharing of management capabilities;
- the presence of external threats, e.g., distant water fishing nations (DWFNs), which may consolidate the regional position, and which may require a united front for an effective response;
- intra-regional maritime disputes which threaten security generally, and which motivate formation of a regime for conflict avoidance and/or dispute resolution;
- the existence of significant transnational networks of scientific or other communities which can provide both information on management issues and the stimulus for action;
- public awareness and concern with a given issue or range of issues;
- similar levels of economic development and capacity to fund the regime;
- a regional perception of participation of extra regional states as beneficial, or at least not opposed by major regional leaders; and
- informal arrangements and institutional approaches which avoid the pit-falls of formal ratification.

Caveats and Choices

The choice of management unit is critical, but usually unclear. From an ecological perspective, the effort should include all states which border or impact a Large Marine Ecosystem (LME) or the Geopolitical Marine Ecosystem which also includes States in the hinterland which drains into the semi-enclosed sea. But political reality and efficiency often dictate a more limited scope and membership. Indeed the world community concept of integrated ocean management has become so complex and sophisticated[43] – much more so than in the UNCLOS III era – that the national level of management is inadequate, at least for developing countries. But the regional or macro-regional level introduces too many additional complications and unsustainable costs. So, by default, the best unit for cooperative ocean management, and for ocean regime-building is often the sub-region.

Regarding the scope of activities and functions, a broad interdisciplinary mandate can be perceived as duplicating and competing with the mandates of specific regional or UN bodies and thus engender their opposition. To avoid this situation, a marine affairs organization should lead where there is no competitor, be supportive and cooperative where there are pre-existing relevant activities or programs, and be catalytic in focusing attention and engendering support for others' ongoing efforts. Flexibility is key and a formal prioritized set of activities should be avoided. Similarly, the effort should be initially limited and focused and not move too rapidly towards a structure which important potential participants may resist, but instead maintain a rather informal approach.

Another important choice to be made is the decision regarding participation of maritime powers situated outside the region. On the one hand, these powers undertake maritime activities in the region, e.g., fishing, shipping, oil and gas exploration, and most important, can contribute funds necessary for the regional regime to form and progress. On the other hand, these powers may undermine the jealously guarded leadership role or status of regional powers, and may unduly influence the regime in their favor.

Constraints

The following are serious constraints to regime formation and positive evolution.

- *Use of an inappropriate model.* The original model of regional marine environmental co-operation designed for the Mediterranean was too ambitious to be amenable to effective implementation in other, less well endowed regions.[44] The regional action plans and conventions often did not lead to the adoption of the desired amendments in national legislation, nor did their activities and programs consider a number of root causes of the environmental problems along their marine and coastal areas such as upstream pollution sources, degradation by land-based pollutants and irrational management of resources.
- *Excessive diversity.* The regional scale of the UNEP initiative involved excessive dependency on the diplomacy of groupings of too many countries with differing interests, priorities and capabilities.[45]
- *Low capacity.* The UNEP initiative was too statist in concept, overstretching the capacity of bureaucracies and discouraging "civil society" institutions from seeking a central role as catalyst and manager.[46] Moreover, most developing countries lack professional and technical expertise in ocean management on the scale required to sustain sophisticated regimes.[47]

- *Low priority*. In most developing regions, ocean management, particularly ocean environmental management, still has too low a national priority to justify the large-scale expenditure of scarce financial resources.[48] And aid organizations are increasingly insisting on conversion of their projects to sustainability through indigenous support.
- *No long-term commitment*. Permanent commitment to regime maintenance is unlikely in most developing regions as long as external funding sources are willing and able to support projects only over a medium-length period of 5–10 years.[49]
- *Insufficient public awareness* of the problem and solutions.
- *Redundancy* of both issues and of national and international agencies addressing the issues.
- *Selfish national interest,* in which all countries and their diplomats, often driven by domestic politics, want to gain more benefit than they give.
- *High politics* and a *lack of regional consciousness*. Active opposition from a major regional power, can severely retard regime formation. In the Indian Ocean, India opposed Sri Lanka's leadership and formed a potentially competing but more exclusive organization that included the other two major powers in the Indian Ocean, Australia and South Africa.

Applicability Of Lessons Learned To Northeast Asia

The general premise in the recent literature is that lessons learned in one region are transferable to another.[50] In contrast, these case studies conclude that each region is *sui generis* and that specifics – if not principles – of regimes must be designed *de novo* for each region. Nevertheless, these studies do provide some useful general concepts and *caveats* for regime design in Northeast Asia.

Maritime regime formation in Northeast Asia – at least a formal regime – is retarded by several factors:

- China's opposition to potentially constraining multilateral efforts, its opposition to such initiatives unless it leads, and its relative disinterest in Northeast Asian marine affairs;
- Japan's lack of political will and unwillingness to follow the lead of others such as South Korea;[51]
- the resurgence of traditional sovereignty concerns which undermine efforts at regional identity formation;
- deeply-rooted differences in priorities regarding environmental protection; and
- the lack of a Track Two or Track One forum to discuss such issues.

The difficulties experienced in promoting the formation of ocean regimes in Northeast Asia may be due to the special, if not entirely unique, political characteristics of the region. The region lacks any modern history or tradition of political cooperation. The Northeast Asian states have always been uneasy neighbors at best, and often bitter enemies. Even given the recent warming of relations, the cultivation of trust between governments continues to tax the diplomatic skills of these countries' most enlightened officials and politicians.

Accordingly, the political milieu of Northeast Asia does not seem congenial to a formal initiative for inter-governmental regime-building. Indeed a bold proposal in this regard by one of these countries would almost certainly provoke suspicions on the part of at least two of the others.

There is also a marked degree of distinctiveness in the marine geography of Northeast Asia. Whereas most other marine regions consist of countries that look out at a single sea or ocean that is perceived as a shared, and potentially unifying, environment – as an extension of their land-based economies – the countries of Northeast Asia face either the North Pacific, which is too vast to be perceived as their "shared dominion," or a number of discrete Seas (Yellow Sea, East China, Japan [East]) where sovereignty concerns tend to undermine the concept of shared authority and responsibility. Thus the geography of Northeast Asia seems unfriendly to the ideal of regional cooperation in the semienclosed seas – at least as a linked whole.

The Northeast Asia region is ineligible for UN designation as a developing marine region because of the relative affluence of Japan and South Korea. Only China and North Korea clearly meet the traditional UN criteria for such treatment. Perhaps only the Yellow Sea would qualify as a developing marine area, albeit with South Korea as one of the three littoral states. This anomaly prevented the inclusion of the seas of Northeast Asia in UNEP's "East Asian Seas" Programme, and made it necessary for China to be treated as part of Southeast Asia for this purpose.

Thus it is not surprising that in Northeast Asia there is still considerable resistance to the initiation of a multilateral management regime. Perhaps the most important inducement for a multilateral regime in Northeast Asia would be the evening up of the levels of marine technology and expertise throughout the region. In short, the major trade-off would be the benefit to Japan and South Korea of adherence by China, North Korea, and Russia to a predictable regime with common minimum standards of pollutant discharge, in exchange for training and technical assistance from Japan and South Korea. However, until elites in Japan and South Korea realize that it is in their long-term interest to enhance their partners' capacity, regime formation will be difficult.

The current preference in Northeast Asia is for loose co-operation from which participants can defect without penalty. And this loose environmental cooperation is likely to continue well into the future. It will focus on establishing stronger networks among governments and non-governmental actors in the region and promoting common understanding of what the goals and priorities of action should be. In many ways the kind of cooperation that must emerge in Northeast Asia is similar to that between the European Union and the former East bloc states. There one of the greatest stimulants for improving environmental regimes was the promise of greater economic and social cooperation and integration.

The Way Forward

Given all the constraints, the way forward for maritime regime building in Northeast Asia would include the following elements:

- an influential sponsoring organization;
- a "loose" second track initiative which would build the network from which could emerge national leaders or co-ordinators with some influence within national bureaucracies and which could help convert the effort into a dual-track process of regime-building;
- an initial focus on a subregional sea which is not shared by a major uncooperative power, unless of course that power chooses to lead or support the multilateral effort;
- an initial focus on environmental protection and perhaps related marine scientific research rather than resource management;
- identification of an acceptable leading country and sufficient funding for at least the initial stages of the effort;
- differentiated obligations tailored to the capacity of the different participants; because of the relative affluence of Japan, Taiwan and South Korea, it would be difficult to persuade a Western international development agency to undertake a major funding role in a dual track regime-building effort in Northeast Asia without matching or comparable contributions from these governments;
- a definition of the region which is acceptable to all participants, possibly excluding areas of overlapping claims;
- addressing of the interests of outside powers;
- although the littoral countries would be the core players, other regional countries with interests in the Sea could be invited to participate by the core countries;
- praise for existing arrangements while underscoring the rationale for co-operation;
- encouragement of bilateral discussions and arrangements as complementary to the subregional effort and the goal of a multilateral regime; and
- avoidance of any impression that this is an effort to resolve or mitigate boundary of territorial issues; the effort should emphasize that
  1. boundaries are a matter only for the parties concerned;
  2. this co-operative effort is necessary whether or not boundaries are resolved; and
  3. the goal is to create a positive atmosphere – a sense of community – and a tradition of co-operation.

Co-operative Ocean Management as Confidence Building

It would be enormously helpful if all Northeast Asian countries could appreciate the potential political benefit of co-operative ocean management, such as confidence and security building. Indeed, co-operation in ocean management could have positive spillover effects on naval security co-operation in Northeast Asia. Given the rapid rapprochement on the Korean Peninsula, and the warming of ties among China, Japan, South Korea and Russia, it is not too early to start thinking about multilateral security cooperation in Northeast Asia. And the best place to start may be with maritime affairs.

Indeed, there is a growing need for maritime trust-building initiatives due to the new uncertainties and conflict points created by the 1996 wave of maritime jurisdictional extensions to 200 nautical miles in the region. These jurisdictional extensions and resulting disputes over maritime space and resources were thrust upon an already transitional and unstable political environment. However, these disputes can be mitigated by co-operative ocean management.

Indeed, co-operative bilateral maritime arrangements have been proliferating over the past two years and may provide the basis for possible trust-building *multilateral* agreements. These arrangements include bilateral fisheries agreements between Japan and South Korea, Japan and China, and China and South Korea. But more to the point is the rapid increase in bi- and multilateral naval exercises and exchanges. In 1998, Russia staged a search-and-rescue drill with Japan. In 1999, Japanese and South Korean naval vessels staged a trail-blazing search-and-rescue operation in the northern East China Sea. Russia and China also announced joint naval maneuvers. South Korea has proposed joint maritime search and rescue with China as well as an exchange of visits by naval ships, and it has also asked Russia to join a naval exercise. Meanwhile the United States has proposed that its joint-search and rescue training exercise with Malaysia be expanded to include China and Japan. And Japan and China have resumed their security dialogue, while Russia and North Korea have signed a new treaty of friendship and cooperation.

To build confidence among navies, multilateral initiatives must be realistic and pragmatic, using gradual, methodical approaches with clearly defined objectives. The best way is to begin small, avoid excessive formality, and use the bilateral initiatives as a foundation. The initial focus should be on low-level matters such as bilateral Incidents at Sea (INCSEA) agreements, which already exist between the United States and Russia, the United States and China, Japan and Russia, Japan and South Korea, and South Korea and Russia.

Given this network of INCSEA agreements already in place, and China's tentative agreement with ASEAN on a code of conduct for the South China Sea, a multilateral agreement on a "code of conduct" for Northeast Asian seas would be a natural step forward. Initially, any multilateral arrangement should not be strictly military but address common civil maritime problems like search and rescue, environmental protection, drug trafficking, and smuggling. In particular, multilateral cooperation in ocean management could have positive spillover effects on trust-building among navies.

However, there are still formidable obstacles to any multilateral security arrangement. North Korea has shown little desire to participate in multilateral discussions on security issues that would be necessary for a subregional INCSEA agreement. It has, however, joined the Association of Southeast Asian Nations (ASEAN) Regional Forum as an observer, as well as Track Two discussions in the Conference on Security Co-operation in the Asia-Pacific. And peace is rapidly marching forward on the Korean Peninsula. China and Taiwan, on the other hand, still pose a serious problem. Any attempt to include both in an official agreement would be folly, unless the arrangement was instead considered an informal "understanding." This is another reason why beginning with co-operative ocean management can help build the trust necessary to take further steps.

Given Russia's domestic turmoil, it is not likely to be a steady partner in any cooperative regime for some years to come, but nevertheless to build a foundation for regional peace, it must be included. Including South Korea would be a political signal that the agreement was not exclusive or aimed at facilitating "a new concert of powers." The United States should probably be included because of its long regional naval involvement, its alliances with Japan and South Korea, and its forward deployed troops. Indeed, a U.S. role may be critical because without its intelligence support, Japan and South Korea would probably be reluctant to join any multilateral security process or arrangement. In this context, U.S. Pacific Commander Dennis Blair's recent proposal for multilateral naval exercises in Asia could give the concept a big boost.

Further out to sea – in space and time – an international naval or "self-defense" force might be created to ensure ocean peacekeeping, including safety of navigation. This joint force could focus on the area beyond national jurisdiction and emphasize protection of high seas fisheries, air-sea rescue, and open-ocean environmental monitoring. However, when all is said and done, navy-to-navy arrangements will depend on the quality of political relations. And this can surely be enhanced by comprehensive bilateral and multilateral ocean management.

Notes

1. On this perceptual advantage, see Douglas M. Johnston and Lawrence M. Enomoto, "Regional Approaches to the Protection and Preservation of the Marine Environment" *in* Douglas M. Johnston (ed.), *The Environmental Law of the Sea* (Berlin: IUCN, 1981): 285.
2. See Lewis M. Alexander, "Regionalism At Sea: Concept and Reality" *in* Johnston, ed., *supra* note 1, 10–12, for a summary of regional institutional arrangements existing prior to the *LOS 1982*. See also Loe Kimball, "Part I: The UN Convention on the Law of the Sea: A Framework for Marine Conservation" *in* IUCN, *The Law of the Sea: Priorities and Responsibilities In Implementing the Convention* (Gland: IUCN, 1995) for a summary of global and regional arrangements post-*LOS 1982*.
3. UN Doc. A/Conf.62/122, Dec. 6, 1982, in force Nov. 16, 1994.
4. Lewis M. Alexander "The Co-operative Approach to Ocean Affairs: Twenty Years Later," *Ocean Development and International Law Journal* 21: 105–109.
5. For background, analysis and proposals for co-operation in the Baltic Sea, see Mathew Auer, "Prospects for Environmental Cooperation in the Yellow Sea," *Emory International Law Review* 5 (1991): 163–208; Ton Ijlstra, "Development of Resource Jurisdiction in the EC's Regional Seas: National EEZ Policies of EC Member States in the Northeast Atlantic, the Mediterranean Sea, and the Baltic Sea," *Ocean Development and International Law* 23, 2–3 (1992); Baruch Boxer, "Mediterranean Action Plan: An Interim Evaluation," *Science* 202 (10 November 1978): 585–90; Gunnar Kullenberg, "Long-term Changes in the Baltic Ecosystem," *in* Kenneth Sherman and Lewis M. Alexander (eds.), *Variability and Management of Large Marine Ecosystems*, AAAS Selected Symposium 99 (Boulder: Westview Press, Inc., 1986), B.I. Bybern and S.H. Fonselius, "Pollution in the Baltic Sea" *in* Aoano Voipio (ed.), Elsevier Oceanography Series 30 (Amsterdam: Elsevier Scientific Publishing Company, 1986): 351–82; ICES, *Assessment of the Marine Environment of the Baltic Cooperative Research Report XX* (Copenhagen, 1986); F.B. Pedersen, "The Sensitivity of the Baltic Sea to Natural and Man-made Impact" *in* J.C.J. Nihoul (ed.), *Hydrodynamics of Semienclosed Seas*, Elsevier Oceanography Series 24 (Amsterdam: Elsevier Scientific Publishing Company, 1982): 385–99; Aoano Viopio, *The Baltic Sea*, Elsevier Oceanographic Series (Amsterdam: Elsevier Scientific Publishing Company, 1981).
6. For background analysis and proposals for co-operation in the North Sea, see Sven Andersen and

Brit Flostad, "Sea Use Planning in Norwegian Waters: National and International Dimensions," *Coastal Management* 16 (1988): 183–200; H. Carison, "Quality Status of the North Sea. International Conference on the Protection of the North Sea" *in* John King Gamble (ed.), *Law of the Sea: Neglected Issues*, Proceedings of the Law of the Sea Institute Twelfth Annual Conference, held at The Hague, The Netherlands 23–6 October 1978; Gerard Peet, "Techniques and Methods for Sea Use Planning and Management in Selected Areas," Report of a literature study commissioned by Directie Noordzee, Rijkswaterstaat, 1986, Second Chamber of the State General, The Netherlands, Harmonization of Netherlands North Sea Policy 1989–1992, 44–5, SDU uigevergij; A.J. Smith, Elizabeth Kennet and M.B.F. Ranken, *Britain and the Sea; Further Dependence – Further Opportunities* (Edinburgh: Scottish Academic Press Limited, 1984); H.D. Smith and C.S. Lalawani, *The North Sea: Sea Use Management and Planning* (Cardiff: University of Wales Institute of Science and Technology, 1984); Elizabeth Young and Peter H. Fricke (eds.), *Sea Use Planning* (London: Fabian Society, 1975); Steinar Andresen, "The Environmental North Sea Regime: a Successful Regional Approach" *in* Elisabeth Mann Borgese, Norton S. Ginsburg, and Joseph R. Morgan (eds.); *Ocean Yearbook* 7 (Chicago: the University of Chicago Press, 1989): 378–401; Steinar Andresen. "The 'Effectiveness' of Regional Environmental Co-operation in the Northern Seas." Paper presented at the Annual Meeting of the International Studies Association, Chicago 23–25 February 1995.

7. For background, analysis and proposals for co-operation in the Mediterranean Sea, see Aldo Chircop, "The Mediterranean Sea and the Quest for Sustainable Development," *Ocean Development and International Law Journal* 23 (1992): 17–30; Norton Ginsburg, Sidney Holt and William Murdoch, The Mediterranean Action Plan and the Maritime Development of a Region, *Pacem in Maribus* 111, Proceedings of a Conference, Split, Yugoslavia, April 28–30, 1972 (The Royal University of Malta Press, 1974); Adalberto Vallega, *A Human Geographical Approach to Semienclosed Seas: The Mediterranean Case in Regional Development* (Chicago: The University of Chicago Press, 1988); S.J. Holt, "Mediterranean: International Cooperation for a Sick Sea," *Environment* 16 (1974): 29–3; United Nations Environment Programme, "Activities for the Protection and Development of the Mediterranean" *in Ocean Yearbook* 1 (Chicago: The University of Chicago Press, 1978): 584–97; United Nations Environment Programme, "Recommendation for the Future Development of the Mediterranean Action Plan" *in Ocean Yearbook* 2 (Chicago: The University of Chicago Press, 1980): 547–54; "Protocol for the Protection of the Mediterranean Sea Against Pollution from Land-based Sources" *in Ocean Yearbook* 3 (Chicago: The University of Chicago Press, 1982): 489–96; "MARPOL 73/78: The International Convention Concerning Pollution and the Mediterranean" *in Ocean Yearbook* 6) Chicago: The University of Chicago Press, 1986: 572–73; United Nations Environment Programme, "The Mediterranean Action Plan: Retrospect and Prospect," presented at the fourth Ordinary Meeting of the Contracting Parties to the Convention for the Protection of the Mediterranean Sea Against Pollution and its Related Protocols, Genoa 9–13 September 1985; published as Document UNEP/IG.56/4, 26 June 1985.
8. See E. Miles, "On the Utility of Regional Arrangements in the New Ocean Regime *in* D.M. Johnston, (ed.), *Regionalization of the Law of the Sea* (Cambridge, Mass., Ballinger, 1978): 260–264; also see Mark J. Valencia. "Regional Maritime Regime Building: Prospects in Northeast and Southeast Asia," *Ocean Development and International Law Journal* 31 (2000): 223; Mark J. Valencia, Jon Van Dyke and Noel Ludwig, *Sharing the Resources of the South China Sea* (The Hague: Martinus Nijhoff, 1997): 151–153.
9. This section is summarized from Philip Saunders, "Regional Cooperation and Ocean Management Regimes," Paper presented at the *Planning Meeting for a Possible Project on Maritime Regime Building: Lessons Learned and Their Relevance for Northeast Asia*, 28–30 August 2000, Honolulu, Hawaii.
10. The concept has been extensively applied to international resource management, where the complexity of the instruments, institutions and actors made it particularly appropriate. See, e.g., Oran Young, *International Cooperation: Building Regimes for Natural Resources and the Environment* (Ithaca: Cornell Univ. Press, 1989). For similar reasons, the notion of regimes has been widely applied to the oceans; see, e.g., Peter Haas, "Prospects for Effective Marine Governance in the NW Pacific Region", *Marine Policy* 24 (2000): 341; see also Valencia et al., *supra* n. 8: 199–222.

11. S.D. Krasner, "Structural Causes and Regime Consequences" *in* S.D. Krasner, (ed.), *International Regimes* (Ithaca: Cornell Univ. Press, 1983): 2.
12. On the nature and importance of soft law instruments in environmental law, see P.M. Dupuy, "Soft Law and the International Law of the Environment", *Michigan Journal of International Law* 12 (1991): 420.
13. Peter Haas, "Do Regimes Matter? Epistemic Communities and Mediterranean Pollution Control", *International Organization* 43, 3 (1989): 384. As Haas notes, the term was introduced to international relations from the field of the sociology of knowledge. This study of the Mediterranean considered the impact of like-minded scientists in developing the agenda and creating domestic support for international action on the environmental problems facing the region.
14. G. Downs, K, Danish and P. Barsoom, "The Transformational Model of International Regime Design: Triumph of Hope or Experience?, *Columbia Jourrnal of Transnational Law* 38, 3 (2000): 467.
15. *Ibid*: 467. It should be noted that a survey of environmental treaties carried out by Downs *et al.* cast doubt upon the supposed benefits of this approach, in part because of the equal or better success attributed to other strategies for alteration of state behavior, and because the empirical record was not promising. At the very least, they found that while the strategy could be "optimal in some contexts, there are others in which it will not yield all of the benefits that its advocates hope and still others where its application almost certainly will be counterproductive. The problem is that we do not know which context is which." *Ibid*: 508. On the issue of promoting convergence through the operation of regimes, see also Haas, *supra* n. 13: 377.
16. John C. Perneta, "An Overview of the Role of the Global Environment Facility in International Waters with Reference to Marine Capacity Building," *Marine Policy* 22, 3 (1998): 235–246.
17. As, for example, with the following instruments: *Rio Declaration on Environment and Development*, June 13, 1992, UN Doc. A/Conf.151/26/Rev.1 [hereinafter *Rio Declaration]; Agenda 21: Programme of Action for Sustainable Development*, UN Doc. A/Conf.151/5/Rev.1, June 14, 1992 [hereinafter *Agenda 21*].
18. As is arguably the case with large portions of the *UNCLOS 1982*, as well as the more recent UNCED-related treaties: *United Nations Convention on Biological Diversity*, June 5, 1992, in force Dec. 29, 1993 *United Nations Framework Convention on Climate Change*, the World's Forests After Rio "92" *in* L. Campiglio et al (eds.), *The Environment After Rio: International Law and Economics* (1994): 68.
19. The failure of the global level to achieve both consensus and binding obligations on contentious issues has nonetheless led to a certain amount of disillusionment among environmentalists who expected more. This attitude was concisely expressed in the context of forests by an observer who referred to the non-binding *Forest Principles* as the "regressive development of international law". A. Szekely, "The Legal Protection of the World's Forests After Rio "92" in L. Campiglio et al, *supra* n. 18.
20. And possibly, though not necessarily, more closely shared political and legal cultures.
21. The open-ended nature of the definitional criteria has been noted by Lewis M. Alexander, *Marine Regionalism In The Southeast Asian Seas* (East-West Environment and Policy Institute, East-West Center, 1982): 3.

    The distinguishing criteria for the region may be physical in nature, or may represent demographic, economic, political or other elements. In fact no limits exist to the categories that may be used in defining a region, so long as the criteria selected are valid ones and the area in which the criteria occur can be differentiated geographically from other areas
22. There are numerous examples of states which can be considered members of multiple overlapping "regions", including: EU members which are also Mediterranean states; Caribbean states which participate in complementary fisheries programs (with different memberships) through the Organization of Eastern Caribbean States (OECS) and CARICOM; South Pacific island states which have maintained functionally-distinct fisheries programs through SPC and FFA, again with different memberships. Once institutions are created or engaged for the purpose of cooperation, however, a certain amount of rigidity is probably inevitable if only out of convenience.
23. This problem is widespread, but nowhere more acute than in small island states such as those of the Caribbean, southwest Indian Ocean and the South Pacific, which often combine extensive zones with small populations and inadequate management resources.

24. The most notable success being the experience of the Forum Fisheries Agency (FFA) of the South Pacific in dealing with DWFN tuna fleets through cooperative programs and ultimately through the mulitlateral treaty arrangement with the United States. For a summary of FFA activities in dealing with DWFNs in the 1980s and up to the early 1990s, see R. Herr (ed.), *The Forum Fisheries Agency:Achievements Challenges and Prospects* (Suva: ISP, 1990). See also Judith Swan, "Highly Migratory Species: The South Pacific Forum Fisheries Agency" *in* Albert Soons (ed.), *Implementation of the Law of the Sea Convention Through International Institutions* (Honolulu: LSI, 1990): 318.
25. For a review of the role played by regional actors in the drift-net fishing dispute in the South Pacific, which had both regional and global aspects to the negotiations, see A. Wright and D. Doulman, "Drift-Net Fishing In The South Pacific: From Controversy to Management", *Marine Policy* 15 (1991): 303.
26. With reference to the mischaracterization of general bilateral issues as regional in nature see, e.g., Mark J. Valencia, "Southeast Asian Seas: National Marine Interests, Transnational Issues, and Marine Regionalism" *in* Chia Lin Sien and Colin MacAndrews (eds.), *Southeast Asian Seas: Frontiers for Development* (Singapore: McGraw Hill, 1981): 354.
27. An important challenge for the FFA in the South Pacific was to develop funding sources for surveillance and enforcement programs which did not rely on donors from countries with direct interests in the region.
28. The early programs of CCOP/SOPAC (later SOPAC –the South Pacific Applied Geoscience Commission) were heavily concentrated on deep sea research of questionable relevance to many regional states. This was arguably related more to the scientific interests of the major donors of the time than to regional priorities. Later, with the growing independence of the organization, the focus shifted markedly to nearshore and coastal issues.
29. See Valencia *et al*, *supra* n. 8: 151–152.
30. An example of such flexibility is found in the Mediterranean, where the Barcelona Convention of 1995 was amended to allow for extension beyond the waters of the Mediterranean, and protocols can define geographical scope independently. See Douglas M. Johnston and David VanderZwaag, "Toward the Management of the Gulf of Thailand: Charting the Course of Co-operation" *in* D.M. Johnston (ed.), SEAPOL Integrated Studies of the Gulf of Thailand I (Bangkok, SEAPOL, 1998): 101; see also Adalberto Vallega, "Geographical Coverage and Effectiveness of the UNEP Convention on the Mediterranean", *Ocean and Coastal Management* 31 (1996): 199.
31. Johnston and VanderZwaag, *supra* n. 30: 118–122. Other options included non-binding statements of principles, action plans and codes of conduct, and the development of specific dispute settlement procedures. For other examples of flexible approaches to the development of cooperatives measures, see Valencia *et al*, *supra* n. 8: 111–122, on a range of options for the South China Sea, including, *inter alia*, informal workshops, an eminent persons group, "preventive" diplomacy, various confidence building measures and joint research activities.
32. The review should extend to independent regional organizations as well as regional programs of global agencies, which may have been carrying out some of the target functions in the past. See, e.g., the review of this issue in: Western Indian Ocean Tuna Organization (WIOTO), *Background Paper: Development of A Recommendation To Bring WIOTO Into Operation On An Interim Basis* (December 1993). This can become a highly politicized and sensitive process, given the natural tendency for institutions to resist incursions on what is perceived to be "their turf."
33. For an example of such an exercise, see Herr, *supra* n. 24. This collection of papers was the product of a ten year review and re-consideration of the agency's mandate and priority functions.
34. The willingness to take seriously the practical contributions of non-binding instruments is closely linked to the reconceptulaization of "compliance" away from traditional notions of treaty observance and towards a better understanding of how states participate in and, generally, abide by the norms and rules of more complex international regimes. On the issue of compliance, see, e.g., B. Kingsbury, "The Concept of Compliance as a Function of Competing Conceptions of International Law," in T. Schoenbaum, J. Nakagawa and L. Reif (eds.), *Trilateral Perspectives On International Legal Issues* 9 (New York: Transnational, 1998); see also N. Okuwaki, "The Changing Nature of International

Obligations: Can Voluntary Compliance Overcome the Difficulties in the Present Nation-State System", *ibid*: 61.

35. Hanns Buchholz, "The Baltic Sea: Lessons Learned and Their Relevance for Northeast Asia." Paper presented at the *Planning Meeting for a Possible Project on Maritime Regime Building: Lessons Learned and Their Relevance for Northeast Asia*, 28–30 August, 2000, Honolulu, Hawaii.
36. Aldo Chircop, "The Emergence and Evolution of Mediterranean Regional Environmental Cooperation: Lessons for Regime-Building." Paper presented at the *Planning Meeting for a Possible Project on Maritime Regime Building: Lessons Learned and Their Relevance for Northeast Asia*, 28–30 August, 2000, Honolulu, Hawaii.
37. Steinar Andresen, "Lessons from Marine Regional Cooperation: The North Sea and Beyond." Paper presented at the *Planning Meeting for a Possible Project on Maritime Regime Building: Lessons Learned and Their Relevance for Northeast Asia*, 28–30 August, 2000, Honolulu, Hawaii.
38. Hasjim Djalal, "Lessons Learned and Their Relevance for Northeast Asia: The Experience of Managing Potential Conflicts in the South China Sea." Paper presented at the *Planning Meeting for a Possible Project on Maritime Regime Building: Lessons Learned and Their Relevance for Northeast Asia*, 28–30 August, 2000, Honolulu, Hawaii.
39. Douglas Johnston. "Southeast Asia: Lessons Learned." Paper presented at the *Planning Meeting for a Possible Project on Maritime Regime Building: Lessons Learned and Their Relevance for Northeast Asia*, 28–30 August, 2000, Honolulu, Hawaii.
40. Jon Van Dyke, "Maritime Regime Building in the Pacific." Paper presented at the *Planning Meeting for a Possible Project on Maritime Regime Building: Lessons Learned and Their Relevance for Northeast Asia*, 28–30 August, 2000, Honolulu, Hawaii.
41. Hiran Jayewardene, "Indian Ocean Co-operation in the Field of Marine Affairs: Lessons Learned." Paper presented at the *Planning Meeting for a Possible Project on Maritime Regime Building: Lessons Learned and Their Relevance for Northeast Asia*, 28–30 August, 2000, Honolulu, Hawaii.
42. The Pacific Islands have not, however made any governmental moves to create a regional human rights organization. See Jon M. Van Dyke, *Prospects for the Development of Intergovernmental Human Rights Bodies in Asia and the Pacific in* Ellen L. Lutz, Hurst Hannum, and Kathryn J. Burke (eds.), *New Directions in Human Rights* (1989).
43. The UNEP Regional Seas Programme, like UNCLOS III, was the product of the 1970's, when concern over pollution threats occupied center stage in the international arena. To-day, in an age of greater sophistication, it is clear that the oceans are threatened by a much more complicated array of problems and deficiencies that call for an integrated approach to longer-term objectives of ocean management.
44. Any rigorous regime entails substantial costs. It was always the hope of UNEP officials that the countries of each designated regional sea would eventually be able and willing to absorb a growing proportion of these costs, but given the nature of these instruments much of the funding required would have to go into training programs in science and technology, not just for a relatively low-cost inspectorate as in the case of strictly regulatory regimes.
45. The solution to this problem might be to explore the possibility of sub-regional cooperative arrangements with smaller groupings of 3 to 5 neighboring littoral states, as in the Gulf of Thailand.
46. If the UNEP Regional Seas Programme were being designed now, it would probably draw upon the resources and talents of "civil society" institutions on a scale that was unimagined in the mid-1970's.
47. So far as known, no developing region has taken over full financial responsibility for the maintenance of a regional network in the field of ocean law, policy and management.
48. Environment in general still has a low priority in most developing countries, as measured by *per capita* expenditures, despite three decades of continuous global diplomacy to raise environmental standards led by the more affluent states. On environmental initiatives within Southeast Asia, see Douglas M. Johnston, "Environmental Law as "Sacred Trust': Western Values and Southeast Asian Prospects," *in* Douglas M. Johnston, and Gerry Ferguson, *Asia-Pacific Legal Development* (1998): 405–65.
49. This difficulty is becoming less acute, as more and more students graduate from ocean-related programs. But most of these specialists are dependent on foreign universities in developed, mostly Western, countries.
50. Peter M. Haas, "Prospects for Effective Maritime Governance in the NW Pacific Region." *Marine*

Policy, 24, 4 (2000): 341–8; Mark J. Valencia. Comment on "Prospects for Effective Marine Governance in the Northwest Pacific Region" *Marine Policy*, 24, 5 (2000): 439–440.

51. The Kim Dae-jung administration has made environmental protection one of the pillars of Korean diplomacy. Yonemoto Shohei. "Japan's Diplomatic Strategy for Dealing with Acid Rain", *Japan Echo* (August 2000).

INDEX

Publications on Ocean Development

1. R.P. Anand: *Legal Regime of the Sea-Bed and the Developing Countries.* 1976
ISBN 90-286-0616-5
2. N. Papadakis: *The International Legal Regime of Artificial Islands.* 1977
ISBN 90-286-0127-9
3. S. Oda: *The Law of the Sea in Our Time.* Volume I: *New Developments, 1966–1975.* 1977
ISBN 90-286-0277-1
4. S. Oda: *The Law of the Sea in Our Time.* Volume II: *The UN Seabed Committee, 1968–1973.* 1977
ISBN 90-286-0287-9
5. C.O. Okidi: *Regional Control of Ocean Pollution.* Legal and Institutional Problems and Prospects. 1978
ISBN 90-286-0367-0
6. N.S. Rembe: *Africa and the International Law of the Sea.* A Study of the Contribution of the African States to the 3rd UN Conference on the Law of the Sea. 1980
ISBN 90-286-0639-4
7. R.P. Anand: *Origin and Development of the Law of the Sea.* History of International Law Revisited. 1983
ISBN 90-247-2617-4
8. A.M. Post: *Deepsea Mining and the Law of the Sea.* 1983
ISBN 90-247-3049-X
9. S.P. Jagota: *Maritime Boundary.* 1985
ISBN 90-247-3133-X
10. A.O. Adede: *The System for Settlement of Disputes under the UN Convention on the Law of the Sea.* A Drafting History and a Commentary. 1987
ISBN 90-247-3324-3
11. M. Dahmani: *The Fisheries Regime of the Exclusive Economic Zone.* 1987
ISBN 90-247-3374-X
12. S. Oda: *International Control of Sea Resources.* Reprint with a New Introduction. 1989
ISBN 90-247-3800-8
13. D.G. Dallmeyer and L. DeVorsey, Jr. (eds.): *Rights to Oceanic Resources.* Deciding and Drawing Maritime Boundaries. 1989
ISBN 0-7923-0019-X
14. B. Kwiatkowska: *The 200 Mile Exclusive Economic Zone in the New Law of the Sea.* 1989
ISBN 0-7923-0074-2
15. H.W. Jayewardene: *The Regime of Islands in International Law.* 1990
ISBN 0-7923-0130-7
16. D.M. Johnston and M.J. Valencia: *Pacific Ocean Boundary Problems.* Status and Solutions. 1990
ISBN 0-7923-0862-X

17. J.A. de Yturriaga: *Straits Used for International Navigation*. A Spanish Perspective. 1991 ISBN 0-7923-1141-8
18. C.C. Joyner: *Antarctica and the Law of the Sea*. 1992 ISBN 0-7923-1823-4
19. D. Pharand and U. Leanza (eds.): *The Continental Shelf and the Exclusive Economic Zone: Delimitation and Legal Regime / Le Plateau continental et la Zone économique exclusive: Délimitation et régime juridique*. 1993 ISBN 0-7923-2056-5
20. F. Laursen: *Small Powers at Sea*. Scandinavia and the New International Marine Order. 1993 ISBN 0-7923-2341-6
21. J. Crawford and D.R. Rothwell (eds.): *The Law of the Sea in the Asian Pacific Region*. 1995 ISBN 0-7923-2742-X
22. M. Munavvar: *Ocean States*. Archipelagic Regimes in the Law of the Sea. 1995 ISBN 0-7923-2882-5
23. A. Strati: *The Protection of the Underwater Cultural Heritage: An Emerging Objective of the Contemporary Law of the Sea*. 1995 ISBN 0-7923-3052-8
24. A.G. Oude Elferink: *The Law of Maritime Boundary Delimitation*. A Case Study of the Russian Federation. 1994 ISBN 0-7923-3082-X
25. Y. Li: *Transfer of Technology for Deep Sea-Bed Mining*. The 1982 Law of the Sea Convention and Beyond. 1994 ISBN 0-7923-3212-1
26. T.O. Akintoba: *African States and Contemporary International Law*. A Case Study of the 1982 Law of the Sea Convention and the Exclusive Economic Zone. 1996 ISBN 90-411-0144-6
27. J.A. Roach and R.W. Smith: *United States Responses to Excessive Maritime Claims*. Second Edition. 1996 ISBN 90-411-0225-6
28. T. Treves (ed.): *The Law of the Sea*. The European Union and its Member States. 1997 ISBN 90-411-0326-0
29. A. Razavi: *Continental Shelf Delimitation and Related Maritime Issues in the Persian Gulf*. 1997 ISBN 90-411-0333-3
30. J.A. de Yturriaga: *The International Regime of Fisheries*. From UNCLOS 1982 to the Presential Sea. 1997 ISBN 90-411-0365-1
31. M.J. Valencia, J.M. Van Dyke and N.A. Ludwig: *Sharing the Resources of the South China Sea*. 1997 ISBN 90-411-0411-9
32. E.C. Farrell: *The Socialist Republic of Vietnam and the Law of the Sea*. An Analysis of Vietnamese Behavior within the Emerging International Oceans Regime. 1997 ISBN 90-411-0473-9
33. P.B. Payoyo: *Cries of the Sea*. World Inequality, Sustainable Development and the Common Heritage of Humanity. 1997 ISBN 90-411-0504-2
34. H.N. Scheiber (ed.): *Law of the Sea*. The Common Heritage and Emerging Challenges. 2000 ISBN 90-411-1401-7

Publications on Ocean Development

35. D.R. Rothwell and S. Bateman (eds.): *Navigational Rights and Freedoms and the New Law of the Sea*. 2000 ISBN 90-411-1499-8

36. M.J. Valencia (ed.): *Maritime Regime Building*. Lessons Learned and their Relevance for Northeast Asia. 2001 ISBN 90-411-1580-3

Martinus Nijhoff Publishers – The Hague / London / Boston